CXC Principl
Business

W. Armand Layne
Wendell A. Samuel
Kenny D. Anthony

CAMBRIDGE
UNIVERSITY PRESS

Published by the Press Syndicate of the University of Cambridge
The Pitt Building, Trumpington Street, Cambridge CB2 1RP
40 West 20th Street, New York, NY 10011–4211, USA
10 Stamford Road, Oakleigh, Melbourne 3166, Australia

First published 1994

Printed in Great Britain by Scotprint Ltd, Musselburgh, Scotland

A catalogue record for this book is available from the British Library

Library of Congress Cataloguing in Publication data applied for

ISBN 0 521 44766 6

HM

Contents

Acknowledgements

The authors and publishers are grateful to the following for permission to reproduce photographs:

Panos Pictures, pages 38, 197; Neil Sealey, pages 64, 138, 186; David Simson, pages 20, 32, 45, 57, 64, 108, 139, 212, 220, 265, 274, 293, 316; ZEFA, pages 14, 17, 91.

Cover photo: Telegraph Colour Library

The examination questions on pages 41, 207, 306 and 322 were reproduced with kind permission of The Caribbean Examinations Council.

Preface

This book discusses and explains the business, economic and legal foundations on which Caribbean firms conduct their business affairs. The book is based on the CXC syllabus, Principles of Business. It is directed at CXC students but the Caribbean lay person will also find it useful.

Its 20 chapters are arranged around the eight units of the CXC syllabus. Each chapter treats its subject matter in a thorough manner. In some cases we have introduced additional material which is not included in the CXC syllabus. Examples can be found in Chapter 5, where we explain a stock exchange, the importance of a stock exchange, stock exchange listing agreements and disclosure requirements, brokers and jobbers, and in the 'Note on Business Documents', page 144.

A stock exchange is perceived to play an important function in Caribbean economies and students and lay people should know all about it and its related activities. The Note on page 208 emphasizes the reasons why documents are needed in a business. Note too that the legal aspects of business discussed in Chapters 15, 16 and 17 draw attention to the different legal concepts that exist in the Caribbean.

The value of this book lies in its

- easy readability
- detailed but straightforward treatment of its subject matter
- insights into Caribbean business, economic and legal activities and how these compare with those of industrial countries
- focus on educational upliftment and
- philosophical undertones.

Thanks go to the following:

- the Cambridge University Press for publishing the text
- the Cave Hill Campus, UWI Research Fund Committee who provided funds for the retyping of the work
- Dr W. Anderson and Mr J. Cumberbatch, Lecturers in the Faculty of Law, Cave Hill Campus, for making helpful suggestions on the legal section of this book

- an unknown referee who provided sound advice in critiquing the work
- Miss Jacqueline Deane who retyped the work.

In spite of the subeditor's efforts, this book may still contain mistakes. It may also contain ideas not shared by teachers and students. When you have read the work, if you discover mistakes or bizarre ideas, or if you think that clarification of some topic is required or that we have failed to explain an idea lucidly, please write to us at the address shown below, pointing out our mistakes, stating your disagreements and offering suggestions on how the work can be improved. Note that education is always an on-going process and that we too can learn, correct, update and refine our work when circumstances show that such an action is required.

W. A. Layne
W. A. Samuel
K. Anthony

University of the West Indies
Cave Hill Campus
BARBADOS

Chapter 1 The Nature of Business and the Business Environment

If you ask a typical West Indian standing on a street corner what he or she understands by business, the most likely answer that you would get is some activity related to buying and selling of goods. This perception is quite understandable, given the dominance of the wholesale and retail trades in the Caribbean business environment and the late development of manufacturing in the region. Agricultural production is another type of business which is often overlooked.

The street corner respondent would only be partly correct, for business encompasses all the activities which aid the production of goods and services used in the satisfaction of wants. It involves all those activities concerned with the transformation of goods from their natural state to final consumption. These activities include extracting, manufacturing, transport, distribution, banking and insurance.

1.1 Production, exchange and specialization

In the earliest times humans were essentially gatherers. They collected the fruits of nature and used these to satisfy basic human needs of food, clothing and shelter. They collected fruits, hunted and fished to provide food. The skins from the hunted animals could also be used for clothing. Shelter was found in caves or constructed from the leaves of plants. There was no need for exchange as everything gathered was used. Later, humans started cultivating the land and became self-sufficient producers. They produced all the goods they needed to satisfy their wants. This arrangement is usually referred to as *the direct satisfaction of wants*. Life during this time was nasty, brutish and short.

To improve their lot, people progressed from being self-sufficient producers and produced surpluses which they sought to exchange. As opportunities for exchange increased, people began to specialize, to take advantage of special talents. For example, the best farmers specialized in farming, while the best tailors provided clothing. In this mode of production wants are satisfied indirectly since people no longer have to produce everything they need. They simply specialize in the activity in which they have a comparative advantage and exchange the surplus for the other goods they need.

The first type of exchange was one that involved the exchange of goods for goods without the use of money. An economy in which there is no money is called a *barter economy*. The most basic type of barter – direct barter – requires a double coincidence of wants. That is, if I have shoes to exchange and I need corn, in order to make a trade I need to find a farmer who not only has corn to trade but also needs shoes. This type of exchange is very costly in terms of search costs and transport costs.

An improvement on this type of arrangement is *fairground barter*. In this case traders meet in a central location to trade. Although it does not eliminate the double coincidence of wants, the chances of making a trade are greatly increased and some of the transport cost is eliminated.

The chances of making a trade are improved further if traders are willing to make intermediate exchanges in order to get the goods they really need. For example, I could exchange my shoes for a goat, and then exchange the goat for corn, which is what I really need. One can think of much longer transaction chains by which a trader can obtain the goods he needs. This type of *indirect barter* can be very costly if the trader makes a few bad trades along the way, because he or she is not familiar with the goods being traded.

A final type of barter which might emerge is *trading post barter*. In this case trading posts are established for each pair of goods. To exchange my shoes for corn, I simply go to the trading post that exchanges shoes for corn. This arrangement is also inefficient for if there are 20 goods in the economy, 380 trading posts will have to be established, and 2,450 trading posts will have to be established if there are 50 goods. The number of trading posts gets larger as the number of goods increases, and is calculated by the formula $N (N - 1)$, where N is the number of goods.

In whatever form, the barter system was a very inefficient way of effecting exchange and eventually gave way to the use of money as a medium of exchange. The use of money facilitated exchange, since the trader simply exchanged goods for money and used the proceeds to buy whatever was needed.

Initially goods were used for money but some proved to be too cumbersome to be useful, or not durable enough. Some societies used cowrie shells and other objects which seemed valuable to them. As the system evolved, precious metals proved to be the preferred objects for use as money. Later, these precious metals were made into coins by the governing authorities. Precious metals, however, are expensive to produce and gave way to less expensive paper notes and token coins. Today money consists of currency (ie coins and notes) and cheque deposits. Credit cards are also used to facilitate exchange. The characteristics of money are discussed in detail in Chapter 5.

The introduction of money in the system eliminates the double coincidence of wants, and intermediate trades. The exchange of goods is made much easier because all goods are now denominated in a single unit called a *numeraire*.

The high degree of monetization of the economy is only one of the features of the modern economy. Perhaps the most important feature is the degree of specialization made possible by exchange. Workers can specialize in doing a single task and use their wages to buy all they need. This form of organization is called *the division of labour*. It increases with the scale and mechanization of production. For example, in a backyard chicken farm the owner will have to do everything from raising the chickens to cutting them up to be sold as chicken parts. In a much larger, more mechanized plant, people will be assigned one specific job. For example, one person's job may simply be to cut both legs off a chicken as it passes by on a conveyor belt.

A number of advantages are derived from the division of labour:

1 The division of labour increases the skills of the worker, because the same task is performed again and again, and the worker learns by doing. The earning power of the worker increases because he or she becomes more highly skilled.

2 The productivity of the worker increases because he or she is more skilled. Also, less time is lost in changing from one task to the next (as in the case of the backyard poultry producer who performs all of the tasks). The increased output which results benefits the entire society.

3 If the productivity of all of the workers increases then total output of the economy increases, raising the standard of living of the society.

4 As a result of greater output of an industry, the cost of production is reduced and consumers benefit from lower prices.

5 The division of labour also leads to improvement in the quality of the goods produced. The person who has to perform all of the tasks is not expected to be an expert at all tasks. With specialization the person best suited for a task is the one who performs it. Moreover, mechanization facilitates quality control. The consumer receives the benefit of higher-quality products.

6 Less time is spent on training the worker. Under specialization the worker is trained to perform just one or a few tasks. With no specialization the worker has to be trained to perform all of the tasks. The firm can therefore reduce its training costs.

7 Specialization in management is also possible, which in the modern organization of production is a very important ingredient for increased productivity. This increases the profitability of the firm.

There are, however, some disadvantages of specialization:

1 The work can be monotonous. Doing the same thing over and over can become tiresome. When you think about it, cutting the legs from a chicken day after day is not very exciting. The monotony can be alleviated by rotating workers where possible.

2 The work environment can become very impersonal, especially in large organizations. Workers become alienated from management and the relationship between them can deteriorate. This situation is not good for a firm, since the efficiency of the organization is reduced.

3 The worker can lose pride in the work, because he or she cannot point to a final product that is the fruit of a single worker's labour.

Limitations on the division of labour

The extent to which division of labour can be practised depends on the nature of the industry. In the agricultural industry not all the tasks are repeated day after day. In this case the agricultural worker will need to have more than one skill. The level of demand for the product also determines the extent of the division of labour. Minute division of labour is only possible where demand is large, while production for a small market restricts division of labour. Therefore the small domestic markets that exist in the Caribbean islands do not encourage division of labour. Above all, as noted earlier, specialization is only possible if there is the opportunity to exchange.

1.2 What is business?

We can define business as *the production of goods or services with a view to making a profit or operating surplus*. Businesses may have other goals like maximizing sales, the growth of the firm's assets or simply satisfying the owners' desire to be in business. However, although firms do not single-mindedly seek to maximize profits, a firm cannot continue doing business for an extended length of time if it is making losses.

The profit–making motive is very important for it distinguishes businesses from other types of organization. For example, social clubs and other non–profit organizations are not businesses. Although some of these non–profit organizations perform services which are similar to those performed by businesses, their motivation is different. They perform services for their members and may simply aim to cover their costs. Making profits is a major function of businesses.

From the definition of a business, the most important activity undertaken by businesses is the production of goods and services. Goods are tangible objects which are used to satisfy human wants. The term 'goods' does not carry a moral meaning, for something which can be bad for the human body is still called a good if it satisfies a want, for example alcohol. Services are intangible, but the provision of these services satisfies wants either directly (as in the case of a haircut), or indirectly (as in the case of advertising).

In order to produce goods and services, businesses have to employ resources. One of these resources is labour. Thus the establishment of a business creates jobs for the society. Hence another of the functions of business is job creation.

In the Caribbean, growth and development of the economy is very important in the fight against poverty. To the extent that the growth of the business contributes to the growth of the economy, they are partners in the development process. Thus a business should view contributing to the growth of the economy as another of its functions.

1.3 Economic systems and their characteristics

Every society, no matter how rich it is, has to solve the problem of scarcity. Every society has a limited amount of resources which it has to allocate, in some form or fashion, to satisfy the unlimited wants of the members of that society. There are three things involved in this problem: unlimited wants, scarce resources and scientific know–how.

There are three basic wants of a society: food, clothing and shelter. After these are satisfied, then the society can look towards the satisfaction of its less pressing needs, like entertainment and cultural needs. The important thing about wants is that they are unlimited. As one want is satisfied, more and more less essential wants are found. The ultimate goal of economic activity is the satisfaction of wants.

Resources, on the other hand, are limited or scarce. There are four major resources: land, labour, capital and enterprise. *Land* refers to all of the natural resources with which nature provides the society, for example gold, iron ore, bauxite, oil, fish (on the beaches, in the rivers and seas). *Labour* refers to all of the human resources in the society, including skills and education. *Capital* is manufactured resources, like tools and machinery which are used to facilitate the production of goods and services. The fourth factor of production is *enterprise* or *entrepreneurship*. This can be defined as *the ability to organize business and take risks*.

All the resources identified above are available to the society in limited quantities. In the Caribbean, which is a region of mainly small island states, resources are even more scarce. Thus the countries find it more difficult to satisfy the wants of the members of the society.

The third element of the problem of scarcity is technology, which is scientific know-how. Improvement in technological know-how can increase the amount of goods and services produced from the scarce resources. Thus the same amount of resources would satisfy a greater amount of wants if there were improvements in technology. The invention of tractors increased agricultural production and the use of computers in the Japanese car industry increased the production and quality of Japanese cars.

Improved technology enables these robots to be programmed by computers to assemble cars

To satisfy the wants of the society given its scarce resources, three questions must be answered:

1 What to produce?

2 How to produce?

3 For whom to produce?

The answers to these questions depend on the economic system that exists in the society. There are three types of economic system: the free enterprise system, the planned economy and the mixed economy.

The free enterprise system

The free enterprise system or *market economy* is a system in which the resources of the economy are owned by private individuals. The answers to the three questions posed above are provided by the *price system*. The price system directs economic activity. The consumer expresses a personal choice for a good by the price he or she is willing to pay for it. If more of a good is demanded than is available, the price will rise. So will the profits of the firms producing these goods and more firms will be attracted to produce the goods. On the other hand, if consumers do not demand these goods their prices will fall. The firms producing these goods will make losses and stop producing them. In this way the price system determines what to produce.

The prices of resources determine how they are combined in the production process. The firm tries to minimize its cost of production and will therefore combine resources in the cheapest possible way. If the wage rate (the price of labour) rises relative to the price of capital, then the firm will try to reduce the amount of labour and increase the amount of capital used in production. The opposite happens if the wage rate falls relative to the price of capital. Thus the price system determines how to produce.

The resources which are in great demand get higher prices and the owners of these resources receive more income. If the owners receive more income, they are able to buy more of the goods and services produced. In this way the price system solves the question: For whom to produce?

The system does not always work smoothly and some problems arise:

1 Social goods, for example defence, police, education and health services, cannot be adequately provided via the market mechanism because 'free-riders' cannot be excluded. For example, if defence is provided by the private sector, people cannot be excluded from the security provided by the defence force if they refuse to pay. Once defence is provided, everyone is protected from invasion. In this case very few people will pay and defence will not be provided.

2 The free market can lead to monopolies which can exploit consumers by demanding higher prices for certain goods and services because they are the only seller in the market.

3 A free enterprise system can lead to a more unequal distribution of income. The rich can bid up the prices of luxuries, and resources will be used to produce these items rather than necessities.

4 Too much money may be spent on advertising to attract customers.

5 The price mechanism may work sluggishly and as a result suppliers will react slowly to demand changes.

6 The profit motive may not always lead to maximum welfare for the society. For example, the effect of production on pollution and destruction of the environment may not be considered.

7 Resources can remain unused if it is thought they will not yield a profit.

The planned economy

In the case of the planned/command economy, all of the resources are owned by the government. The decisions about what to produce, how to produce and for whom are made by a centralized planning agency. The planning body determines consumer demands and makes decisions about how these goods are to be supplied and in what quantities.

The advantages of the planned economy are related to the problems with the free enterprise system. The planned economy is not driven by profit, so there is greater employment of resources and the social cost is taken into consideration. Planners can ensure that adequate resources go into the production of social goods, and advertising can be limited to providing information only. The monopoly power of the state can be used for the welfare of the society as a whole.

There can be problems with the planned economy:

1 It is impossible to estimate accurately the needs of the consumers. This leads to shortages of some goods and a glut of other goods. Moreover, the government of the country can impose its choices on the rest of the society, for example producing more military goods and fewer consumer goods.

2 When the needs of the society are determined, their provision has to be arranged by politicians and bureaucrats (civil servants) who may not be trained in the management of large organizations. Moreover, large organizations are unwieldy and difficult to manage efficiently. This leads to coordination problems. For example, in the former Soviet Union, in spite of good harvests there were episodes of food shortages because there were not enough trucks to transport the food.

3 Many more officials are required to do the planning in this system than are required in the free market system.

4 The state ownership of resources reduces the incentives of the members of the society to work harder. Since they are working for the state and not for themselves, their effort will not be as great.

Food shortages in the former USSR led to public protests

The mixed economy

The two systems described above are extremes, and there are no true examples of these in the real world. The United States is the closest to the free enterprise system, but there is some government ownership of resources. The former Soviet Union was the closest to a planned economy, but there was some private ownership of resources. In recent times the Soviet Union and the rest of Eastern Europe have been moving towards becoming market economies.

Most of the countries of the world have not chosen either of the two extremes. They have adopted the middle ground, trying to obtain the advantages of both systems. Countries differ only in the extent to which they adopt one system rather than the other. This middle ground is called a *mixed economy*. All of the Caribbean countries have mixed economies, with a higher level of private ownership than government ownership.

The main characteristic of the mixed economy is that the public and the private sectors exist side by side. The private sector consists of all operations that are privately owned and, for the most part, is profit oriented. The public sector, on the other hand, includes those operations that are government owned and their motive may not be strictly profit making. They respond to the needs of the society rather than demand (ie wants that are backed by purchasing power). These operations include government departments, statutory corporations, nationalized industries and other government-owned enterprises.

The size of the public sector is a measure of the extent to which the country has a mixed economy. The private sector is one minus the fraction of the economy represented by the public sector. For example, if the government sector is one-quarter, then the private sector is three-quarters. In most of the Caribbean islands the public sector is fairly large and in most cases the government is the largest employer.

Comparison of the three economic systems

The goal of all three economic systems is the efficient allocation of the society's scarce resources between competing wants. The market economy also tries to preserve individual choice in the allocation of those resources. Market economies usually have democratically elected governments.

Planned economies strive for equality in the distribution of resources among members of the society, in addition to their efficient allocation. They also try to produce adequate amounts of social goods which would not be produced by the pure market economy.

The mixed economy recognizes the weaknesses in both the planned and market economies and tries to solve this by leaving those activities which can be efficiently done by the private sector in their hands. The activities which the private sector cannot undertake efficiently are handled by the government.

1.4 Differences between private and public sectors

The major differences between the public and private sectors are these:

1 The government is the ultimate source of funds for the public sector. The government raises these funds through taxation, borrowing at home – either by raising bank loans or issuing government securities – and borrowing from abroad. In the Caribbean a large proportion of the funding for government enterprises is obtained from abroad. The funds for the private sector come from the owners of the firms and can be supplemented by borrowing.

2 The public sector responds to the needs of the society, providing social goods and services. The private sector, on the other hand, responds to the demand.

3 The main motive of the private sector is creation of profit for the owners of the firm. The general welfare of the society is hardly considered. The public sector is not driven by profit, so social services are provided even if there is no profit.

4 The public sector is not profit-oriented, so the pricing policy is different. In some cases prices are set only to cover the cost of production. In the case of some essential services like water and public transport, the government subsidizes the production of these

services and charges a price less than the cost of production. The private sector will always try to set prices which result in profits.

5 Employment can also be higher in the public sector than in the private sector. The public sector does not look at profit narrowly defined in terms of money. The government may think that it is better to employ more people and make a loss than to keep them unemployed.

1.5 The classification of productive activities

Productive activities can be classified into four categories: extractive industries, manufacturing, construction and services. An *industry* is defined as a number of firms producing closely related goods or services. It is not very difficult to view extractive industries (agriculture, mining and quarrying), manufacturing and construction industries as productive activities. However, it is a little more difficult to view the provision of services as an act of production. To the extent that services satisfy human wants directly, as in the case of doctors and teachers, or indirectly by being aids in the production of goods, they are classed as *productive activities*.

Extractive industries

Extractive industries are industries which are engaged in obtaining goods from the natural environment. These include agriculture, fishing, mining and quarrying. Although in some cases these industries produce final products like bananas and mangoes, the main function of these industries is to provide raw materials for the manufacturing, construction and, to a lesser extent, the service sectors. For example, agriculture provides canes for the manufacture of sugar, mining provides bauxite for the manufacture of aluminium products, quarrying provides stones for the construction of houses, and agriculture provides food for the tourist industry.

Manufacturing industries

Manufacturing industries are involved with the transformation of goods so as to increase their value. For example, the raw materials from the extractive industries are made into final products which satisfy the consumers' wants. This is the case in the manufacture of sugar cane into sugar.

However, not all products produced by manufacturing firms are used by consumers. The output of some firms is bought by other firms to produce final products. For example, some of the sugar produced by a sugar factory is used in the production of soft drinks, chocolates, cakes and pastries. When the output of one manufacturing firm is used by another, the output of the first firm is called an *intermediate good*. The output of some manufacturing firms is also used as tools or machines by other firms. For example, the tractor used in agriculture is produced by a manufacturing firm. This type of product is called a *capital good*.

Refining is a major manufacturing activity undertaken by some Caribbean countries. In Trinidad & Tobago, crude oil is refined into petroleum and other petroleum-based products like motor oil and lighter fuel. Jamaica and Guyana also refine bauxite into alumina.

An oil field in Barbados

Another aspect of manufacturing is assembling. Although it does not involve the physical transformation of the good it is still regarded as manufacturing. Many of the industries in the Caribbean are assembly-type industries. The various parts are imported from the rest of the world and the final product is assembled in many of the industrial estates across the Caribbean.

Construction industry

The construction industry combines the output from the manufacturing and extractive industries to produce structures like houses, factories, roads and bridges. For example, in the construction of a house the builder uses timber, cement, concrete blocks, etc from the manufacturing industries, and stones and sand from the extractive industries. Some of the output of the construction industry – houses, factories and warehouses – is used by consumers and businesses.

The government also creates a demand for the output of the construction sector, ie bridges, roads, airports and seaports. These structures are referred to as the *infrastructure* of a country.

Service industries

Services are late-comers to the categorization of industries. However, in the modern economy, services are becoming increasingly more important. Services can be divided into two broad groups: direct services and commercial services. *Direct services* are services which directly satisfy human wants. They include those services provided by professionals like doctors, barbers and lawyers, government-provided services (like health and education), and tourism.

Commercial services are services which are concerned with trade and the aids to trade. They do not directly satisfy human wants, but are useful in the production of goods which satisfy these wants. For example, transport is required to bring the goods to the final consumer, and advertising to inform consumers about the goods which are available.

Trade can be defined as the exchange of goods and direct services. It can be divided into domestic trade and foreign trade. Domestic trade or home trade can be divided into wholesale trade and retail trade; these are discussed in Chapter 14. Foreign trade is the exchange of goods and services between countries. It can be divided into import and export trade; these are discussed in Chapter 9.

The aids to trade are those services which are necessary to facilitate the exchange of goods and services. These include banking, insurance, transport, advertising, communications and information services. The relationship between production of goods and services can be seen in Figure 1.1.

Information services is a relatively new area. It only became popular with the widespread use of computers and has grown quite rapidly to be a multimillion-dollar industry. It is concerned with the processing and communication of data. It requires a large amount of labour, a resource which is very abundant in the Caribbean. Information services is one of the fastest-growing industries in Barbados and Jamaica. Data for American firms are processed in Barbados and sent to the United States by computer via the telephone system.

The extractive activities are sometimes referred to as *primary industries*. The construction and manufacturing industries are called *secondary industries*, and services are referred to as *tertiary industries*. This is an alternative way of classifying economic activities and is displayed in Figure 1.2.

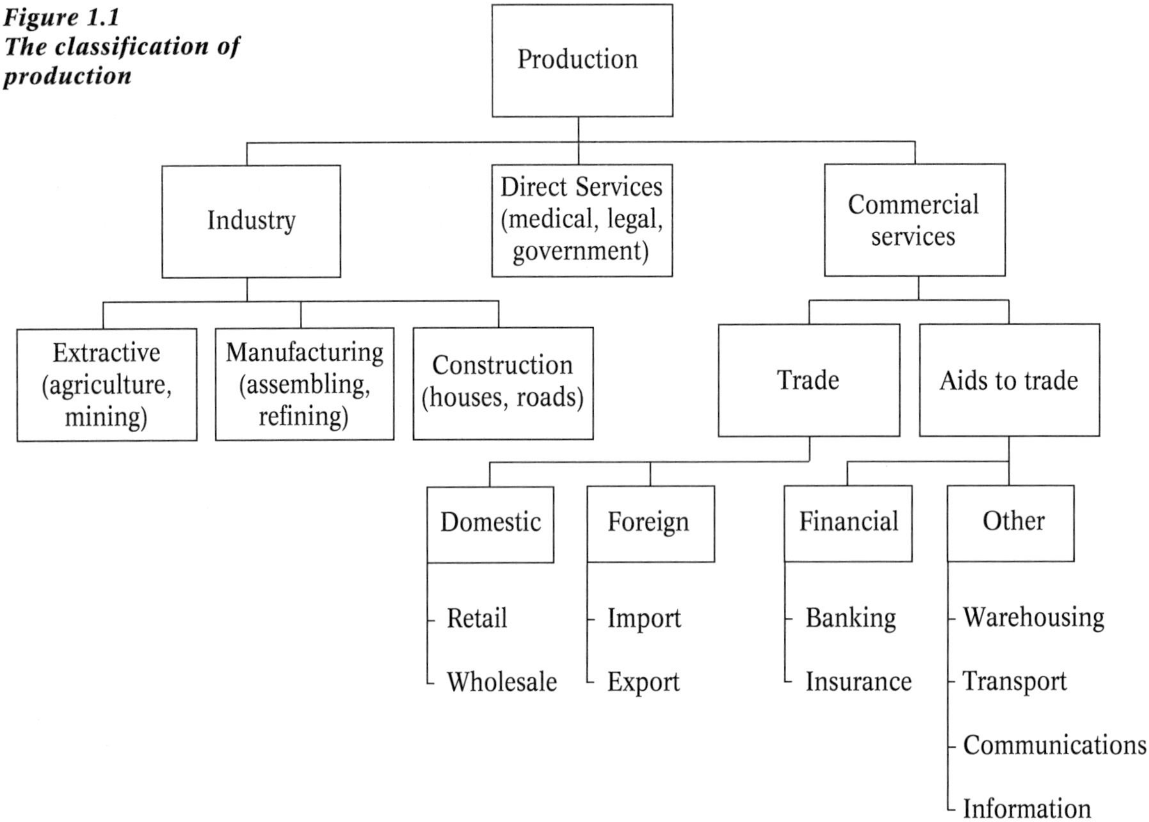

Figure 1.1
The classification of production

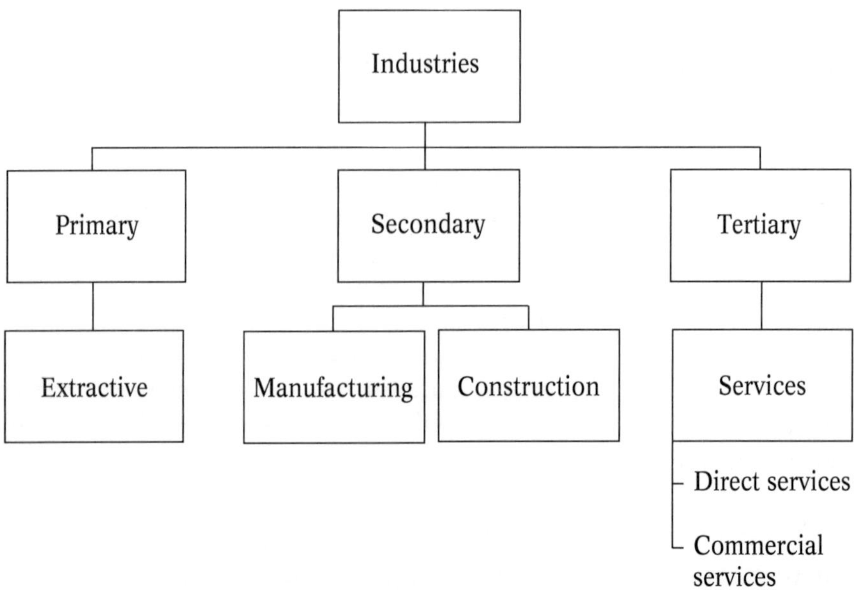

Figure 1.2
Alternative classification of production

1.6 Productive activities in the Caribbean

All of the major branches of production exist in the Caribbean. However, some are more important than others. Table 1.1 shows the relative importance of the major productive activities in some of the Caribbean countries. The table shows that the service sector is the largest sector in all of the countries listed, except Guyana. In most of the countries, distributive services (wholesale and retail) is the largest component because most businesses in the Caribbean are involved in buying and selling. Tourism also forms a large proportion of the service sector in most of the Caribbean countries. This is especially so in Antigua, Barbados, The Bahamas and Jamaica, which have large tourist sectors.

The next largest sector is extractive industries. This sector includes agriculture, fisheries, mining and quarrying. Agriculture is the oldest activity in the Caribbean. The islands were colonized by the Europeans to provide agricultural products, especially sugar for the European markets. Today many of the Caribbean countries have stopped producing sugar but agriculture still plays an important part. Some of the agricultural products in the region other than sugar are bananas (the Windward Islands), citrus fruits (Dominica, Jamaica and Trinidad), rice (Guyana and Trinidad) and nutmeg (Grenada). In the

Table 1.1 Percentage share of the major productive activities in total output, 1987

	Extractive	Manufacturing	Construction	Services
Antigua	6.9	3.7	11.7	77.7
Barbados	9.1	9.5	14.9	66.5
Dominica	30.6	6.6	5.3	57.5
Grenada	19.2	5.4	9.4	66.0
Guyana	41.9	14.1	4.8	39.2
Jamaica	15.5	18.9	9.8	55.8
Montserrat	5.7	6.0	12.0	76.3
St Kitts	9.7	14.4	7.7	68.2
St Lucia	15.0	7.8	8.1	69.1
St Vincent	21.1	8.3	10.5	60.1
Trinidad	27.5	8.5	10.7	53.3

Sources: OECS Economic Affairs Secretariat; Central Bank of Barbados, *Annual Statistical Digest*, 1990

area of mining, bauxite is the most important (Jamaica and Guyana) along with mining for oil and natural gas (Trinidad and Barbados).

Other minerals mined in the Caribbean are gold and diamonds (Guyana), asphalt (Trinidad) and gypsum (Jamaica).

The construction industry is also quite important in the Caribbean because it generates employment and uses a large quantity of local raw materials. The manufacturing sector in the Caribbean is small – less than 10 per cent of total output in most of the countries shown in Table 1.1. However, there is a diversity of manufacturing activities in the region and the sector is increasing its contribution year by year.

Production in the Caribbean compared with the rest of the world

The Caribbean countries are small, so the scale of production is much smaller than in developed countries like the United States, Canada, Japan and the countries of Western Europe. This means that the level of mechanization in the Caribbean is not as high as in the developed countries.

Apart from sugar, the manufacturing sector in the Caribbean has only emerged in recent times. Many countries are at the early stage of manufacturing. The Caribbean does not have an advantage in the production of manufactured goods, so the sector has to be protected and given special incentives. One of these incentives is the provision of factory shells in industrial estates, also known as industrial parks, and many of the manufacturing concerns in the Caribbean are located in industrial parks.

The Caribbean does not have many natural resources, and most of the raw materials have to be imported. Nor do the Caribbean countries produce many capital goods and intermediate goods; these also have to be imported. As a result the manufacturing sector produces mainly light manufactured goods (like processed foods) and goods assembled from imported components. Many high-tech electronic products are assembled in the industrial parks in Barbados, Jamaica and St Kitts, although they do not have the technology to produce the components.

Where the raw materials exist, they are not processed in the Caribbean. For example, raw sugar is sent to the United Kingdom to be refined, bauxite is exported for the final stage of processing and cocoa is exported to be made into chocolate and cocoa powder. The final products are then re-imported at very high prices. The Caribbean therefore concentrates more on the extractive activities. For the development of the region the emphasis will have to be shifted to processing the raw materials from the extractive industries into final manufactured products.

The establishment of the European single market threatens the existence of the sugar and banana industries, two major industries in the Caribbean. Protected markets are likely to be eliminated and countries will have to face greater international competition. In the future countries will have to try to diversify their agricultural exports to include fresh fruit and vegetables and manufactured products which require high levels of skill. The services industry will also become more important. In addition to tourism, information services and other telecommunications-based services will need to be developed to service the United States and Canadian markets.

Key Points

- The ultimate aim of economic activity is the satisfaction of wants. They can be satisfied either directly by self-sufficient production, or indirectly through exchange.
- The functions of businesses are to produce goods and services, to create jobs, to make profits or operating surpluses and to contribute to economic development.
- There are three types of economic system: the free enterprise economy, the planned economy and the mixed economy. In the free enterprise economy, resources are privately owned and production responds to price signals. In the planned economy, resources are government owned and production is planned by the government. The mixed economy is a combination of both.
- Productive activity can be categorized into four groups: extractive (agriculture, fishing, mining), construction (building), manufacturing (assembling, refining), and services (advertising, communications, tourism, transport).
- All the different types of productive activity exist in the Caribbean in varying degrees in all of the countries. The provision of services is the most important activity, especially distributive services (wholesaling and retailing) and tourism.
- Production in the Caribbean is on a much smaller scale than in the developed countries. This limits the amount of specialization and division of labour. Manufacturing is a relatively new activity in the Caribbean but its importance is growing.

Questions

1 Explain what is meant by (a) *direct satisfaction of wants* and (b) *indirect satisfaction of wants.*

2 What is a *barter economy*? What are the limitations of such a system?

3 Explain what is meant by *specialization* and *division of labour.* What factors create limits to the division of labour in the Caribbean?

4 What are the advantages and disadvantages of the division of labour?

5 What is a *business organization*? What are the functions of business organizations in developing countries like the Caribbean?

6 Describe the different types of economic system, and explain how they solve the problems of *what to produce* and *how to produce.* Do they offer different solutions to the question, *for whom to produce*?

7 Compare and contrast the advantages and disadvantages of (a) the free enterprise system and (b) the planned economy.

8 Explain the differences between the public and private sectors.

9 List the different types of economic activity and give examples of these activities in the Caribbean.

10 Distinguish carefully between *industry* and *commerce.* Which of these activities is more important in the Caribbean?

11 Compare and contrast production in the Caribbean with production in the developed countries of the world.

12 Explain what is meant by *production.* Describe the activities that are performed by (a) primary industries (b) secondary industries and (c) tertiary industries.

Chapter 2 The Organization of Production

In Chapter 1 we looked at the different types of productive activity. In this chapter we look in greater detail at the organization of production by the individual firm.

Production can be defined as the *change of inputs into outputs*. For example, in order to make sugar we need sugar cane, workers and machinery. Sugar cane, workers and machinery are the inputs needed to make sugar. The inputs to the production process are land, labour and capital. The outputs are goods and services which are used either directly or indirectly in the satisfaction of wants.

2.1 The levels of production

In the earliest times, people satisfied their wants directly by producing all the goods they needed. This form of production was called *subsistence production*. People still produce in this way in just a few remote communities in some Caribbean islands and in parts of Africa and Asia. They grow most of what they need on a small plot of land. This type of agricultural activity is called *subsistence farming*. In some cases the people in a community may specialize in the production of certain goods and exchange the surplus in the local marketplace, but the community as a whole is self-sufficient. This form of production does not contribute significantly to the economy in the Caribbean.

In a second type of production, the producer specializes in the production of a good or service and sells it on the local market. Production in this case is entirely for local consumption. If the entire economy operates in this way the economy is self-sufficient. A totally self-sufficient economy is said to operate under *autarky* (ie an economy in which there is no international trade).

It is very difficult for any country, no matter how large, to be self-sufficient in all goods and services. Any country needs to import essential goods and services. To do this, the country produces surpluses in those commodities it is best suited to produce, and exchanges these surpluses for the goods it is unable to produce. However, some countries try to be self-sufficient in the production of certain essential commodities. The United States and China try to be self-sufficient in food and steel so that if there is a war the country is not at a disadvantage.

Caribbean countries are small islands, so are unable to be self-sufficient. They cannot produce all of the goods and services they need, given their resources. Most of the islands produce cash crops like sugar, nutmeg, bananas, coffee and rice. These are exported and the earnings then used to buy those goods that the countries do not produce, or do not produce enough of.

A more frequent arrangement in the Caribbean is the peasant farmer who owns a small piece of land on which he or she grows a cash crop like bananas, nutmeg or coffee. At the same time the farmer grows food crops to feed the family. Thus the peasant farmer practises both cash crop and subsistence agriculture. In many of the Caribbean countries peasant farming contributes significantly to the economy, especially in countries like Dominica, St Vincent and Grenada where there are very few large plantations. It has been estimated that the peasant farmer is responsible for about 80 per cent of the food production in the Caribbean.

2.2 The factors of production

In 1776, in his book *The Wealth of Nations*, Adam Smith identified three factors of production: land, labour and capital. *Land* includes all the natural resources of the land and the seas. *Labour* includes the skills and training acquired by the workforce. The third factor of production is *capital*, ie buildings, machinery and equipment which are used in the production process. Another factor, *enterprise* or *entrepreneurship* – the ability to take risks and manage firms – is essential if production is to take place.

The other three factors of production are harnessed in various combinations by entrepreneurs to produce output of goods and services. They are all important to the production process. No goods can be produced without all three inputs. For example, the production of carrots requires land in which the seedlings can be planted. Labour is necessary for planting, weeding and harvesting. The workers need implements (capital) for planting and harvesting the crop. Enterprise is also needed to organize the whole production process. A small farmer supplies both labour and entrepreneurship. Similarly, in the production of motor cars, natural resources are used to produce the components using special machinery (capital). Human resources are used to operate the machinery and manage the firm.

2.3 Natural resources in the Caribbean

The natural resources of a country are its land, forests, minerals and marine resources. The Caribbean countries are not rich in natural resources, but there is a wide variety of natural resources which form the basis of many of the region's industries. These industries range from agro-processing to the production of alumina.

All Caribbean countries have arable land which is suitable for agriculture. This is the basis for agro-processing industries in the region. The oldest industry in the Caribbean is the manufacture of sugar. At one time all Caribbean countries produced sugar. Today it is produced mainly in Jamaica, Guyana, Trinidad & Tobago, Barbados and St Kitts. A by-product of sugar production is molasses which can be used for making rum. Some Caribbean countries like Antigua, St Lucia, St Vincent and the Grenadines no longer produce sugar but do still produce rum, which is made from imported molasses.

The region's agricultural production forms the basis for other types of agro-processing, including the production of dairy products from milk, various types of canned juices from local fruits, bottled jams, jellies and preserves, packaged meat and fish products. These industries are found in all of the Caribbean countries, although not all require a factory to produce them.

Guyana and Belize have large forest reserves, while countries like Dominica and St Vincent have smaller forested areas. In these countries teak, greenheart and mahogany are plentiful. Teak and greenheart are used in the construction industry, and mahogany is used in the furniture industry.

The mineral resources of the Caribbean are quite small compared with those of other countries in the world (see Figure 2.1). The main mineral resource is bauxite, which is found in Jamaica and Guyana. The bauxite ore is mined and processed into alumina. The manufacture of aluminium from alumina requires large quantities of cheap electricity which is not available in these countries, so the alumina is exported to be made into aluminium products.

An important mineral is crude oil which is found in Trinidad and in small quantities in Barbados. Trinidad produces about 1 per cent of the world's crude oil. This resource is very important to the Trinidadian economy, as it contributes more than 60 per cent of the income of Trinidad & Tobago and employs many people. Crude oil is refined and used in the manufacture of a wide range of consumer products. Some of the industries associated with oil are the manufacture of gasoline, kerosene, lubricating oil and aviation fuel. Trinidad and Barbados also have deposits of natural gas which is used mainly for cooking.

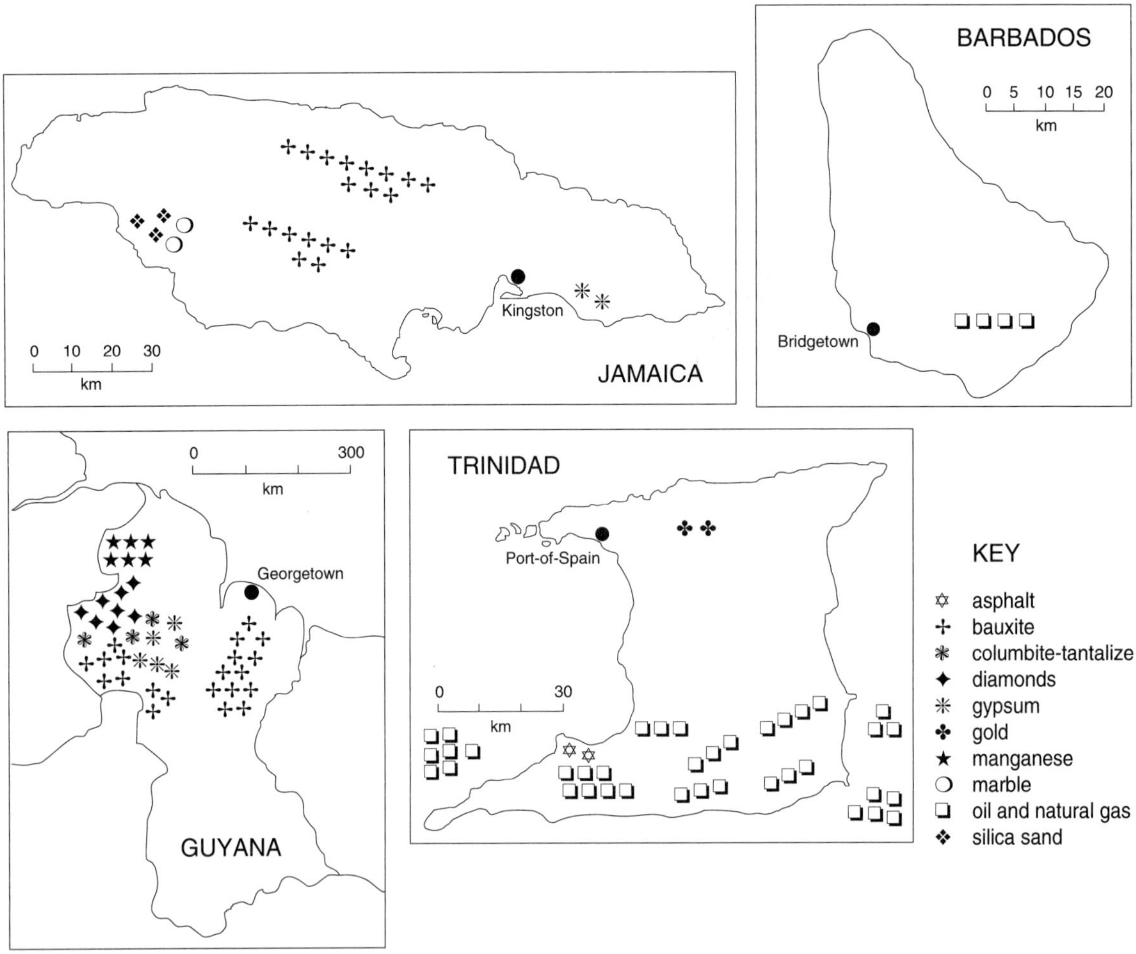

Figure 2.1 Minerals in the Caribbean region

Other mineral deposits in the Caribbean countries are gold and manganese in Guyana, gypsum in Jamaica and limestone in Barbados. Most countries also have quarries which provide material for the construction of houses.

Most of the Caribbean countries are completely surrounded by sea. The sea is our most abundant natural resource. The marine resources include fishes, lobsters, shrimp, seamoss and salt. The most important industry based on marine resources is fish processing. The harvesting of seamoss to make beverages is a growing industry. In some islands like The Bahamas and Anguilla, salt is extracted from the sea water.

The natural beauty of the Caribbean islands is also a valuable natural resource. The white sand beaches of islands like Barbados and Antigua and the rugged mountains of St Lucia and Grenada attract visitors to these islands. This, along with a very agreeable climate, makes the tourist industry one of the most important industries in the Caribbean.

Tourism is a major source of foreign exchange earnings for most of the Caribbean countries. It has transformed countries like Barbados and St Kitts from being single crop (sugar) economies to economies that are more diversified. It has improved the standard of living in most of the Caribbean countries. Tourism revenues come not only from payments for hotel rooms and food but also from money spent on taxis, handicrafts, hairdressers and water sports, for example. Employment is also created for the people who provide these services.

Table 2.1 lists the mineral resources of the Caribbean countries and the industries associated with them.

***Table 2.1* Mineral resources and their related industries in the Caribbean**

Resource	Related industry	Location of resource
Asphalt	Asphalt mixing	Trinidad & Tobago
Bauxite	Alumina	Guyana, Jamaica
Columbite	For export	Guyana
Crude oil	Petroleum, petrochemicals	Barbados, Trinidad & Tobago
Diamonds	Jewellery	Guyana
Gold	Jewellery	Guyana
Gypsum	Construction	Jamaica
Iron ore	Steel	Trinidad & Tobago
Manganese	For export	Guyana
Marble	Construction	Jamaica
Natural gas	Cooking gas	Barbados, Trinidad & Tobago
Platinum	For export	Guyana
Sand and gravel	Construction	All countries
Silica sand	Construction	Jamaica
Tentalite	For export	Guyana

2.4 Human resources and their importance

Labour is needed to combine with the other factors of production to produce output. The quantity of labour a firm needs depends on the quantity of output of that firm, the other factors employed, and the price of labour (the wage rate).

If a firm needs to produce a larger volume of output it must employ more labour, and perhaps more of the other factors of production too. For example, if a farmer wishes to double the output of bananas, he/she must use more land, more labour and more capital (eg spray cans, forks and cutlasses).

In some cases the producer can choose to use more capital and less labour, for example in the sugar industry in Barbados where production is mechanized. The mechanized cane harvester has reduced the demand for labour needed to cut cane.

If the wage rate is low, firms can employ more labour than if the wage rate is high. As the wage rate increases, firms are likely to employ less labour. The relationship between the wage rate and the level of labour used by a firm is called the *demand for labour.*

Human resources – the labour force and skills – is one of the most abundant resources in the Caribbean. The populations of the countries are large relative to their size. People are also well educated and can be trained easily. Barbados boasts a 98 per cent rate of literacy, and the other islands are not too far behind. Since human resources are abundant in the Caribbean, it is necessary to develop these resources to the full, and to manage them efficiently.

Factors affecting the supply of labour

The rate of growth of the population This depends on the birth rate, the death rate and the amount of migration. A high birth rate increases the population. The death rate and outward migration reduce the population. In most Caribbean countries there is a high rate of population growth owing to an increasing birth rate and a lower death rate. However, this is partly offset by the high rate of outward migration.

The age at which people enter the labour force The younger people are when they enter the labour force, the larger is the supply of labour. In all Caribbean countries the law prohibits children under the age of 16 from entering the labour force.

The retirement age If people are allowed to remain in the labour force longer, there is a larger supply of labour, but if the retirement age is reduced, the supply of labour is smaller. In most Caribbean countries the age of retirement for government workers is 60, while workers in the private sector may retire at 65.

The wage rate This is the reward people receive for working, expressed as dollars per hour or dollars per day. As the wage rate increases, more people will be willing to work for higher pay. However, if people prefer leisure to income, as their income rises as a result of an increased wage rate they work fewer hours.

The participation rate At any one time, all of the people who are able to work will not be willing to work. Those who are not willing to work are not counted as part of the labour force. The labour force participation rate is the percentage of the employable population that is in the labour force. (See below.)

Religious and cultural practices Certain religions do not encourage women to work outside the home. This reduces the supply of labour. In the Caribbean more and more women are entering the labour force as they become better educated.

The mobility of labour If people do not mind moving from one place to another to find jobs, the supply of labour will be greater. However, if people are unwilling to move, then the supply of labour comes only from the local area. This means that in one area there may be labour shortages, while in another there is surplus labour.

Transport is also important: an efficient transportation system widens the area from which labour can be drawn.

The productivity of labour

An important aspect of the labour supply is the productivity of labour – the output per worker, or the quantity of output divided by the number of workers used to produce it. The same number of workers can produce more goods if they are more productive. An increase in labour productivity lowers the cost of production and increases the standard of living of the society.

The productivity of labour depends on the following:

The capital that the worker has to use The more and better machines the worker has, the greater is the output.

Education and training The better educated and trained the workers, the greater the productivity.

Health A healthy, well-fed worker is more productive than an unhealthy one.

Work ethic Conscientious workers are more productive than idle ones. Workers with a strong work ethic are likely to have higher productivity.

Motivation Motivation of workers plays an important part in productivity. One of the roles of management is to motivate the workers (see Chapter 13).

Human resource development

Human resource development involves improvement in the education, skills, health and nutrition of the labour force.

Education Improved basic education increases the trainability of workers and makes them more productive. Basic education is acquired in schools and universities.

Skills Improvement in the skills of workers also makes them more productive. Skills are more job-related and are acquired in technical colleges, on skills training programmes and during on-the-job training.

Health The health of workers is also very important, because unhealthy workers are not as productive as healthy workers. Disease eradication and greater attention to environmental health are critical to the maintenance of a healthy labour force.

Nutrition Improvement in the nutritional standards of the workers contributes to their overall health and hence their productivity.

2.5 Self-help and community work

In small, developing economies like those in the Caribbean, the government is unable to provide all of the social goods and services needed by the society. Self-help projects and community work are important ways of providing these goods and services. To improve the skills of unemployed young people, communities can establish centres to help them acquire skills like needlework, handicrafts, leathercraft and the making of other small items. Training can be provided at a reasonable cost by members of the community who have these skills.

Community work can also provide some necessary facilities like playgrounds, hard courts for sporting activities, roads and public baths. These efforts can be coordinated by the government ministries responsible for community development, which can provide the raw materials. Members of the community may provide the labour free of cost.

As well as providing necessary social goods and services, self-help projects bring members of a community closer together. They make people more aware of their civic duties and develop a spirit of healthy cooperation within the society.

2.6 Migration

Migration is the permanent movement of people between societies. This movement is usually in search of better jobs or better educational opportunities, but may also be the result of political or racial persecution. Migration can be either between countries, or domestic migration as in the case of the rural-urban migration in many of the less developed countries of the world since 1950. The Caribbean countries have not been exceptions. Many thousands of people have moved from the rural areas to seek a better life in the cities.

International migration has been significant in the Caribbean countries. A person who leaves the home country is called an *emigrant*. In the country to which the person migrates he or she is referred to as an *immigrant*. The entire history of the Caribbean countries records both *in-migration* (immigration) and *out-migration* (emigration). When slavery ended, thousands of East Indians were brought to the Caribbean to provide labour for the plantations. In more recent years Caribbean people have migrated to Panama, the United Kingdom, Canada and the United States, and many are still doing so.

The migration of workers has both negative and positive effects on the economy.

Negative effects of migration

1 Workers migrate with the skills they have acquired. These skills are needed in the less developed countries, but when a worker leaves, those skills are lost. The movement of skilled workers from one country to another is called *the brain-drain.*

2 Usually it is young people in a society who migrate, so the society loses some of its most energetic and healthy citizens.

3 As people leave, the country has to pay more for training new workers. For example, many nurses in the Caribbean are trained here, then are recruited by hospitals in the developed countries which attract them with higher wages and better conditions of service.

The advantages of migration

1 Migrant workers usually send remittances in the form of money or goods to their relatives in the home country. These can improve the welfare of the society as a whole and bring in much-needed foreign exchange.

2 In countries that have a large population relative to the size of the country, migration is a way of easing the population pressure on the scarce resources of the country.

2.7 Trade unions

A trade union is an association of workers established to try to improve the wages and working conditions in an industry or group of industries. The union acts as a representative of the workers in all important matters between the workers and the employer. The trade unions negotiate on behalf of the workers and their negotiating power is backed by the threat of strikes. However, strikes are the weapons of last resort and are only used when the negotiations break down.

The first trade unions were founded in Europe in the 19th century to combat the low wages and poor working conditions which existed there after the industrial revolution. The unions were met with hostility by the employers and at first were outlawed. A similar hostility greeted the establishment of trade unions in the Caribbean during the 1930s. Today unions are respected representatives of the workers and are protected by the laws of the country. Many political parties in the Caribbean have their roots in the trade union movement and are closely allied with some unions.

The Caribbean labour laws guarantee that workers have a right to be represented by a union. The laws also allow for *arbitration* in the event of a deadlock in negotiations. This arbitration is usually done by the Department of Labour or the minister responsible for labour. In Trinidad & Tobago, arbitration is by an industrial court. The government can also pass laws to protect unions from being sued for loss of profits due to strikes, minimum wage laws and laws prohibiting strikes in certain essential services.

There are several types of trade union depending on the type of workers they represent. For example:

Industrial workers unions These represent workers of a particular industry or group of industries. The Oil Field Workers Union in Trinidad and the Farmers Union in St Lucia and St Vincent and the Grenadines are examples.

General workers unions These represent workers who are not connected to a particular industry. The Barbados Workers Union is an example.

Government workers unions They represent groups of government workers like teachers and civil servants. The Teachers' Union, found in most Caribbean countries, and the regional body the Caribbean Union of Teachers (CUT) are examples of this type of union.

Professional unions These represent workers in certain professions like engineers and other skilled workers. Membership of these unions is restricted to those with qualifications in the particular area.

Performing arts unions These represent workers in the performing arts like actors, calypsonians and other entertainers – an example is the Calypsonians' Association.

The main aims of trade unions are to increase wages and improve the working conditions of their members. Their effectiveness depends on the union's strength, negotiating skills and discipline of members. Unions therefore try to get as many members as possible.

Subscriptions are collected so that the executive has sufficient funds to carry out its functions. Union representatives (shop stewards) are elected for each workplace so that matters affecting the workers can quickly be brought to the attention of the leaders of the union and resolved.

Trade union workers in Grenada take part in a celebration march

Worker education is a major activity of the unions. The workers are educated about their rights, and the importance of solidarity, or working together. The leaders are also educated in negotiating skills and business evaluations.

The functions of the unions

- To negotiate improved wages and conditions of service for the workers. These include pensions, holidays and number of hours worked.
- To protect workers from unfair dismissal.
- To improve the physical working conditions of the workers – that is, to guard against dangerous and unhealthy working conditions.
- To educate the workers in job-related activities.
- To present the workers' point of view to management and government agencies.
- To provide unemployment and sickness benefit schemes where government-sponsored schemes are inadequate.

In seeking to improve the position of the workers, trade unions must not lose sight of the effects of their action on the country as a whole. High wage demands are only possible in the long term if the productivity of the workers is increasing. Higher wages that are not accompanied by increased productivity will reduce the profits of the businesses, which will have to lay off workers or close down the business entirely. Higher wages can also result in inflation in the country as firms increase their prices to offset wage increases. The higher prices which result can also lead to the products of the country becoming uncompetitive in foreign markets, thereby reducing the country's exports.

2.8 The role of capital in production

There are several forms of capital. The two most common are financial capital and physical capital. *Financial capital* refers to the money capital of a company and is divided into share capital and loan capital (see Chapter 5). *Physical capital* refers to manufactured goods which are combined with natural resources and human resources in the production process. Natural resources and labour can be distinguished from capital because they are not manufactured. Here, capital refers to the plant and machinery which the firm uses, and any other equipment that is used in production.

The use of physical capital increases the productivity of labour. Increasing the amount and quality of the machinery increases the amount of output. For example, if plantation workers are given tractors rather than hoes to plough the land and harvest the crop, their output will be much greater. Similarly the output of clothing manufacturing workers will be increased if they use machinery for cutting the cloth rather than doing it by hand.

The amount of capital that a firm employs depends on the size and type of the industry and the price of capital relative to the price of labour. A small firm cannot employ much capital because its output is too small to justify the use of expensive machinery. The type of output produced by the firm is also important. The production of cars, for example, requires a large factory and special machinery, while the production of leather goods can be done in a small shop with very little capital equipment. The use of capital also facilitates the division of labour (see page 11).

2.9 Entrepreneurship

One of the important functions of the entrepreneur is to combine the factors of production – natural resources, human resources and capital – to produce goods and services. The most important function of the entrepreneur or manager is the ability to spot profitable opportunities and to take advantage of them before anyone else does. A manager must therefore be astute. The opportunities to make a profit do not always turn out favourably and can result in losses. The entrepreneur must therefore be a person who is willing to undertake risks. Profits are the reward for the risks.

In the free market and in mixed economies, the entrepreneur is the one who responds to the signals provided by the price mechanism. By responding to these signals, the correct amount of goods and services are produced and the factors of production are combined so that the lowest cost is achieved. Without the organizing skills and instincts of the entrepreneur, today's complex economic systems could not satisfy the needs of society as efficiently as they do.

Key Points

- There are four factors of production: land, labour, capital and enterprise. Land can also be called *natural resources* and labour can be defined as *human resources*.
- Natural resources are land, minerals and marine resources. There are many industries based on these resources including agro-processing and petrochemicals.
- Human resources include the labour force and all the skills acquired by workers. They also include entrepreneurship which is necessary to manage the factors of production.
- Capital refers to the tools and equipment used in the production process. It helps to increase the productivity of labour.
- The entrepreneur combines the other factors of production to produce goods and services. An entrepreneur must be willing to take risks, and for this is rewarded with profits or losses.

Questions

1 Explain the different levels of production. Why is it difficult for Caribbean countries to be self-sufficient?

2 Name the factors of production and explain how they are used in the production process.

3 What are *natural resources*? Identify some of the natural resources in the Caribbean and the industries associated with them.

4 Define *labour supply*, and discuss the factors that affect the supply of labour.

5 What do you understand by the term *productivity of labour*? What are the factors that determine labour productivity?

6 Explain what is meant by *human resource development*. What factors contribute to human resource development?

7 Distinguish between *immigration* and *emigration*. What are the advantages and disadvantages of the migration of people from the Caribbean?

8 What are *trade unions*? List the different types of trade union. What are their functions?

9 (a) List *five* of the major resources of the Caribbean region.

(b) Select one of the resources you have named and explain how it has helped in the development of the country in which it is found.

(c) Outline two problems experienced in the development of the resource, and show how you would deal with one of these problems.

(CXC June 1985)

Chapter 3

The Scale and Location of Production

In this chapter we look at businesses of different sizes – cottage industries, small businesses and large-scale enterprises – and discuss their role in the economy. We also look at the effects of mechanization and automation, and at the linkages between industries, and the location of industries.

3.1 Cottage industries

Cottage industries are manufacturing activities which take place in people's homes or in small workshops close to or adjoining the house. For example, many people make jams, jellies and preserves in their homes and sell their output to supermarkets and grocery shops. Some aspects of the garment industry are also operated along the line of cottage industries. A firm usually provides the raw materials for people to make the products at home. For example, the smocking industry in Barbados and St Vincent is organized in this way. The yarn is provided to the workers who make the clothes and they are paid according to how many garments they make.

The advantages of a cottage industry:

1 There is no need for factory space, so costs are reduced.

2 The workers (many of whom are women) can do the job at the time that best suits them.

3 It provides self-employment for people who would otherwise be unemployed.

4 It provides extra income for people who may have a regular job and do the cottage activity in their spare time.

5 The equipment used is simple and inexpensive.

The disadvantages of cottage industries:

1 The business is quite small and cannot take advantage of economies of scale (see section 3.3).

2 The simple equipment does not provide the benefits of mechanization and automation.

3 The product may not be such good quality because of the equipment that is used. Where an employer gives out the work to different people, the quality can vary and the product will be difficult to standardize.

3.2 The role of the small business in the Caribbean economy

One step up from the cottage industry is the small business, which shares many of the characteristics of cottage industries. Small business can play a very important role in the development of the Caribbean countries. Because of the size of the economy of these countries, firms are not able to raise sufficient capital to establish large businesses, so the small to medium-sized business is the most important type of business organization. Their contribution to the generation of income in the economy and employment is recognized by the government. Most Caribbean governments have policies that encourage the establishment of small businesses.

Small businesses survive in the Caribbean for the following reasons:

1 They are family owned and operated, open longer hours and provide a more personalized service to their customers.

2 The owner of the small business is self-employed and works harder to make the business a success.

3 Large businesses grow out of small ones. Entrepreneurs usually establish a small firm initially because they have a limited amount of funds. Small businesses are also a way of trying out new ideas.

4 The small business may be the only viable business organization in many small towns and villages. The size of the market cannot support a big business. Also, certain types of business are difficult to manage on a large scale. If a firm becomes too large, it can become difficult to coordinate the activities of heads of departments and deal with rivalries among them. Rapid decisions may have to be made, for example in fashion-conscious industries, and the company's structure slows down the process.

5 Small businesses provide competition, and prevent large businesses from using their size to charge higher prices for their goods and services.

6 Like cottage industries, some small businesses are established to earn extra income for the owner or to provide self-employment and employment for the family.

7 Small businesses are actively encouraged by governments because they help to bring about a more equal distribution of income and wealth in the economy.

In spite of the merits of small businesses they have some disadvantages when compared with large firms (see below).

3.3 Large-scale production

As a firm expands, the cost of producing each unit of output declines. These reductions in cost are called *economies of scale*. Those economies that are due to changes in the internal structure of the firm as it expands are called *internal economies*. The cost reductions that arise because the entire industry grows are called *external economies*.

Internal economies

There are five types of internal economy:

Technical economies As the firm expands, it becomes more mechanized. For example, a soft drinks manufacturing firm may introduce machinery that handles two sets of bottles at the same time, so that the plant doubles the amount of soft drinks produced in the same period of time. However, the cost of operating the machinery will not double. Thus the average cost is reduced. The nature of technical economies depends on the goods that are produced. For example, technical economies will be achieved more easily in the manufacture of motor cars than in retailing.

Managerial economies Division of labour can be applied to management. The most suitable person will perform various management functions. For example, the small retailer who operates his own shop needs to perform management functions like ordering goods and keeping accounts as well as other functions like cleaning and selling goods. As the firm expands, the owner can specialize in the management functions, for example personnel and finance. If the firm becomes very large there can be further division of labour in management, with people responsible for sales, marketing, administration and purchasing. The gains from specialization would far outweigh the extra costs involved.

Commercial economies There are various types of commercial economy:

(a) *Purchasing* – as the firm expands its purchases it will receive discounts for buying in bulk.

(b) *Transport* – the firm can purchase its own trucks to do its collections and deliveries.

(c) *Selling economies* – if the sales staff are not fully utilized, sales can be increased at little extra cost. The firm can also reap economies on advertising by publicizing all of its products.

Financial economies A large firm is able to negotiate loans at more favourable rates of interest. It can also obtain money at lower cost in the financial markets.

Risk-bearing economies The large firm is in a better position to diversify its activities to guard against risk. For example, the large firm can produce a variety of products, so that if sales in one product decline, the other products can still contribute profit. In a large country a firm can have branches in different parts of the country, so if one makes losses it is unlikely that all will make losses at the same time. In the Caribbean some firms like Goddards Ltd (a Barbados-based firm) operate in different countries. The large firm can also diversify its sources of raw materials so that if there is a strike it can continue production.

External economies

Internal economies arise from the firm's deliberate action and are under its control. External economies arise out of the expansion of the industry as a whole and cannot be controlled by the individual firm.

External economies may arise from different sources. For example, if a large number of similar firms are located in the same area they can benefit each other. A skilled labour force is created, they can share common information services, roads can be improved and trade schools and better social services can be provided.

As the industry expands, specialist firms may be established to provide necessary services. For example, firms may be established to manufacture components, or provide transport and communications services. These services will be supplied at lower cost because they are provided by specialist firms. The specialist firms would be able to produce the services at lower cost because they are able to specialize in the activity they perform and hence reap the advantages of specialization and division of labour (see Chapter 1). For example, if trucking is performed by a specialist trucking firm, it can reduce costs by transporting the products of several firms at the same time.

Diseconomies of scale

Increases in cost as the firm expands its output are called *diseconomies of scale*. There are some disadvantages of large-scale production:

1 As the firm expands, it becomes so large that the general manager is unable to control the various activities of the firm properly. There can be disagreements between departments and information will not flow smoothly, resulting in higher costs.

2 Because of the size of the firm and the large amount of machinery, production becomes inflexible. As a result, the firm will be unable to respond readily to changes in demand for its products.

3 As the firm expands, the management loses touch with its customers.

4 As the firm expands its market share, more people know about it. It becomes more visible and as a result can, for example, be subject to government regulation like price controls, and closer scrutiny to prevent pollution. These measures may be costly to the firm.

3.4 Mechanization and automation

One of the consequences of an expansion in the size of a firm is greater mechanization and automation. *Mechanization* refers to the replacement of human and animal muscle power by machines to perform certain tasks in the production process. For example, people using hoes or animal-drawn ploughs may be replaced by a tractor to prepare the land and reap the crops. Mechanization is often very costly, but the benefits in terms of higher output per worker usually outweigh the costs.

Automation, on the other hand, refers to a process in which a number of tasks are performed by machines with a minimum of human interference. For example, in a soft drinks bottling factory the machines automatically wash the bottles, then move them along a conveyor belt where they are filled with soft drinks. The filled bottles are moved to another machine which puts on the cap. All the workers have to do is start the machinery. The increasing use of computers in the production process has resulted in more automated processes. It only needs someone to program the computer and the machinery will perform a variety of tasks and make minor corrective adjustments without human intervention.

The advantages of automation and mechanization:

1 Labour cost is reduced because fewer workers are needed to operate the machinery.

2 Output increases because the production process can be speeded up and there are fewer rejected products.

3 The increased output, along with the reduced labour cost, reduces the cost of the product to the consumer.

4 The tasks are performed more accurately because there is a reduction in human error. This results in a more standardized product.

5 Automation encourages further research and development (R & D) which can result in further improvements in technology.

The disadvantages of automation and mechanization:

1 They can lead to increased unemployment. As workers are replaced by machines, the workers who are made redundant may not be able to find new employment, especially if they are unskilled or the machines have eliminated the demand for their skills. For example, the increasing use of robots in the manufacture of cars in the USA has thrown many people out of work.

2 The machines need skilled technicians to install, operate and repair them. These skills are in short supply in the Caribbean.

3 Sophisticated machinery is very expensive, and firms have to make a large investment to install it.

4 Machinery is expensive, and many installations require a large output to operate efficiently, which may lead to a decrease in the number of small firms.

5 The technology is always changing and machinery can become obsolete quite quickly. Business people may not want to take the risk of buying expensive machinery which could become obsolete in a few years.

Some production processes use a large amount of capital and very little labour. This type of production is called *capital intensive* production. For example, the assembly of cars requires much capital and very little labour. On the other hand a production process that uses a large amount of labour and very little capital is called *labour intensive* production. For example, the growing of bananas is a labour intensive activity. The use of capital intensive techniques in Caribbean economies, which have an abundance of labour, would lead to greater unemployment. They could also lead to an unequal distribution of income since fewer workers will be employed at higher wages. An example of this is the production of oil in Trinidad, which is highly capital intensive. Only a limited number of workers are high wage earners. The combined effects of high unemployment and unequal distribution of income in any society can result in social unrest.

3.5 Industrial linkages

When one industry depends on the output of another industry there is an industrial linkage. For example, the tourist industry depends on the output of the agricultural industry to provide some of the food served to the tourists. There can be backward and forward linkages. For example, the production of dairy products depends on the agricultural industry. The agricultural industry in turn depends on feed mills to provide feed for the cows. These are examples of *backward linkage.* On the other hand the dairy sells its output to the ice-cream factory. The ice-cream factory in turn sells its output to restaurants. These are examples of *forward linkage.*

Industrial linkages are very important. The stronger they are, the greater is the effect on income of an increase in purchases by the final consumer. Strong linkages mean that the money spent by the consumer filters down to other producers in the economy. These are called *multiplier effects* because the increase in spending results in an increase in income which is larger than the original expenditure. Assume, for example, that more tourists come to a particular Caribbean country and spend more in restaurants on ice-cream. This would lead to greater demand for ice-cream from the ice-cream factory, which would demand more milk from the dairy. This increases income for the ice-cream factory and for the dairy. The dairy would have to demand more milk from the farmers, who would have to increase the number of cows and demand more feed from the feed mills. This increases income for the farmers and the feed factory. On the other hand, if the ice-cream has to be imported then there will be no increases in income for the dairy, the farmers and the feed mill because there are no linkages.

In the Caribbean the linkages between industries are not well developed because the countries import most of their raw materials. For economic development of the region it is necessary to develop better industrial linkages. However, there are some activities in which there are strong industrial linkages. These include:

1 The *sugar industry* which supplies molasses for making rubbing alcohol, rum and sugar for the candy industry. The bagasse from the sugar cane factory is also used to generate electricity and to make hardboard.

2 Several industries are linked to *oil production*, including plastics, vinyl, lubricating oil, kerosene, lighter fluid and aerosol sprays.

3 The output of the *cement factories* is used in the construction industry to build houses, bridges, roads and factories.

4 The output of the *forestry industry* is used in the furniture industry and the construction industry.

5 In the *agriculture industry*, dairy products are supplied to the tourist industry, although most of the milk processed by the dairies in the Caribbean is imported in powdered form (see above).

The development of industrial linkages between industries in the various Caribbean countries is very important. It would help the countries to utilize more effectively the limited resources they have. For example, the oil resources in Trinidad & Tobago can be used to provide energy to process Jamaican and Guyanese bauxite into aluminium products. Small-scale production of processed agricultural products in the Organization of Eastern Caribbean States (OECS) can be made internationally competitive, if raw or semi-processed materials from the various countries are produced into final products in one location. The countries have to produce goods in sufficiently large quantities if they are to break into international markets.

3.6 Industrial location

One of the important decisions the owner of a business has to make is where to locate the business. The firm has to weigh the advantages of a site over the costs of location. It does not make sense to locate a flour factory on a busy city street, because the rent will be too high and traffic congestion would make it difficult for the trucks transporting the unmilled wheat and the flour which is produced. On the other hand it would be advantageous to locate a department store on a busy city street, because there would be plenty of possible customers passing by.

Several factors influence the location of an industry:

Geographical Geographical factors like climate and the relief of the land are important. Certain crops need a special type of climate to grow well. For example, bananas need a lot of rainfall which explains why bananas are grown extensively in Grenada, Dominica, St Lucia and St Vincent, but not in Antigua and St Kitts. The slopes of the Blue Mountains in Jamaica are well suited for the production of high-quality coffee.

Raw materials In some industries the raw material is more bulky than the final product. For example, 6 tonnes of bauxite produces 1 tonne of alumina, so it would be more economical to locate the industry near to the raw material and transport the final product to the market.

Closeness to the markets For perishable and fragile products, and where the final product is bulkier than the raw material, it is more economical to produce them closer to the market. In the case of fragile products like glassware and china, the longer the distance over which they are transported the greater the chance of breakage. Perishable products like fresh fruits and vegetables may spoil if they are too far from the market.

Energy (power) Long ago, when coal was the most important source of energy to drive the machines in factories, it was necessary to locate industries near to the coalfields. Coal is very bulky and costly to transport. However, electricity can now be transported, and other sources of energy are used, so a location near to a source of energy is less important.

Infrastructure If an area does not have good roads and reliable water and electricity supplies, production will not be located there. Frequent power reductions and cuts and water shortages mean loss of production when the machinery stops. Breaks in power may also damage expensive equipment.

Cost of land Rent or the price of land close to populated areas is high and in the middle of a city can be very high. A firm must weigh the advantage of being close to the market against the rent it has to pay. If the benefits are not very great the firm may prefer to locate further away from the market to a place where rent is lower.

The supply of labour A readily available supply of industrial labour is an advantage to a firm, so it will try to locate close to a town where there is a good supply of industrial labour, especially if skilled labour is needed. Most of the industrial estates in the Caribbean are close to the cities.

External economies of scale Firms may choose to locate close to similar firms to reap external economies of scale (see section 3.3).

Government incentives Caribbean governments offer incentives to both local and foreign firms to set up in certain areas. The government offers tax incentives to firms to set up in an area where unemployment is high. Governments have built industrial parks (industrial estates) where factory spaces are provided for industries. In order to protect the environment, a government may also place restrictions on areas where certain firms cannot be established.

Although the other factors influencing industrial location are important, government incentives and restrictions may be the deciding factor in the choice of industrial location by a firm. Government restrictions cannot be ignored, and the incentives may have a significant effect on the profitability of the firm.

Key Points

- *Cottage industries* refers to production in the home, and like small businesses they help to increase the level of income and reduce the unemployment rate in the Caribbean.
- Large-scale production has many advantages which are referred to as *economies of scale*. There are internal economies due to the expansion of the firm and external economies which result from the expansion of the industry as a whole.
- The *diseconomies of scale* increase the average cost of the firm as it expands. These are the major disadvantages of large-scale production.
- Industrial linkages occur when one industry is dependent on another industry for its raw materials. When industrial linkages are strong, the effect on income of an increase in final demand for the product is greater. These effects on income are called *multiplier effects*.
- A number of factors influence *industrial location*. These include infrastructure, closeness to markets, raw materials and labour supply. In the Caribbean, the most important influence on industrial location is government restrictions and incentives.

Questions

1. What is a *cottage industry*? List the advantages and disadvantages of cottage industries.
2. Compare and contrast small business and large-scale production in the Caribbean.
3. Distinguish between *internal* and *external* economies of scale. Explain the different types of internal economies of scale.

4 Explain what is meant by *automation* and *mechanization*. What are the advantages and disadvantages of mechanization?

5 Explain the difference between *cottage industries* and *small businesses*. Give two examples of each of these in your country. Discuss the importance of one of these to the development of your country.

6 Distinguish between *backward* and *forward industrial linkages*. Identify industries and discuss the types of linkage that can be found in the Caribbean.

7 Discuss the factors that determine *industrial location* in the Caribbean. Identify three specific government incentives to influence the location of industry in your country.

8 (a) State *five* factors which would determine where an industry is to be located.

(b) Explain how two of these factors have influenced the location of any *one* industry in your country.

(c) Identify three problems which may result if the industry named in (b) is poorly located.

9 (a) Explain the term *small business* as used in the Caribbean, and give three examples to illustrate your answer.

(b) (i) Identify *three* problems affecting the development of small businesses in your country.

(ii) State *two* activities that have contributed to the development of small businesses in your country.

(c) Select two of the problems which you identified in question (b)(i) and for each problem suggest *two* measures you would recommend for dealing with it. Show how the economy would benefit from *one* of your suggestions.

Chapter 4 Business Organizations

A business organization is made up of a group of people who have pooled their talents and money to form a business. The business employs people with various educational and technical abilities to exploit commercial ventures for non-profit or profit motives. A business organization is goal-oriented. It monitors, controls and coordinates its activities.

4.1 Departments in a company

The major functional departments in a company are personnel, production, finance and marketing. These departments are headed by managers who perform special duties in the sense that they coordinate and execute the agreed policies of the board of directors of a company.

Personnel department

The personnel department is managed by a personnel manager whose functions include the following:

- to advise the company directors on all matters relating to the employment of staff
- to assist in the formation of company policies relating to staff, for example terms and conditions of employment, wages and salaries, health and safety at the workplace, recruitment and staff development
- to implement staff promotional policies agreed by the board of directors
- to select, train and advise a firm's employees
- to see that personnel records and employment statistics are maintained
- to represent the company on external committees and to state the company's position at wage bargaining negotiations with unions
- within limits set by the board of directors, to conduct on the company's behalf all negotiations dealing with wages, salaries, terms and conditions of employment
- to interview, screen and select employees for the various company jobs
- to dismiss employees formally from the company, with the board of directors' approval, whenever a situation warrants it.

Production department

The production department is engaged in the manufacturing or the transformation of raw materials into a saleable, social product. Production involves time, place, machinery, materials, labour, organization and knowledge.

In the Caribbean, the manufacturing of goods for sale is carried on in houses or factories. The making of goods in houses can be called *small-scale production*, for example of bread, sugar cakes, embroideries, leather sandals, chairs and paintings.

The making of goods in factories can be called *large-scale production*. Examples are car assembling, the processing of bauxite, cement and cement blocks, sugar, rum, paper and book publishing.

Finance department

In a company, finance is the concern of the finance or accounting department. The head of the accounting department is called a *financial controller*. Healthy business financing is the basis of economic activities. It is vital to the smooth operation and success of a business.

Business finance has two functional aims: executive and incidental. The *executive* finance function is responsible for the following:

- formulation of suitable policies for the management of assets and cash requirements
- determination of operational profit results
- evaluation of financial performances to judge how the firm has used its funds.

The *incidental* finance function deals with the following:

- the supervision of business transactions
- the safety of cash and securities
- the implementation of financial plans (budgets)
- the maintenance of records and the creation of financial reports for internal and external evaluations.

It is the combined practices of the executive and incidental finance functions that create growth or non-growth in firms in market economies.

Marketing department

What is marketing? Marketing is a process directed at satisfying customers' needs and wants through exchange transactions. It is also a process that seeks to identify, anticipate and satisfy customers' wants profitably.

The marketing department of a company is responsible for many interrelated activities:

1 Identifying marketing opportunities, through market research which seeks to find out the requirements and needs of the different types of customer.

2 Managing the product or products – the marketing department is responsible for forecasting and managing the rate of supply and distribution of the company's existing products. The department is also concerned in finding out what new products should be developed by the company and marketed in various places.

3 Choosing and motivating the channels of distribution – that is, the retailers who stock and sell the firm's products.

4 Advertising and promoting the firm's products – the aim is to encourage the potential buyer to become interested in buying the firm's products.

5 Setting prices and terms of supply, agreeing and setting market prices and credit terms which are negotiated with retailers, so that retailers are given adequate credit to encourage them to stock and sell quantities of goods.

6 Planning the market activity – the planning process will cover the following areas:

   (a) product development and market launching

   (b) yearly sales forecast which is linked to the firm's budgetary plans

   (c) yearly cash flow expenditure on advertising and promotion

   (d) the rates at which customers can be encouraged to pay for the goods they have received.

4.2 The forms of business organization

The main forms of business organization are:

- the sole trader or proprietor
- partnerships
- cooperatives

corporations or companies which can be classified as:

- private companies
- public companies
- conglomerates
- multinationals
- nationalized industries
- local and municipal authorities
- government departments.

The sole trader

A sole trader or proprietor is someone who owns his or her own business. Examples are shopkeepers, street vendors, plumbers, barbers, electricians, dentists, medical doctors, opticians, fishing boat owners, horticulturists.

The advantages of a sole trader's business:

1. It is usually small. It does not require a great deal of paper work to carry out its business affairs.
2. Capital is contributed by the sole trader to start up the business.
3. The sole trader is responsible and accountable only to him or herself.
4. The profits from the business at times are not subject to taxation. Any taxation is at the lower, personal income tax rates.
5. The sole trader interrelates with customers in a businesslike but friendly way.
6. The sole trader adopts a conservative, risk-minimizing strategy in all business dealings.
7. Decisions can be made quickly.

A sole trader

The disadvantages of the sole trader:

1 Unlimited liability for business debts – this means that a sole trader can be sued for any amount of money beyond that which he or she puts into a business. This can be compared with the principle of limited liability which means that a person can only be liable to the extent of the capital (money) he or she has contributed to the business.

2 Bank borrowing is restricted. Many Caribbean sole traders – for example the shopkeeper, street vendor, plumber, barber, the fishing boat owner – do not keep a formal set of accounts. This restricts their bank-borrowing ability, because banks and financial lending institutions require projections of cash flows, income and balance sheet statements before a decision is made on the repayment ability of the borrower.

3 The business usually ceases to exist at the sole trader's death.

4 One person carries out all tasks – that is, there is no division of labour.

5 Working hours are long.

6 Sickness may mean that the business runs into difficulties.

Partnerships

A business partnership is an agreement between two or more people who have consented to the same thing under a legal contract to operate a business with a view to making a profit. Examples of business partnerships can be found in the building, electrical and motor mechanical trades and in the accounting, legal and medical professions.

The advantages of a partnership:

1 It is easy to organize.

2 It is less expensive to form than a company.

3 It brings together more money, expertise and talent than is possible in a single proprietorship.

4 A partnership does not have excessive governmental supervision.

5 It is easier to dissolve and wind up than a company.

6 Decisions can be made quickly.

7 Duties can be specialized.

8 There are tax advantages.

9 A partnership is a good form of business organization for professionals.

The disadvantages of a partnership:

1 By law, each partner must contribute equally to losses unless the partnership agreement says otherwise.

2 Partners are not entitled to remuneration for their services unless this is stated in the partnership agreement.

3 Interest on the partners' capital – the money they contribute to form the business – is restricted by law to a fixed percentage.

4 Partners may disagree.

5 A partner cannot change the firm's policies fundamentally without the consent of the other partners.

6 There is unlimited liability for at least one partner.

Cooperatives

Cooperatives are formed by people who want to promote the economic interest of their members. They are of two types:

1 Members try to eliminate the profit of a middleman by combining the resources of the society to fix prices for social products and sell them direct to their members at prices that do not include a profit mark-up

percentage. Examples of this type are police and teachers' cooperatives.

2 Members pool their finances for the purpose of lending funds to their members for investment purposes. An example of this type is a credit union.

The advantages of a cooperative:

1 It is owned by those people who actually operate the cooperative whether it is a consumer or producer cooperative.

2 A person becomes a member of a cooperative by buying shares in it.

3 The cooperative is run by a management committee elected from among its members.

4 A cooperative may help in bringing order and control to volatile markets.

5 It is a medium through which government aid can be channelled.

The disadvantages of a cooperative:

1 It has a limited capital base.

2 It may be unable to attract highly qualified people.

3 As a result, it may suffer from amateurish direction and management.

Private companies

There are private limited and unlimited companies. It is rare to find unlimited companies in the Caribbean, so what follows refers to *limited* companies.

Private and public limited companies (see below) require at least two but not more than fifty people to form a company. These companies have a document called a *Memorandum of Association* which governs the company's relations with the outside world. It gives details of the company, for example its *name*, the *address* of its registered office, the company's *objectives*, a statement that the *liability* of its members is limited, the amount of the *share capital* to be issued and the *types of shares*. Such companies also have an article of association which controls the internal affairs of the company, for example meeting procedures, duties of the managing director, and borrowing powers of the company.

Private limited companies are owned by families. In such companies the family businesses and philosophies are passed on to descendants. Examples of Caribbean private companies are sugar plantations, the retail stores on the main streets of Caribbean cities, and country shops.

A private company has the following features:

- It excludes employees from membership.
- Its shares are not traded on the stock exchange (see below).
- Its owners are personally liable, in a limited way, for the debts of the business.
- It is unable to undertake major growth and investment plans because of its limited capital base.

The advantages of a private limited company:

1 It has limited liability.

2 The death of a shareholder does not affect the company.

3 Capital can be obtained from its members.

4 It has some privacy in its affairs.

The disadvantages of a private limited company:

1 Its shares are not transferable without the consent of the directors.

2 Its shares are not offered to the general public.

3 Because of the family structure of such companies, their entrepreneurial talent is drawn from a restricted pool.

4 Caribbean private limited companies do not engage in research – ie the continual search for improvements in current technology, and product or service improvement.

Public limited companies

A public limited company is one whose shares are listed on a stock exchange. It is owned by shareholders. The advantages of a public limited company:

1 It has continuous existence.

2 It is independent of its owners.

3 It is controlled by directors.

4 It has powers and limited liabilities distinct and separate from its owners.

5 It can only raise capital by a *flotation*, ie issue of shares to the public
6 It has plenty of expertise and talent at its disposal.
7 It is accountable to shareholders and to the society in which it operates.
8 The individual investor is safeguarded against unlimited liability for the company's debt.
9 The different types of shares attract a variety of investors.
10 Control and ownership are separated. Specialist and knowledgeable managers and directors are employed.
11 Small savers and employees are encouraged to invest in the company.
12 The shares of public companies are quoted on the stock exchange, so they can easily be converted to ready cash by investors who might want to sell them.
13 Such companies can enjoy economies of scale in their financial, managerial, marketing and technical functions.
14 Risk is spread over a wide number of people instead of one or two people (as is the case with the sole trader or partnership).

The disadvantages of a public limited company:

1 Some public limited companies grow too large, which can result in administrative difficulties and lack of coordination between departments.
2 Departmental politics and competition between departmental heads for leadership roles can hinder the company's progress.
3 Decisions are made by central management, and people at lower levels of management have no say in influencing company policy.

Conglomerates

A conglomerate is made up of a group of companies, each of which operates in different industries and markets. It has no common identity or purpose except in the pursuit of profit. Caribbean examples of conglomerates are the Barbados Shipping and Trading Company Ltd, Neil and Massey Holdings in Trinidad, the Eastern Caribbean Group of Companies in St Vincent, TDC Ltd in St Kitts-Nevis, and Grace Kennedy and Company Ltd in Jamaica.

Advantages of the conglomerate:

1 It spreads the risk of group failure over a range of industries.

2 It allows other companies to draw on the expertise and services of other companies in the group.

3 It enables the holding company to offset the tax losses of any of its companies.

4 It has a good cash position, since it is unlikely that all of its companies would be undergoing financial strain at the same time.

5 It provides opportunities for the training and transfer of staff between industries and functions.

6 It boosts morale among employees since there is scope for promotion.

7 Industries can advertise under the group name.

The disadvantages of a conglomerate:

1 It lacks a common objective.

2 Its diversified structure prevents sensible, comparative analysis between its constituent companies.

3 There may be resentment by subsidiary management of their performance evaluations by head-office staff.

4 Conglomerate executives may fail to evaluate subsidiary management decisions properly.

Multinationals

A multinational company has diverse activities and its subsidiaries operate in many other countries besides its country of origin. There are no multinationals based in the Caribbean but there are multinational companies operating in the Caribbean, for example Barclays Bank plc, Booker Tate plc, Cable and Wireless Co. Ltd, Geest Industries plc (all British companies), and also the Canadian Imperial Bank of Commerce, the Royal Bank of Canada, and the Bank of Nova Scotia (all Canadian).

The advantages of a multinational company:

1 It brings capital, technology and expertise to less developed countries.

2 It creates employment.

3 It implements sensible working techniques and budgets.

4 It provides markets.

The disadvantages of a multinational company:

1. It makes business decisions in a global context. This is considered a disadvantage because it may ignore the economic effects that such decisions will have on a particular country.
2. It may leave a country whenever the country's tax laws or political philosophies are in disagreement with its beliefs.
3. It may distort the indigenous culture of the host country by its business practices.
4. It repatriates a legally allowable part of its profits from the host country.
5. Its executives control the decision-making process in countries in which the multinational company operates.
6. It may manipulate transfer prices across borders. For example, it is in the interest of a multinational company to make as much as possible of its total gross profit in a country where taxes are low, and as little as possible in a country where taxes are high.
7. Multinationals may exploit the natural resources of small countries.

Nationalized industries

In a legal sense, nationalized industries are companies that control vital areas of an economy. The private management of such companies was taken over via government legislation, in order to achieve certain economic and political aims. Nationalized industries exist in some form in nearly all Caribbean countries. Examples are the bauxite industries in Guyana and Jamaica, sugar industries in Trinidad and St Vincent, electricity services in nearly all Caribbean countries, and Barbados Port Authority.

The features of nationalized industries

The duties of each industry are set out in separate nationalization statutes. These are generalizations on the social, industrial and commercial needs of the country. Each industry has a board of directors which is responsible for its day-to-day operations.

The composition of the board is decided by the government minister concerned. The board is required to present annual reports and accounts to the minister who in turn presents them to Parliament. That policy helps to make the industries accountable to the public.

Bauxite extraction in Jamaica

The government provides finance in the form of loans and grants to nearly all nationalized industries. This policy removes the threat and stigma of bankruptcy from managers of nationalized industries.

The advantages of nationalized industries:

1 If it is left in the hands of private firms, the production of some industries – for example water, gas, airport and port authorities – will be carried out in a haphazard way.

2 The key industries of a country, for example defence and police forces and industries which make weapons and ammunition, should not be managed by private companies but rather by nationalized firms operating under government supervision and control.

3 Government can coordinate production which results in economies of scale.

4 Unlike private, competitive firms, nationalized industries do not incur high advertising costs. Such high costs are a waste of resources.

5 Nationalized industries obtain better borrowing terms than private firms (mainly because of government guarantees).

The disadvantages of nationalized industries:

1 Many policies of nationalized industries lack initiative to improve products through the implementation of new techniques. Their major objective is to carry on business, not to make a profit.

2 Since most nationalized industries are monopolies, consumers are forced to accept whatever product or service is given.

3 Sensible cost comparisons cannot be made with similar private firms in the industry.

4 Stewardship accountability is lacking in nationalized industries.

Municipal authorities

Municipal authorities are enterprises run by locally elected councillors to operate such units as municipal swimming baths, theatres and community centres. Municipal authorities are found in Jamaica and in Trinidad & Tobago.

Municipal authorities obtain their capital by borrowing against the security of the rates they impose on households. They price their goods or services at a rate that recovers the operating costs, interest and capital repayments based on the life of the physical assets.

Government departments

From the point of view of business and general welfare concepts, government departments are involved in the following activities:

- activities that must be performed by the state
- activities that have been found to be best carried out by the state
- activities to help business people in their business affairs
- activities to maintain prosperity and economic well-being.

The first two concepts have already been discussed. Caribbean government departments which help businesses are the civil and aviation, finance and health departments respectively.

4.3 Government regulatory practices for setting up various forms of business

Any business organization that operates in the Caribbean must perform its duties in line with the legislation of Caribbean countries. Government regulatory practices pertain to the laws, rules and regulations which govern the setting up of Caribbean businesses. The sole trader in Barbados – for example the hawker, rum-shop keeper, fish-cake seller – only needs to acquire a licence to ply his trade, and this directs him or her where to trade. A sole trader in these categories acquires funds either by savings or loans from friends, since the capital outlay is small, in order to start up a business. Professional proprietors, for example accountants, architects, dentists, doctors and concrete block proprietors, in many cases start up their businesses by borrowing from banks or financial lending institutions. They obtain permission to operate their businesses by registering with their professional bodies. Examples of professional bodies in the Caribbean are the Barbados Medical Association, Jamaica Association of Certified Accountants, Bahamas Hotel Association, and the Bar Association of Trinidad & Tobago. Such bodies are given permission by governments to regulate and control their organization.

As a sole proprietorship grows, it may seek partnership status. This requires the pooling of funds, share issues to each partner and formalized partnership agreements. The funds that are needed to form the partnership will be obtained from each partner's contribution.

A partnership can be formed into a private or a public limited company. In this case the steps it takes to commence trading are as follows:

1 The promoters need to find one other person who is prepared to sign a Memorandum of Association.

2 The company must be given a name. The terms *Limited (Ltd), Private Ltd* or *Public Ltd* must be used after its name.

3 The address of the company's registered office must be given.

4 The objects of the company – what the company will do – must be stated. The objects form the legal basis for the company's activities. The company will have to keep its trading activities within the fields specified (usually the objects are many) or the courts may rule them *ultra vires* (beyond the powers). The place where the company is established must also be stated.

5 A statement must be made that the liability of the members is limited.

6 The promoter should state the amount of share capital to be issued, and the type of shares. Private limited share capital will be restricted to the company's members. Public limited share capital will be issued to the public.

7 An undertaking must be given by the signatories that they do desire to be formed into a registered company. They must also undertake to purchase the number of shares against their names.

8 The company must have an *Article of Association*. This is a document that controls the internal affairs of a company.

9 Together with the Memorandum of Association, the Article of Association, and a statement of its nominal capital, the company must be registered with the Registrar of Companies, who in turn will

issue a Certificate of Incorporation. That document bestows upon a company a separate legal personality.

Before a company can begin trading it must secure the capital it needs. With a private limited company the capital will be contributed by the founder members. With a public limited company, the capital will be contributed by the general public.

Figure 4.1 shows the stages of a sole trader's development into a public limited company.

Figure 4.1 The stages of a sole trader's development into a public limited company

Sole trader establishes business. Works hard. Is aided by spouse. Sells goods or services at a profit. Banks some of the profits.

↓

Decides to form a private limited company.

↓

Issues shares to him or herself, relatives and friends after explaining to them and convincing them of the product's or service's growth potential.

↓

The business expands. The company now diversifies into the making of other products.

↓

A decision is taken to form a public limited company.

↓

The new company seeks a stock exchange quotation.

→

The stock exchange agrees to a quotation of the company shares after its rules are complied with.

↑

Company issues prospectus inviting the public to buy its shares.

↑

Shares are issued.

↑

Sales and profits are made. Dividends are declared and paid.

↑

At annual general meetings, directors report on their stewardship.

↑

The results are reflected in the rise or fall of share values in the market via stock exchange quotations.

For cooperative societies there is the Cooperative Societies Act which generally provides for the following:

1 The word *cooperative* shall form part of the name of every society and the word *limited* shall be the last word in the name of every society with limited liability.

2 Every registered society shall have perpetual succession and a common seal and power to hold real and personal property.

3 In the case of a society registered with unlimited liability, a member shall not transfer any share held by him or his interest in the capital of the society or any part thereof, unless (a) he/she has held such share or interest for not less than one year, and (b) the transfer or change is made to the society or to a member of the society or to a person whose application for membership has been accepted by the Committee.

4 The policies and practices of cooperatives should be in harmony with the overall economic development goals of the country.

5 Cooperatives should carry out their functions in accordance with the sensible business conventions.

6 The executive members should be accountable to the cooperative's members.

7 There should be rotation of the cooperative's directors, to guard against the monopolization of power by a group of members.

8 Timely, yearly accounts of cooperative societies should be presented to the Registrar of Cooperatives and members.

9 Qualified auditors should be appointed to verify the validity of the accounts.

10 An amount of money should be carried to a reserve fund from the cooperative society's yearly net profits.

11 The remainder of such profits and any profits of previous years available for distribution may be divided in a specified manner among the members by way of dividend or bonus.

12 The amount of money that a cooperative society can contribute to any charitable purpose is specified.

13 There is a limit on the amount of share capital that a member should have.

4.4 The daily operating procedures of organizations

The methods of running the various forms of organization differ in detail and even in substance. For example, the daily operation of a small proprietary firm differs from that of a company. The small proprietor conducts business mainly by word of mouth and relies on memory as to what was agreed, disagreed, ordered, arranged and paid for.

The daily operating procedures of a partnership will depend on its business. In a medical partnership, for example, the operating procedures of the partners will depend on their specialism. In a trading venture partnership of two people, there can be divisions of labour where, for example, a partner can act as an executive manager, ordering goods and looking after the daily financial side of the business, while the other partner performs general duties, for example serving customers.

Important daily operating procedures in any partnership are the recording of monetary business transactions in formal accounting books. This is done not only to have a record of current transactions for stewardship purposes, ie accountability, but also to enable the profit or loss of the business to be apportioned between the partners at periodic intervals.

The daily operating procedures of cooperatives will also depend on the kind of work in which they are engaged. A consumer cooperative will deal with the provision of items such as food or timber for its members in an effective way. A financial cooperative will advise members on credit arrangements and make investment decisions about the members' funds it has at its disposal. The recording in formal accounts of the funds received from members and the investments made with their monies will also be a daily operating procedure of a financial cooperative. In other cooperatives, for example service and workers' cooperatives, daily operating procedures will be based on their specific functions.

The daily operating procedures of private and public limited companies, conglomerates, multinationals, government departments and nationalized industries have similar features. Such companies make many daily transactions, so they place people in authority to do their business, for example to answer correspondence, receive and sell goods, pay wages and do their accounts. The head office of a multinational company will also contact its dependencies on a daily basis to ensure that their production plans are in line with its overall production strategy. Such action is necessary in order to plan effectively.

The daily operating procedures of municipal authorities are ensuring that the business activities undertaken by them are carried out sensibly and in accordance with their rules.

4.5 The calculation of traditional accounting profit or loss

Profit or loss as described here relates to the *traditional accounting* (also known as *historical cost accounting*) concept of its calculation, where no adjustments are made to a firm's accounts for inflation or deflation. A profit or loss of a business is usually calculated at discrete time periods. The profit or loss calculations by a business or proprietor are based on transactions with external parties as a result of operational activities. The transactions relate generally to revenues received from the sale of goods or services and the various costs incurred in achieving those sales. The recorded costs are analysed and segregated and those costs which can sensibly be attributed to the revenue of the period are matched with it. Those costs which cannot be matched are carried forward to future periods to be matched with the associated revenues. An allocation process also takes place, for example the writing off of depreciation in the profit or loss statement of some value of the physical assets (machine cars, equipment). Figure 4.2 shows in a simple way how traditional accounting profit is calculated.

Figure 4.2 Calculation of traditional accounting profit

Profit statement, Period 1

	$	$
Sales		10,000
Less operating costs	7,000	
Depreciation	500	(7,500)
Accounting profit		2,500

Notes The statement is also called a revenue statement or a profit or loss statement.
A loss would be shown if the sum of operating costs and depreciation charge was greater than sales.

4.6 Procedures for profit or loss distribution in various forms of business

When small proprietors – for example hawkers, butchers, kitchen gardeners – make a profit via cash transactions, it is kept. No taxes are deducted from it. Losses on trading are borne by them.

Professional proprietary firms – for example florists, doctors, dentists, minibus owners, concrete-works owners and accountants – by law are required to keep a formal system of accounts. When such firms make a profit on trading, part of it is distributed to the government tax department, to banks or financial institutions, in the form of interest charges and the repayment of principal. Part of it is also distributed to savings accounts. Losses on trading are borne by them.

Partnership businesses distribute a part of their profits to the partners in agreed profit sharing ratios, and to the tax department.

Partnership losses on trading are also shared in the agreed sharing ratios in every case except one. The exception is that if a partner is insolvent, the loss on the personal account of the insolvent partner must be shared between the solvent partners not in the normal profit/loss sharing ratios but in proportion of their last agreed capitals.

Profit distribution in private limited and public limited companies goes

(a) to their shareholders (both ordinary and preference and founding members) in the form of dividends

(b) in some cases to employees in the form of bonuses and cash for the buying of company shares

(c) in taxes to government tax departments, and in interest charges to banks or financial institutions

(d) to revenue reserves for precautionary, speculative or re-investment purposes.

Losses are borne by the company, ie shareholders.

Not all the profits made by cooperatives are distributed to their members. This is so because of the law which regulates the activities of cooperatives. For example, Section 35(1) of the Barbados Cooperative Act 1951 states:

> 'at least one-fourth of the annual net profits of every registered society, as ascertained by the audit prescribed by Section 36, shall be carried to a fund to be called a reserve fund, which shall be employed as prescribed by the rules.'

Section 35(2) states:

> 'The remainder of such profits and any profits of previous years available for distribution may be divided among the members by way of dividend or bonus or allocation to any fund constituted by the society to such an extent or under such conditions as may be prescribed by the rules of bye-laws, provided that, in the case of a registered society with unlimited liability no distribution of profits shall be made without the general or special order of the registrar.'

Section 35(3) states:

> 'any registered society may, with the sanction of the registrar, after one-fourth of the annual net profits in any year has been carried to a reserve fund, contribute an amount not exceeding 10 per cent of the remaining net profit to any charitable purpose.'

The losses of cooperatives are borne by their members. Other Caribbean countries have their own legal Acts.

Profit distribution in nationalized companies goes to the government treasury departments where it is pooled with other funds. Government funds are used for the general welfare of society. Losses of nationalized industries are borne by the state.

Multinationals' profit distributions go:

(a) to the taxation department of the country in which the multinational is trading

(b) to its headquarters in the form of dividends

(c) to its employees in the form of bonuses and loans and

(d) to charitable institutions in the countries in which they operate.

Losses are borne by the company's shareholders.

4.7 Formal and informal organizations

Organizations are structures that achieve their objectives via human effort and communication. Human organization is not strictly homogeneous (ie consisting of people of like nature), so both formal and informal organization exists in businesses.

Formal organizations are represented by static organization charts, by official standards, statements and procedures. Further, they are characterized by hierarchical structures, status relationships and defined objectives. Examples of formal organizations are the army, business firms, colleges, churches, hospitals and universities. Organizations can also be characterized as normative, instrumental and coercive. Examples of *normative* organizations are charitable organizations and professional bodies. Examples of *instrumental* organizations are business organizations, travel clubs and mercenary armies. Examples of *coercive* organizations are prison, or a conscript army.

Informal organization is the unofficial, social interaction, behaviour, relationships and agreements that exist between some members of an organization at the workplace. Informal organizations arise from the inadequacy of the formal organization to satisfy every human whim within an organization. Informal organization can also arise from a group having different educational, ideological and social backgrounds from those people who maintain the formal system. Examples of informal organizations include groups of trade union members who ignore union rules, and employees who restrict their output.

An inevitable feature of an organization, especially an instrumental one, is its hierarchical structure, with people placed in positions of authority to carry out organization objectives. Their function is to encourage interdepartmental coordination, control and planning. Hierarchical relationships which operate perpendicularly – that is, orders for pursuing organizational goals are given through authoritative channels, for example from an executive director to a head of a department who in turn gives the order to a superintendent – are known as *line relationships*. An organization which operates in such a way is known as a *line organization*.

Line organizations

The term *line organization* describes functions that contribute directly to the provision of goods and services to the customer, for example production and sales. It also describes the authority and relationships – the chain of command within an organization.

The advantages of line management:

1 The problem of authority is defined so that each person in the organization knows the superior to whom he or she reports and takes instructions from, and the superior knows the subordinate for whom he or she is responsible.

2 The various organizational activities which need to be done repeatedly are systematically allocated throughout the organization to ensure that the whole is integrated and that there is no duplication.

3 Obstacles to sensible communication are avoided because there is a clear line through which each item of information must pass.

4 Duplication of information is avoided as each person receives only data which are relevant to his or her function.

The disadvantages of line management:

1 Executives are over-burdened with administrative work.

2 Specialization of duties is ignored.

Figure 4.3 shows an organization chart based on the line concept. It shows a chain of command and the direct lines of delegation and responsibility. For example, the works manager is responsible to the managing director for all activities within his or her sphere. The work for which the works manager is responsible is delegated to those people who are answerable to him/her – the production controller, production manager and works engineer. The last two also delegate work to the shop foremen and the service foremen.

All authority and responsibility rests with the managing director who is accountable to the board of directors. A board of directors is concerned with organizational policy, the managing director with planning and control, and the managers with work execution and accomplishments.

Figure 4.3 Organization chart based on the line concept

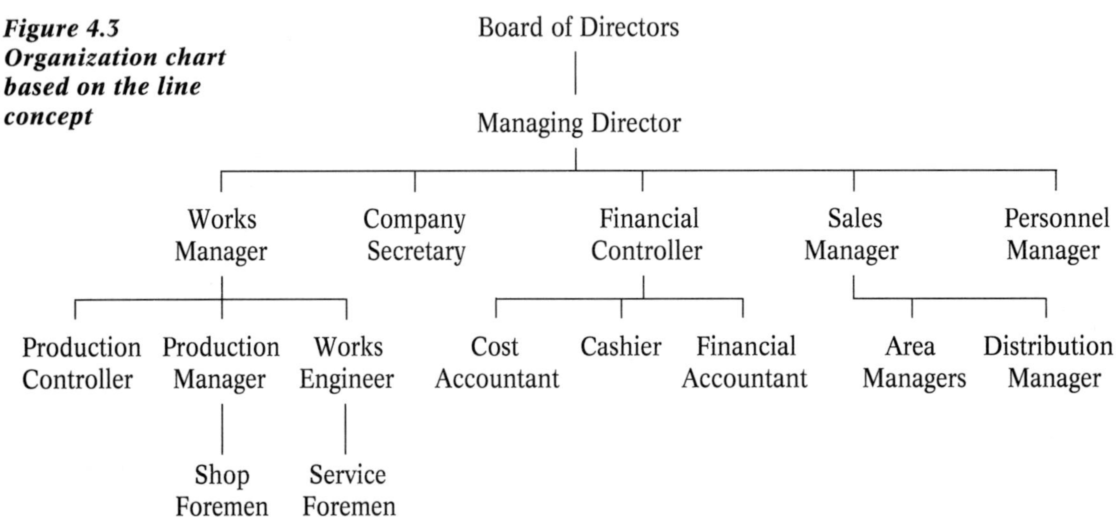

Functional organizations

Functional organization structures are based on a downward flow of authority for each specialized activity or function. Functional authority means that a specialist manager can exercise authority over others, including other managers, in respect of his or her specialist area of responsibility. A good example of a department that exercises functional authority is the personnel department which has functional responsibility for many people and for industrial relations within an organization.

The advantages of a functional organization:

1 It obtains the benefits of specialization.

2 Expert advice is available.

The disadvantages of a functional organization:

1 Employees have more than one supervisor.

2 There may be conflicts owing to the overlapping of authority.

Figure 4.4 shows the situation where a company is organized functionally for financial control purposes.

Figure 4.4
A functional chart for financial control

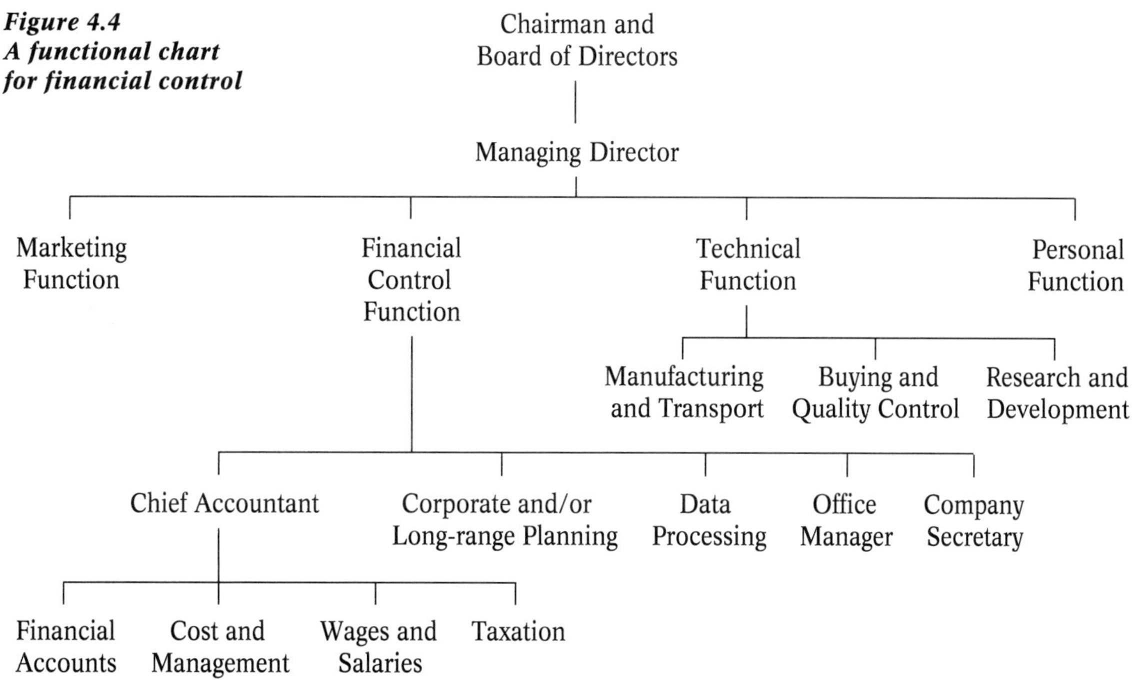

Staff functions

As they grow, all organizations require the services of a variety of experts to carry out advisory duties. These *staff functions*, while they are necessary to an organization, are not all directly connected with production, distribution or marketing of the organization's goods or services. Some examples of staff people in an organization are:

- cost and financial accountants, who analyse cost and financial information and make recommendations to managers
- architects/consultants, who give advice on the construction of buildings
- the maintenance engineer in a chemical plant
- economists, who advise managers on economics
- legal counsels, who advise managers on legal matters.

Staff people advise line managers. A staff person does not have the authority to direct subordinates unless a line manager delegates that responsibility to him or her.

The advantages of staff in an organization:

1. They provide a service from which the whole organization benefits.
2. Staff departments have a control function. In such a capacity they will introduce a system and ensure that the system is used sensibly throughout the organization.
3. Specialists advise the line managers, but employees report to the line manager.

The disadvantages of staff in an organization:

1. There may be conflicts between line and staff unless relationships are made clear.
2. Line managers' authority and responsibility are curtailed by the appointment of specialists.
3. Specialists speak a different language and use sophisticated techniques that are not understood by the layman.

Figure 4.5 shows a line and staff organization chart.

Figure 4.5 Line and staff organization in a firm

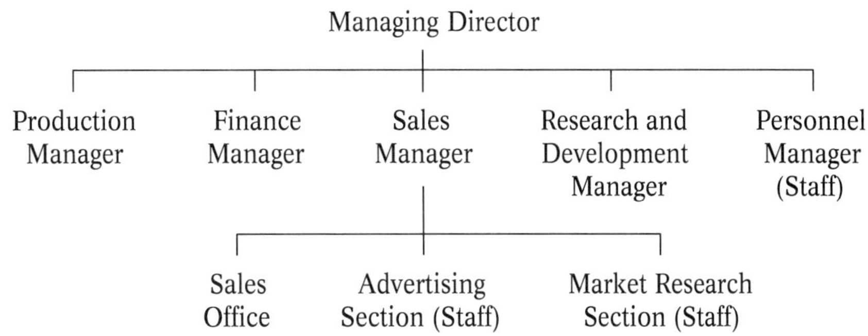

Committees

A committee is made up of a group of people who have been formally appointed to examine a problem and to suggest solutions to the problem. It is a form of delegation. A committee has authority and responsibility. Committees are widely used in businesses, churches, government departments and universities. A committee is usually headed by a Chairman.

A *standing committee* has a permanent role within an organization. It meets at regular intervals, for example weekly or monthly. An *ad hoc committee* is set up for a specific purpose. It has no routine work. When its task is finished the ad hoc committee is disbanded.

The advantages of committees:

1 They allow specialists to come together and their diverse knowledge can be applied to a problem.

2 Working in a group can stimulate creativity. An idea put forward by one member can generate a different idea in another member.

3 They provide an avenue through which the views of subordinates can be known.

4 They allow members to participate in the decision-making process.

The disadvantages of committees:

1 They are slow in making decisions.

2 Committee decisions are arrived at through compromises or by a dominant group rather than by a rational route.

3 They use specialists' time ineffectively and are costly.

4 Committee members are able to avoid individual responsibility for the outcome of a decision.

Span of control

The term *span of control* refers to the concept of how many subordinates should report to a manager or superior. The current attitude is that there is a limit in each management field to the number of subordinates that a supervisor can manage.

The span of control is *wide* where the need is to supervise a large number of subordinates carrying out routine tasks in one place. The span of control is *narrow* where the need is to supervise a specialized group of subordinates who are working in different places. Mass assembly operations located in one factory result in a wide span of control. A highly technical organization has a narrow span of control. Figures 4.6 and 4.7 show these forms.

Figure 4.6 An organization where the span of control is wide

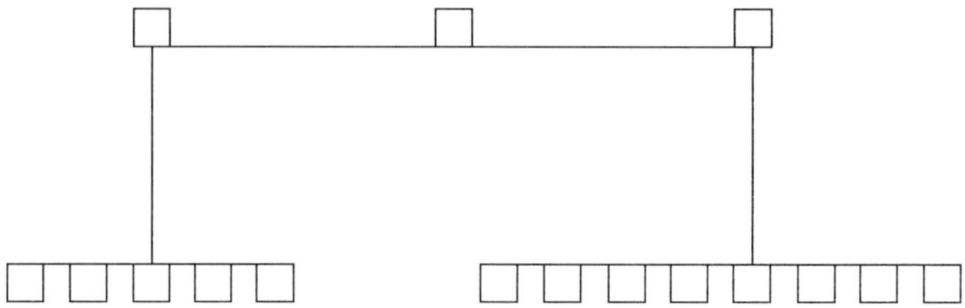

Figure 4.7 An organization where the span of control is narrow

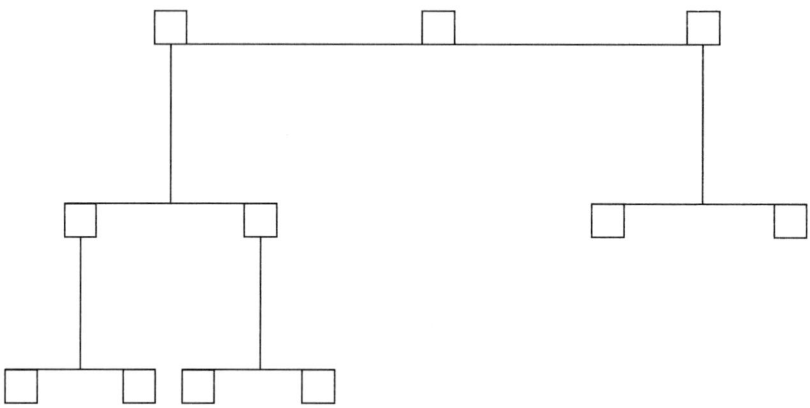

4.8 Growth effects in an organization

Growth means expansion. For example, a small proprietor might want to expand his business, or a large firm may want to capture additional markets. Some firms are motivated to expand because growth brings prestige and additional profits, and is a protection against contraction and decay.

Growth in an organization creates the need for the following:

1 An increase in capital investment – the buying of physical assets, for example buildings, land, machinery.

2 New functional departments such as accounting, engineering, personnel, legal, marketing, production and research to perform specialized duties.

3 The specialization or division of labour associated with the new functional departments.

4 An increase in control. New duties and authoritative positions will be given to management personnel who will exercise control over the organization and who will be held accountable for their actions.

Growth in an organization creates the need for delegated authority. Continual communication on business matters will have to take place between the new functional departments mentioned in order to ensure sensible coordination of organization activities.

Key Points

- A business organization is made up of a group of people who have pooled their talents and money to form a business. The business employs people with various educational and technical abilities to exploit commercial ventures for non-profit or profit motives.
- The major functional departments in a company are personnel, production, finance and marketing.
- The forms of business organizations are sole trader or proprietor, partnerships, cooperatives, corporations or companies, nationalized industries, local and municipal authorities, and government departments.
- Any business organization that operates in the Caribbean must perform its duties in line with the legislation of Caribbean countries.
- The daily operation of a small proprietary firm differs from that of a company. The small proprietor conducts business mainly by word of

mouth and relies on memory as to what was agreed, disagreed, ordered, arranged and paid for.

- The daily operation of a partnership depends on its business. The daily operating procedures in any partnership are the recording of monetary business transactions in formal accounting books.
- A consumer cooperative's daily operating procedures are taken up with the provision of services for its members. A financial cooperative's daily operating procedures are taken up with advice to members on credit arrangements and with investment decisions on the members' funds.
- The daily operating procedures of private and public companies, of conglomerates, multinationals, government departments and nationalized industries are taken up with correspondence, receiving and selling goods or services, accounting and production planning.
- The daily operating procedures of municipal authorities are ensuring that the business activities undertaken by them are carried out sensibly and in accordance with their rules.
- The profit or loss calculations by a business or proprietor are based on transactions with external parties as a result of operational activities.
- When a small proprietor makes a profit, he or she keeps it. No tax is deducted from it. Losses on trading are borne by the proprietor.
- When professional proprietary firms make a profit on trading, part of it is distributed to government tax departments, to banks or financial institutions in the form of interest charges and the repayment of principal.
- Partnership businesses distribute a part of their profits to the partners in agreed profit sharing ratios, and to the tax department. Partnership losses on trading are also shared in the agreed sharing ratios in almost every case.
- Profit distribution in private limited and public limited companies goes to

  (a) shareholders (both ordinary and preference and founding members) in the form of dividends

  (b) in some cases to employees in the form of bonuses and cash for the buying of company shares

  (c) in taxes to government tax departments, and in interest charges to banks or financial institutions

(d) to revenue reserves for precautionary, speculative or re-investment purposes.

Losses are borne by the company shareholders.

- Not all the profits made by cooperatives are distributed to their members because the law regulates the activities of cooperatives. The losses of cooperatives are borne by their members.
- Profit distribution in nationalized companies goes to the government treasury departments where it is pooled with other funds. Losses of nationalized industries are borne by the state.
- Profit distributions of multinationals go

  (a) to the taxation departments of the country in which the multinational is trading

  (b) to its headquarters in the form of dividends

  (c) to its employees in the form of bonuses and loans and

  (d) to charitable institutions in the countries in which they operate.
- Organizations are structures that achieve their objectives via human effort and communication.
- Formal organizations are represented by the static organization chart, by official standards, statements and procedures.
- The informal organization is the unofficial social interaction, behaviour, relationships and agreements that exist between some members of an organization at the workplace.
- Informal organizations arise from the inadequacy of the formal organization to satisfy every human whim within an organization.
- An inevitable feature of an organization, especially an instrumental one, is its hierarchical structure with people placed in positions of authority to carry out organization objectives.
- Hierarchical relationships which operate perpendicularly are known as *line relationships*.
- *Span of control* refers to the concept of how many subordinates should report to a manager or superior.
- Some firms are motivated to expand because growth brings prestige and additional profits, and is a protection against contraction and decay.

Questions

1 What is a business organization?

2 List the major functional departments in a company and explain their functions.

3 Explain the function of the personnel manager.

4 What does *production* mean? Give examples.

5 Explain the function(s) of the finance department.

6 State the main objectives for the evaluation of marketing activities.

7 List the advantages and disadvantages of the following types of organization:
(a) sole trader
(b) partnership
(c) companies
(d) cooperative societies
(e) nationalized industries
(f) conglomerates
(g) multinationals.

8 (a) Explain the various ways in which businesses are started.
(b) Discuss the role played by the rule of law in their start-up and business activities.

9 Explain why the daily running of a proprietary firm differs from that of a company or a municipal undertaking.

10 Briefly explain how traditional accounting profit is calculated.

11 Explain the procedures for profit or loss distribution in the various forms of business.

12 What are formal and informal organizations? Explain.

13 What does the term *functional specialization* mean?

14 What are the advantages and disadvantages of line management?

15 Distinguish between *line* and *staff* relationships.

16 What does the term *span of control* mean?

17 Draw a chart of a marketing department which shows the following lines of authority:

(a) the sales department reporting to the sales manager

(b) the sales office reporting to the sales administrator

(c) the market research, market analysis and forecast departments and advertising departments reporting to the marketing manager

(d) the managers and sales administrator of the divisions reporting to the sales director.

18 Modify the chart drawn in question 17 to show the following:

(a) the sales director reporting to the managing director

(b) the sales department and sales office reporting to the sales director

(c) the marketing department reporting to the marketing manager

(d) the sales director and marketing manager reporting to the managing director.

19 It has been stated that organization charts are caricatures of organization structures. Do you agree? Discuss.

Chapter 5 Money, Capital and the Financial Sector

Money, capital and the financial sector create a great deal of business and non-business activity which influences all human behaviour. They are very important in the Caribbean economy.

5.1 The characteristics, functions and importance of money

> 'Money is nothing other than a transferable acknowledgement of a debt, a promise to pay, arbitrarily created and usually with an indeterminate maturity and exchange value. Any such acknowledgement of debt which is put into circulation and used directly as a means of payment for goods or services is money.'
>
> Jacques Ribout, *The Mechanics of Money*, St Martin Press, 1980

> 'For money gives no information about itself, except that it is money. In revealing itself as money it is nothing more than a cultural tautology.'
>
> Thomas Crump, *The Phenomenon of Money*, Routledge and Kegan Paul, 1981

Money in its earliest form was a ritual which became institutionalized. Thus money can be seen as an institution. Because the circulation of money represents a system of social and economic interaction, money can be regarded as a symbolic system.

The use of money can be seen from its payment function. Payment is the transfer from one person (the *payer*) to another person (the *payee*) of an interest which is always expressed as a multiple of a recognized unit with its own name. Money is the means which represents this interest and enables payment to be made. It is the nature of money to be used for an indefinite succession of payments, ie to circulate freely without being subject to any sort of loss of function.

Money is made of some recognizable substance which has certain attributes such as durability, divisibility, portability, uniformity and inelasticity of supply. *Inelasticity of supply* means that the total money supply held by all transactors is maintained at a constant level with only a small increase of new money.

Money is the most generally recognized token of wealth. It is the universal medium of business transactions. It is a prized possession with many social implications. Its main characteristics and functions are as follows:

It is a means of payment This function is essential to any system based on the circulation of money.

It is a standard of deferred payment The money system provides a standard of deferred payments which enable individuals and companies to record debts and eventually to collect them either in one payment or in a series of payments.

It is a unit of account The function of money as a unit of account is to relate transactions to a numerical scale. The object of doing so is to establish the relative monetary position of different transactions, in which case the unit of account provides the basis for scriptural money. Scriptural money is simply the amount of money held by any transactor recorded in a book-keeping system. It has many advantages over actual physical money (coins, notes) when it comes to dealing with large sums of money over long distances.

It is a medium of exchange Different classes of things may be exchanged with each other. If exchange lies at the foundation of any economic system, then the function of money as a medium of exchange is essential to any economic use of money. It is claimed that this function developed in response to the demands of long-term trade. This function establishes a relationship between things. It is credit which establishes a bond between people.

It is a store of wealth The function of the store of wealth represents the future potential of money for making payments. Money between payments is a store of wealth for whoever happens to hold it.

It is a measurement tool Measurement is not only the assignment of values (eg dollars) to objects but also involves monetary calculations about past (*retrospective*) conditions and events, about present (*contemporary*) conditions and events and about future (*anticipatory*) conditions and events. Obviously money measurements enable individuals, companies and corporations to know their financial position at a point in time. Money measurements also enable comparative financial positions to be made among companies and individuals. Seen in this light it can be used to show status relationships. Note that past and present monetary calculations are verifiable and can provide beliefs on which a decision may be made but that hypothetical monetary calculations are always non-factual.

5.2 The functions and services of commercial banks

What is a commercial bank? It is an institution that deals with money matters. It satisfies the central bank of a country (see section 5.8) as to its reputation, confidence and ability in carrying out sensible financial policies which have a favourable effect on a country.

Commercial banks play a vital role in a country's economy. They receive money deposits from customers and are responsible for the circulation of the money supply.

1 Commercial banks provide the following services:

A bank is a safe place in which customers can place surplus funds in the form of personal saving accounts and fixed deposits. Fixed deposits receive a rate of interest and must be deposited for a specific time period. Interest is also given on savings accounts. The interest rate of a deposit account is greater than that of a savings account.

2 Through their current accounts system, commercial banks act as agents of payment for customers. Holders of such accounts are provided with cheque books from which they issue cheques for various sums when paying creditors.

3 Commercial banks lend to customers after obtaining some form of security or collateral in one of two ways:

(a) loans for the purchase of items such as cars, land and household appliances

(b) overdrafts – these permit a bank customer to overdraw a specified sum on his/her current account. A customer is required to pay interest on the exact amount overdrawn, for the number of days that it is overdrawn.

4 Commercial banks assist the business estate by discounting bills of exchange for traders. By discounting bills – that is, making payment to a creditor – the bank enables the creditor to be paid at once and at the same time allows the debtor a period of credit. This is another form of bank lending.

5 Commercial banks offer credit card facilities to trustworthy customers. These cards enable holders to obtain credit up to a certain limit in terms of goods or services from certain specified places.

6 Commercial banks also provide night-safe facilities to special customers, for example shopkeepers, restaurateurs and night-club owners who are unable to go to the bank during its normal working hours.

7 Commercial banks maintain a standing order system by which fixed monthly or yearly amounts can be transferred regularly to a named creditor of a current account holder on a given date. For example, on a customer's request through signed documents, the banks will pay insurance premiums, mortgages, gas, electricity and telephone bills and hire purchase instalments at regular intervals.

8 Commercial banks provide banker's draft facilities in making payments for a customer to foreign creditors (see page 173).

9 Commercial banks negotiate investments for customers through their brokers (see page 94).

10 Commercial banks act as executors and trustees for people who wish to leave their possessions to other people.

11 Commercial banks provide a service for customers by keeping for them in their vaults important documents, for example title deeds to property, wills, codicils, trust deeds, life insurance policies and expensive jewellery.

12 Commercial banks have a specialist section which deals with foreign exchange. This section (a) assists customers with foreign exchange rates – that is, the conversion of a country's currency to foreign currency and vice versa and (b) arranges for foreign currency (with central bank approval) to be made available to business people who are negotiating business deals abroad.

13 Commercial banks buy government securities. In this way they provide government with finance.

14 Commercial banks provide credit rating reports to customers. A credit rating is a certificate as to a firm's or an individual's solvency position. Commercial banks are able to do that as a result of the accumulated data they have.

15 Commercial banks operate a cash dispenser service which pays out a controlled sum of cash to current account customers from a cash dispensing machine. The machine is linked to a computer in an on-line system. Automatic money transfers can also be made between customers' accounts and those machines.

5.3 Sound money management

Sound money management is *a sensible way of spending and investing money*. The Caribbean adage 'to cut and contrive' is apt. At a personal level this means that one's money payments (assuming one is earning money) should be less than or equal to one's wages (income). In relation to a company it means that a company's payments (expenses) should be less than or equal to its income (receipts from sales and services).

Sound money management involves putting money accumulated from savings and from company profits into worthwhile projects, successful businesses and accredited business ventures.

A cash budget is essential to sound money management, whether for an individual, a company or a government. A personal cash budget is a carefully thought-out plan, documented or existing in one's mind, on how you plan to use your money during a specific period. A company's cash budget is a quantitative plan of sales and expenditures which a company plans to incur for a specific budgetary period. A cash budget has two goals:

1 It provides a standard against which the actual results of the plan can be judged.

2 It helps the individual or company to monitor and even, if plans are proceeding badly, to adjust its actions during the budget period. Table 5.1 is a monthly cash budget for a family that has an income of $12,000 a year.

The table opposite shows that for that particular month the family has exceeded its budget. The difference between the two columns 'Estimates' and 'Actual' is known as an accounting variance, which can either be favourable (see entertainment, for example) or adverse (see food, electricity, telephone, children's pocket money, for example). The global or overall adverse variance is $100.

Table 5.1
A family cash budget (\$ per month)

	Estimates	Actual
Food	340	400
Mortgage	250	250
Land rates	30	30
Entertainment	20	15
Cooking gas	40	40
Electricity	100	140
Insurance and medicals	100	100
Telephone	30	35
Water rates	30	30
Savings	20	0
Children's pocket money	40	60
	1,000	**1,100**

5.4 The sources and types of capital open to businesses and to individuals

The word *capital* is a confusing term. In practice one hears about capital stock, capital gains and losses, capital reserves and working capital, so a working definition is needed here. The term capital as used in this section refers to issue capital, revenue reserves, long-term and current liabilities of a company (see Table 5.2 on page 90). From a proprietary view, capital means the money that a proprietor possesses from savings or borrowed funds from financial institutions or groups of individuals. The raising of capital by a business is crucial to its success and development. The next sections show in some detail the role a stock exchange plays in such a scenario.

Throughout the Caribbean there is an unofficial banking system. It involves a person (banker) who collects weekly or monthly amounts of money from people who have agreed to pool some of their wages. The system works like this: assume that 20 people each pay \$5 each week. Each week the banker pays \$100 to an individual in the group The cycle continues until the system comes to an end through friendly agreement. This unofficial banking system, which had its origin in Africa, is known by many different names, for example sou sou, bou, partner hand, meeting turn.

Table 5.2
The components of a company's capital

Issue Capital	**Revenue Reserves**	**Long-term Liabilities**	**Current Liabilities**
Preference shares	Retained profits	Loans	Creditors
Ordinary shares		Debentures	

(a) The issue capital of a company is the ordinary and preference shares respectively.

(b) The ordinary shares (also called equity shares) are documents that acknowledge investment in a company. A company's ordinary and preference shares can be bought by the general public – individuals, insurance institutions, commercial banks, building societies and credit unions. Note that capital reserves can be created by a company in issuing shares to the public in the form of a premium on ordinary and preference shares respectively, and debentures. A company's reserves (accumulated profits) can also be converted into equity capital by a bonus issue. Interests are paid on preference shares; dividends are paid on ordinary shares.

(c) The long-term liabilities are its long-term loans. (The 'long term' can be defined as a period of ten years or over.) They are usually repaid within a ten-year period.

(d) The short-term liabilities of a company are short-term loans, debentures and creditors. ('Short term' can be defined as a period of less than five years.) Short-term loans are obtained from commercial banks, insurance companies or from financial lending institutions.

(e) Debentures are formal documents acknowledging indebtedness by a company in terms of which the amount borrowed from the public will be repaid on an agreed date or under certain conditions. Debentures can be fixed or floating. A fixed debenture is secured on certain fixed assets of a company. A floating debenture is not secured on the particular fixed assets but floats generally over the assets of a company, particularly the current assets. Interest is paid on debentures at defined intervals. The redeemable period of debentures is stated on the document that advertises the issue.

(f) Creditors (current liabilities) are people or companies to whom a firm owes money for goods or services.

5.5 A stock exchange

A stock exchange is a place where jobbers and brokers who are agents meet to buy and sell company shares and government securities. It is usually situated in a country's capital city. The meeting of jobbers and brokers in one place not only reduces information and transaction costs of finding out about the price of companies' shares and government securities, but also makes it possible for those values to be disseminated from an important institution to interested parties. A stock exchange is therefore a marketplace. Brokers and jobbers play important roles in a stock exchange (see page 94).

The London Stock Exchange

Equity capital can be raised on a stock exchange by the following methods:

Offer for sale This means that a company's shares are offered to an issuing house which then offers the shares to the general public by advertising a prospectus in which is shown the issue price. A prospectus is a document that shows the history of a company and its recent financial results.

Public issue This means that a company's shares are offered direct to the public at an agreed price. This method is generally used for large issues by established firms.

Placing Shares, debentures and fixed interest bonds are said to be placed when they are sold privately to the clients of issuing houses or brokers handling the issue. Insurance companies and pension funds are generally the recipients.

Tender By this method shares are offered to the public and investors are invited to bid the price they are willing to pay. The price at which the shares are issued is the highest price that will dispose of all the shares.

Underwriters The incorrect pricing of shares which can occur with share issues creates the need for underwriters. It is the underwriters (insurance companies and pension funds) who, for a fee, purchase at a discount on the price quoted in the offer for sale, all or a part of the issues not taken up by the market.

The importance of a stock exchange

A stock exchange is important for the following reasons:

1 It enables companies to seek a quotation for which a market price can be established.

2 It assists the capital markets by making shares very liquid.

3 It provides the statistics for gauging industrial and commercial activity of a country since it is believed that share price movements reflect success or failure.

4 It provides a means of valuing wealth held in the form of securities.

5 It serves to direct the flow of new capital since share prices provide prospective lenders with the growth prospects of different firms.

6 It enables comparative analysis between companies to be made by investment analysts via the stock exchange ratios, namely (a) earnings

per share (b) price earning ratio (c) earning yield (d) dividend yield (e) dividend cover and (f) asset cover.

Earnings per share (EPS) is a measure of what a company is actually earning on behalf of its shareholders regardless of what it chooses to distribute as dividend.

$$\text{EPS} = \frac{\text{net earnings}}{\text{number of ordinary shares}}$$

Price earnings (PE) ratio is a measure of how expensive a share is.

$$\text{PE} = \frac{\text{market price of one ordinary share}}{\text{EPS}}$$

Earnings yield (EY) is a measure of the underlying annual yield of an investment (share).

$$\text{EY} = \frac{\text{EPS x 100}}{\text{same share}}$$

$$\textit{Dividend yield} = \frac{\text{dividend per share x 100}}{\text{share price}}$$

It is a measure of the cash yield of an investment (share).

Dividend cover (DC) is a measure of the security of the dividend.

$$\text{DC} = \frac{\text{EPS}}{\text{dividend per share}}$$

Asset cover (AC) attempts to show the underlying value of the business assets employed.

$$\text{AC} = \frac{\text{net assets}}{\text{number of ordinary shares}}$$

Stock exchange listing agreements and disclosure requirements

Caribbean companies that wish to go public make applications to their country's stock exchange for listing. Listing means that a company's shares are on a stock exchange list and can be traded. A company is called a listed company when its application is successful.

On being admitted to a stock exchange a company must subscribe to its listing agreements. The agreement is effected by the company's board of directors' resolution which must be lodged with the stock exchange before the listing status is granted.

A listed company is obliged to follow certain stock exchange disclosure requirements:

- to make an announcement of profit or loss to the stock exchange immediately after it has been accepted as a listed company
- to issue yearly reports and accounts within six months following the date of the end of the financial period to which they relate
- to prepare half-yearly interim reports to be sent to shareholders or inserted as an advertisement in the daily newspapers not later than six months from the date of the notice convening the annual general meeting of the company
- to circulate with the company's annual report (a) a statement by the directors giving reasons for any significant failure to comply with standard accounting practice and (b) an explanation if the trading results shown by the accounts under review differ materially from any published forecast made by the company
- to provide a statement as at the end of the financial year which shows bank loans and overdrafts and the amounts repayable
- to produce a statement of the amount of interest paid by the company during the year
- to issue a statement as at the end of the financial year showing the director(s)' interest in the share capital of the company and its subsidiaries, distinguishing between beneficial and non-beneficial interest.

Brokers and jobbers

A stockbroker works on the behalf of members of the public who wish to buy or sell shares. A stockbroker acts as an agent. A stockbroker gives expert advice to clients on companies' behaviour and on whether or not to invest in a company or group of companies. The stockbroker also buys and sells shares on a speculative basis.

Jobbers act as wholesalers in the stock exchange market. Jobbers specialize in selected types of shares. They buy and hold stocks and shares in large quantities and sell them whenever they see that profits can be made.

When brokers and jobbers act in speculative capacities they are given names. The name 'bear' is given to those optimistic share speculators who buy shares believing that prices will rise in the near future and which they will readily sell at a profit whenever their beliefs are evident in the marketplace. 'Bulls' are those pessimistic share speculators who expect share prices to fall and who sell their shares at a profit before that happens.

5.6 Insurance

Insurance became institutionalized as a result of industrialization and the associated society's craving for security from risks. It involves the payment of premiums (money), which are determined from actuarial principles, to insurance institutions for the eventuality or non-eventuality of expected happenings. It involves the pooling of risk funds where those who suffer loss can recover from the risk pool.

What is the purpose of insurance in the Caribbean business world? It enables a proprietor or company to disregard a number of measurable risks, for example fire, burglary, sabotage, the dishonesty of employees and creditors, for fixed annual premiums which ensure peace of mind.

The benefits of insurance

Insurance benefits society as follows:

- It releases funds for investment purposes.
- The accumulated insurance fund is an important source of finance for both industry and government.
- A country's balance of payments benefits from the export earnings of the insurance industry.
- The cost of loss which would otherwise be borne by society through the social services is met by insurance institutions.
- By their advice and actions in raising premiums to wayward insureds, insurance companies play a motivating role in loss reduction. For example, in motor and industrial accident insurance respectively, where regular accidents are the norm, bad drivers and wayward management are forced to reconsider their ways by being asked to pay higher premiums.

The benefits of an insurance policy can only be obtained if an individual enters into a contract of insurance with an insurance company. The legal aspects associated with such contracts are discussed in Chapter 17.

In nearly all Caribbean countries there are national insurance statutes which give an employer authority to deduct national insurance payments from employees' pay. The deductions are sent to the country's national insurance department and are therefore pooled funds. The essence of national insurance is that employees who have been made redundant are paid unemployment benefits for a specified time period. That, of course, is a buffer against the pain of unemployment.

5.7 Central bank functions, and its relationship with commercial banks

A central bank in the Caribbean is an institution which is controlled by government. It is concerned and entrusted with monetary policy, the issue of notes and the replacement of dirty notes and worn-out coins. A central bank does not compete with commercial banks in their type of business. The functions of the central bank are as follows:

1 It is the sole issuer of bank notes. This aspect is closely controlled by government because note issuing is a key to the success or failure of all economic activities within a country.

2 It acts as a banker to (a) government (b) commercial banks and (c) financial institutions.

3 It keeps two principal accounts for government: (a) a receipt and expenditure account and (b) a national loan fund account – that is, the government's capital account for borrowing and lending.

4 It manages the national debt and pays interest on government debentures and stocks.

5 It supervises exchange controls. It can give instructions to the commercial banks to restrict the amount of a country's currency being exchanged for foreign currency.

6 It looks after any borrowing from and repayment to the International Monetary Fund (IMF) and the World Bank.

One of the most important functions of a central bank is the control of a country's monetary policy. This control is exercised for the following reasons:

- to bring about full employment
- to keep down the inflation rate
- to encourage economic growth
- to improve a country's balance of payments position.

5.8 The pursuit of monetary goals

The central bank attempts to achieve the above goals via certain monetary instruments which are described below.

Minimum reserve liquidity ratio

The central bank dictates to the commercial banks and other lending institutions, the minimum liquidity ratio which they must maintain.

Central bank directive

The central bank's management, when it perceives that an economy is experiencing stress, instructs the commercial banks and other lending institutions to place a limit on loans or to discriminate in their lending policies to customers.

Special deposits

The central bank has the power to demand that the commercial banks deposit a certain percentage of their total deposits with it. In essence, these special deposits are frozen with the result that commercial banks' liquidity is reduced.

Minimum lending rate

With this instrument the central bank can deter or encourage investment and credit in the economy (depending on the goals of the government), since increases or decreases in the rate have an effect on commercial bank rates.

Open market operations

The Caribbean financial markets are not well developed. This precludes the use of open market operations. Even where stock markets exist in the Caribbean, the level of trading is insufficient to cause any significant impact on the domestic economy. The central banks can increase the money supply by lending to government through buying government securities, bonds or treasury bills.

Discount rate

The discount rate or bank rate is the rate at which the central bank lends to the commercial banks. An increase in the discount rate has two effects. First, it is a signal that the central bank is going to pursue a tighter monetary policy. Thus all the other interest rates will rise in sympathy. The effect of a rise in interest rates is to reduce the demand for credit.

The second effect is that commercial banks will find it more costly to borrow funds to lend to customers. They will therefore borrow less from the central bank and reduce credit to their customers. The money supply will also fall.

Selective credit controls

The Caribbean central banks have developed the following selective credit controls in an effort to control the economy where there is a balance of payments deficit:

- limits on credit
- instalment credit controls
- mortgage controls
- sectoral credit limits
- interest rate control.

To limit the amount of credit, the central bank can place quantitative limits on the amounts of credit given by the commercial banks. For example, a central bank can decree that the total amount of credit given in a current year is to be no more than 80 per cent of the credit given in a previous year.

If the central bank wants to reduce spending on consumer durables, it can raise the initial down-payment and shorten the repayment period. The effect of this is to exclude some customers because they cannot meet the initial down-payment or meet the higher instalments implied by the shorter repayment period.

This tool can also be used to increase spending on local goods at the expense of imported goods by making the payment terms more favourable on domestic goods.

Mortgage controls work in a similar way to instalment credit. The initial deposits can be varied as well as the repayment period. In addition, the interest rate on mortgages can be altered and funds can be set aside exclusively for mortgages.

The central bank, by decree, can also require that commercial banks allocate credit in a discriminating manner to the various sectors of an economy, for example to agriculture or industry. Firms that operate in both sectors can circumvent these restrictions. For example, if a firm operates in both the manufacturing and distributive sectors, it can obtain credit through its manufacturing section and simply transfer the funds to be used in its distributive section.

Minimum interest rates on savings and maximum interest rates on loans can also be used to influence the cost of credit. If the central bank wants to encourage investment it can reduce the maximum rate that banks charge on loans. If investment is that responsive to interest rates, investment will increase. Note that the availability of credit rather than the cost of credit is the greater constraint on investment in the Caribbean.

Key Points

- Money, capital and the financial sector play very important roles in the Caribbean economy.
- Money in its earliest form was a ritual which became institutionalized.
- The use of money can be seen from its payment function.
- It is the nature of money to be used for an indefinite succession of payments, to circulate freely without being subject to any sort of loss of function.
- Money is made of some recognizable substance which has certain attributes such as durability, divisibility, portability, uniformity and inelasticity of supply.
- Money is the most generally recognized token of wealth. It is the universal medium of business transactions. It is a prized possession with many social implications.
- The main characteristics and functions of money are: means of payment, standard of deferred payment, unit of account, medium of exchange, store of wealth and a measurement tool.
- Commercial banks play a vital role in a country's economy.
- A cash budget is essential to sound money management.
- The capital of a business refers to the issue capital, revenue reserves, long-term and current liabilities of a company.
- The long-term liabilities of a company are its long-term loans, for example debentures.

- The short-term liabilities of a company are short-term loans, and creditors.
- The raising of capital by a business is crucial to its success and development.
- A stock exchange is a marketplace where shares are bought and sold.
- Brokers and jobbers play important roles in a stock exchange.
- A stock exchange provides the following methods for raising equity capital: offer for sale, public issue, placing, tender, underwriters.
- A stock exchange has listing and disclosure requirements.
- A stockbroker works on behalf of members of the public who wish to buy or sell shares.
- Jobbers act as wholesalers in the stock exchange market.
- Insurance involves the payment of premiums, which are determined from actuarial principles, to insurance institutions for the eventuality or non-eventuality of expected happenings.
- Insurance benefits society in many ways.
- The benefits of an insurance policy can only be obtained if an individual enters into a contract of insurance with an insurance company.
- A central bank is concerned and entrusted with monetary policy, the issue of notes, the replacement of dirty notes and worn-out coins.
- A central bank does not compete with commercial banks in their type of business. It has several specific functions.
- A central bank has control of a country's monetary policy, which involves the creation of full employment, the keeping down of the inflation rate, the encouragement of economic growth and the improvement of a country's balance of payments position.
- The central bank attempts to achieve the monetary goals via certain monetary instruments: minimum reserve liquidity ratio, central bank directives, special deposits, minimum lending rate, open market operations, bank rate and selective credit controls.

Questions

1 What are the characteristics, functions and importance of money?

2 What are the functions and services of commercial banks?

3 What are the commonsense principles involved in sound money management?

4 What sources and types of capital are open to businesses and individuals?

5 What is a stock exchange? Discuss its role and functions in a Caribbean setting.

6 List the stock exchange agreements and disclosure requirements.

7 Distinguish between brokers and jobbers.

8 'Insurance plays a meaningful role in the Caribbean business world.' Discuss.

9 Explain the objectives of national insurance.

10 What are the duties of a central bank?

11 What monetary instruments does a central bank have:

(a) to bring about full employment

(b) to control inflation

(c) to encourage economic growth

(d) to improve a country's balance of payments position?

Explain your answers.

Chapter 6 Marketing

Marketing is a human activity. It is a process that informs buyers and sellers about social goods and services, and provides a mechanism of communication between buyers, sellers and customers. Marketing links the production and consumption functions of a society. From a business viewpoint, the marketing activity aims to satisfy society's needs through a monetary exchange process between buyers and sellers.

A market is made up of a group of individuals, organizations or institutions who wish to own the social product or service being offered and have the purchasing power to buy that item (*buyers*), and those people or institutions who wish to sell the item (*sellers*).

6.1 Marketing activities

The major activities in marketing are market research, sales and distribution. An objective of market research is to discover the customer and to find out what the customer wants. Large-scale production enables goods to be produced cheaply if the demand is large, but a misjudgement of the size of the market and of the demand for the goods by consumers can be costly. While the costs are an essential input in the launching of a product, they will be wasted if the product fails to find acceptance from a large number of people.

Another object of market research is to monitor changes in public taste. A product may be left unsold unless its packing and presentation are suitably adjusted to current consumer tastes. New products emerge from technical advances, or existing ones are made obsolescent, so market research ascertains the existence and size of the new markets for the new product, or finds alternative outlets for the old one.

In general, market research activities aim to find answers to some of the following questions:

- How is the market made up?
- How is the market divided?
- What products or services are wanted by the public and in what quantities and qualities?
- What are the patterns of market demand?
- What is the size and economic viability of markets?

Market research can be undertaken in a number of ways. These are set out below.

Salesmen's reports

Sales records are compiled, maintained and subjective assessments are written down, kept and ranked by salesmen. This information may include customer sales records and customer payment records. Business enterprises usually have much of that kind of information which may be useful to market research.

Government reports

These include census data, for example family and expenditure surveys, national income statistics, trade and manufacturing trends. The Caribbean central banks usually produce statistical and economic information on a monthly basis. Such information suffers from a high level of aggregation and time lags, but it can be used as a basic input in market research, since the reports are concerned with demographic (population) distribution and market trends related to income levels.

Market surveys

Market surveys are based on primary research undertaken within the market. They may involve *field research*, in which teams of researchers interview samples of respondents on the streets, or in their homes. Questions are asked by an interviewer and are designed to obtain specific answers to specific questions. There are four ways by which this kind of research is carried out: (a) by personal interview (b) by telephone interview (c) by postal survey and (d) by panel.

Personal interview

The personal interview is a face-to-face (direct) form of questioning, structured around a formal questionnaire, which is conducted by an interviewer. The interviewees' answers are recorded instantaneously on the questionnaire. All answers are later analysed together.

Advantages of the personal interview method:

1. It yields a high percentage of responses.
2. The interviewer can assess cases when lies are told.
3. Via observation, the interviewer can assess the characteristics, age, social position and gender of the respondent.

Disadvantages of the personal interview method:

1 They are costly (salary and travel expenses).

2 The interviewer may influence the answers given by the interviewee.

3 Inaccuracies in recording replies may occur in spite of the instantaneous nature of the recording process.

4 The time taken for interviews is constrained by the time taken to contact interviewees and by the length of the interview.

The telephone interview

This method is restricted to telephone subscribers who are asked a set of questions based on the research questionnaire. The results are recorded and analysed with the other results.

Advantages of the telephone method:

1 The method is satisfactory where the sample of people to be interviewed consists of telephone subscribers.

2 The cost per interview is low.

3 A large number of interviews can be conducted within a short time.

Disadvantages of the telephone method:

1 Observation of the interviewee is impossible.

2 Telephone subscribers may not be representative of the general population.

3 Limited number of possible calls.

4 Because of the impersonal form of communication, and the limited time available for interview, the interviewer is unable to gauge the accuracy of interviewees' replies to questions.

The postal survey method

Self-addressed envelopes are sent to a sample population from whom information is requested, together with a questionnaire and letter requesting completion and return. A follow-up letter is usually sent along with the questionnaire to those who have not replied after a specified time period has passed. Postal questionnaires may also be enclosed in periodicals or attached to a product purchased by a consumer.

Advantages of the postal survey method:

1 A large sample may be reached.

2 The postal survey is less costly than the personal interview survey.

3 The interviewees can consider their answers at leisure.

Disadvantages of the postal survey method:

1 The refusal rate is high.

2 Questions may be misinterpreted and as a result misleading answers may be given.

3 The answers given on the returns may not be those of the person to whom the letter was addressed.

4 Questions are short and interviewees will not reveal additional information about themselves.

Consumer panels

Two kinds are examined here: consumer purchasing and consumer product testing. Consumer purchasing panels are mainly made up of housewives who are asked by a research agency, either by interview, postal questionnaire or via diaries, to report on their buying patterns, purchase intentions and attitudes towards products. The members of product testing panels are asked to test products and report on their reaction to them. The importance of panels is that they allow the researcher to study the same people continuously over a long period of time.

Advantages of consumer panels:

1 They are useful for research into market trends over a period of time since the respondents are the same individuals.

2 Case histories of panel members can be established to give suitable background material to responses.

Disadvantages of consumer panels:

1 There will be losses of panel members through ill-health, death, loss of interest or members moving to other areas.

2 Illiterate people are unrepresented on panels.

3 Continuous membership of a panel makes its members self-conscious.

4 Panel members must be visited from time to time to monitor their activities and reliability. This is expensive.

5 Incentives in the form of gifts are given to panel members.

6.2 Distribution channels

Distribution channels are economic institutions through which a producer delivers social goods so that the goods may be conveniently obtained via purchases by customers. That process creates three utilities:

1. *Place utility*, when the goods are moved to the point of consumption.
2. *Ownership utility*, when the transfer of title to the goods passes from the producer to the buyer.
3. *Time utility*, when the goods are available to the customer whenever the goods are needed.

Marketing channels serve society in many ways:

1. Routine decisions are made which result in not excessive distribution costs.
2. The distribution of goods is financed by the group.
3. They influence the pricing of goods.
4. They act as intelligent, communicative agents between producers and customers.

6.3 Promotion

Promotion is applied communication used by marketers to exchange persuasive messages and information between buyers and sellers.

A firm promotes its products or services in order to influence consumers to buy its products or services. Promotion serves as a conveyor of news about products, prices and the locations in which the goods are to be found.

The basic purposes of promotion are to inform, to persuade and to remind. Promotional efforts – advertising – involve direct communication on a face-to-face basis or indirect communication via some medium like television, radio, highway signs and billboards. Advertising includes any persuasive message, image or picture carried by any of these media. In general, promotion and advertising seek to change people or to confirm them in a desired attitude.

Promoting sales

The functions of sales promotion are to create sales and to help a firm to sell its product or services to the consumer. Sales promotion has incentive devices, for example trading stamps, premiums and special offers. Sales promotion also utilizes exhibitions, point-of-sale displays and sponsorships.

Trading stamps or coupons are given to buyers of goods in order to encourage them to buy more of a firm's goods on a continuous basis. The accumulation of a stipulated number of trading stamps is redeemed by the firm for gifts or other goods. This device is aimed at reinforcing brand loyalty and encouraging repeat purchases.

Premiums, also associated with give-aways, usually take the form of 'buy two items and get one free'. Alternatively, the customer may receive another item once he/she has made a standard purchase, or the customer may receive a specified product or service if the required number of proofs of purchases is presented. Premiums are effective when they relate to the product and enhance its image.

Exhibitions are a form of sales promotion. They create awareness and recall of the exhibition itself and of the promotional messages linked to a product. Exhibitions offer scope and creativity. They give an individual supplier the chance to inspect and evaluate competitors' products and promotional strategies.

Sponsorship is also a technique of sales promotion. It involves a number of interrelated elements:

1 Direct funding of an event or activity.

2 Guarantee of a minimum level of media advertising when the event is taking place.

3 Guaranteed association of the sponsor's name with the event.

The objective of a sponsorship is to promote the sponsor's product and company name in a direct and positive way and to gain by association with the activity. In the Caribbean, sponsorship is associated with sports.

Sales promotion is also concerned with the presentation, display and the location of the product where it is sold. This is called *point-of-sale* (POS) display. Sensible POS display attracts customers' attention, encourages would-be buyers to approach, inspect, touch the product and hopefully to purchase it. POS display is important in the distribution/retailer merchandising mix. POS should be designed to coordinate with the shape and form of the item being promoted.

Some multiproduct companies do price their products from the concept of a range of products rather than on each individual product.

Point-of-sale display material

For example, some products are priced relative to expected demand and consumer sensitivity to price to earn a large unit contribution. Such products are used to support others which carry a lower unit contribution. The object of such a policy is to cover the fixed costs and profit requirements of the product line as a whole.

In some cases, products called *loss leaders* may yield little or no contribution, but encourage the buying of more profitable lines. Loss leaders are a feature of retail operations. They attract people and encourage them to buy other products.

Methods of promoting sales, and their advantages and disadvantages

Firms promote their goods or services to the general public through several controllable and non-controllable promotional methods – advertising, personal selling, publicity, exhibitions. Non-controllable promotional methods communicate marketing messages via word of mouth, by information dissemination or by individual personal recommendation. Controllable methods communicate via the broadcasting media, printed media, cinema, outdoor media, and by personal selling and publicity.

Broadcasting media (radio and television)

Advantages of broadcasting media:

1 Radio and television are powerful tools of communication. A firm that advertises its products or services regularly through such media builds and maintains public and consumer awareness of its products or services.

2 Radio and television advertisements are creative and of a high standard. These qualities have a dynamic effect in persuading people.

3 Promotional messages on the broadcasting media are lively. They have voice, feeling, colour, movement, attractiveness.

Disadvantages of broadcasting media:

1 Television advertisements are expensive.

2 There are some restrictions on what can be broadcast, for example tobacco and tobacco products cannot be promoted.

3 It is not easy to target the promotional message on a specific market segment, so some of the advertising is 'wasted'.

4 Viewers/listeners may switch off when advertisements are broadcast.

5 The desire to watch television or to listen to the radio depends upon the quality and attractiveness of the scheduled programmes.

6 There is increasing competition, for example from satellite broadcasting.

Printed media

The printed media include national daily papers, magazines and periodicals (both for children and for adults) and professional journals.

Advantages of the printed media:

1 They target promotional messages accurately.

2 The printed word is durable – it can be referred to conveniently and read repeatedly.

3 An advertisement may take on some of the prestige of the publication, for example advertisements in medical journals.

4 Printing is a flexible medium and updates of market changes can be made easily.

Disadvantages of the printed media:

1 The reader is not obliged to read the advertisement.

2 Newsprint limits the use of colour and its attractiveness.

3 An advertisement in the printed media is static, not lively.

Cinema

A cinema is any building or theatre in which motion pictures are publicly shown.

Advantages of the cinema:

1 An advertisement on the cinema screen can be made vivid so that its impact on the captive audience is effective.

2 The cinema makes possible the targeting of promotional messages on specific customer segments.

Disadvantages of the cinema:

1 Cinema audiences can fluctuate widely with the type of film being shown.

2 Cinema is subject to much competition from other media, for example radio, television, hi-fi and video.

Outdoor media

Outdoor media include fixed posters and show cards, posters on the inside or outside of public transport vehicles (buses, trains), and electric and neon signs.

Advantages of outdoor media:

1 Fixed posters and billboards are looked at and create a strong impact.

2 Electronic and neon signs have a strong visual impact, especially after dark – just look at any Caribbean city after dark during the Christmas season!

Publicity

Publicity can be through the printed media, the broadcasting media, the cinema, films and by direct communication. It can include the following:

- editorial comment, feature articles, films and pictures
- consumer affairs programmes on radio and television

- documentary films shown to special interest groups
- talks to interested groups.

Advantages of publicity:

1 Publicity, if done by an established institution, appears to be objective.

2 Television and radio programmes have some influence in shaping people's purchasing behaviour, for example in tourism.

Disadvantages of publicity:

1 People may not agree with the ideas that are put forward.

2 Publicity will not always be presented in a favourable way.

6.4 Packaging

In relation to marketing, packaging is the way in which a saleable product is wrapped, displayed and presented to consumers. A package serves several functions:

1 It has to contain the correct quantity of the products.

2 It has to be durable so that transporting, storing or displaying it will not damage its contents.

3 The package must identify the products.

4 It has to be protective (for example of razor blades or harmful sprays).

5 The feel and appearance of the package creates sensations in customers.

Nowadays, some packaging is ecologically oriented – that is, it is designed not to create waste disposal problems.

Packaging also has promotional value which can be effected by the sensible display of goods in appropriate locations.

6.5 The brand name

A brand name is a name given by a firm to one or a number of its products or services. The choice of a brand name calls for great skills from the marketing function, simply because a brand name of a product can convey pleasant or unpleasant sensations in consumers, manufacturers or suppliers. A brand name is a permanent thing. If it is changed frequently it will suggest to consumers that the product is inferior. Once a product has been branded it can be packaged and advertised. The advertising of a brand product repetitiously seeks to create habit buying on the part of consumers.

There are several advantages to a firm that makes and sells its own brands:

- They help customers to recognize and differentiate a firm's products from those of another firm.
- They enable the firm to plan its future production in a sensible manner.
- They make cost control possible.

6.6 Techniques of selling

The quality of the sales force is an important feature of marketing. It is the continual cash from sales that creates a kind of satisfaction in the firm. A firm's selling techniques should be coordinated with its marketing function.

The ability to obtain orders, meet sales targets, acquire and keep customers depends on the skills of the sales function. This in turn depends on the recruitment, training, incentives and supervision of the sales staff.

6.7 Public relations

The public relations function of a firm is concerned with the creation of a pleasant understanding between the firm, its customers and the public. The function attempts generally to present a firm's economic activities in a favourable way.

The public relations objective is to remove any hostility towards a firm or its products. Such hostility may arise when, for example:

- a brand name is difficult to pronounce
- a product seems to be too highly priced
- an advertisement offends a section of the community
- a sales promotion scheme is unsuccessful
- people are ignorant of a firm's products or services.

The public relations function of a firm is concerned not only with painting a pleasant picture of a firm's economic activities, but is also concerned with admitting or confessing that something has gone wrong, or went wrong, in a firm or institution. A high point of the function's efforts is the creation of goodwill for the firm.

Public relations activities

Public relations activities include the following:

1 *Identifying specific interest groups*: for example investors, trade associations, chambers of commerce, then assessing their resources, power, influence and attitudes towards the firm and formulating and implementing public relations strategies which may influence their behaviour.

2 *Counselling*: that is, providing general advice to a firm's management function about what is happening in a particular society or environment, and giving advice derived from forecast information about anticipated events, together with suggestions about what the firm should do if the predicted events occur.

3 *Product publicity*: publicizing the products and services offered by the firm to the general public and targeted groups.

4 *Media relations*: seeking media coverage of newsworthy information of the firm's product/s, activities and services so as to attract attention. Media relations can also be used to correct any bad effects of misinformation of a firm's products or services.

5 *Corporate communication:* addressed to internal and external parties and which is intended to create awareness, understanding and a positive attitude towards the firm.

6 *Lobbying*: trying to dissuade legislators and government officials from implementing laws which may retard the growth prospects of the firm.

6.8 After-sales service

The after-sales service is a follow-up by sales staff to customers on the completion of a sale. It is done to find out whether customers are satisfied with a firm's products or services. The after-sales service also provides the customer with maintenance and repair services at timely intervals. Instruction leaflets or manuals are an important part of the after-sales service. An after-sales service can also come about as a result of a note on a package which requests the consumer to write to the firm stating whether or not its product was satisfactory.

Key Points

- Marketing is a process that informs buyers and sellers about social goods and services and provides a mechanism of communication between buyers, sellers and customers.
- The major activities in marketing are market research, sales and distribution.
- An object of market research is to discover the customer and to find out what the customer wants.
- Market research can be undertaken in a number of ways: salesmen's reports, government reports, market surveys and consumer panels.
- Government reports include census data, family and expenditure surveys, national income statistics, trade and manufacturing trends.
- Market surveys are based on primary research undertaken within the market. There are four ways by which this kind of research is carried out: the personal interview, the telephone interview, postal surveys and panels.
- Distribution channels are economic institutions through which a producer delivers social goods so that the goods may be conveniently obtained via purchases by customers.
- Marketing channels serve society by making routine decisions, by group financing of the distribution of goods, by influencing the pricing of goods, and as agents of communication between producers and customers.
- A firm promotes its products or services in order to influence consumers to buy its products or services. Promotion serves as a conveyor of news about products, prices and the locations in which the goods are to be found.
- In general, promotion and advertising seek to change people or to confirm them in a desired attitude.
- Sales promotion has incentive devices.
- Exhibitions are a form of sales promotion for consumer goods as well as for industrial goods.
- The objective of a sponsorship is to promote the sponsor's product and company name in a direct and positive way and to gain by association with the activity.
- Point-of-sale (POS) display attracts customers' attention, and encourages would-be buyers to approach, inspect and touch the product and, hopefully, to buy it.
- Products called *loss leaders* may yield little or no contribution but encourage the buying of more profitable lines.

- Loss leaders are a feature of retail operations.
- Packaging is the way in which a saleable product is wrapped, displayed and presented to customers.
- A brand name of a product can convey pleasant or unpleasant sensations in consumers, manufacturers and suppliers.
- The advertising of a brand product repetitiously seeks to create habit buying on the part of consumers.
- A firm's selling techniques should be coordinated with its marketing function.
- Public relations activities include identifying specific interest groups, counselling, product publicity, media relations, corporate communication and lobbying.
- The ability to obtain orders, meet sales targets, acquire and keep customers will depend on the skills of the sales function.
- The public relations function of a firm is concerned with the creation of a pleasant understanding between the firm, its customers and the public.
- The public relations function is also concerned with admitting or confessing that something has gone wrong in a firm or institution.
- The after-sales service provides the customer with maintenance and repair services at timely intervals for a firm's products.

Questions

1. Explain, in your own words, what marketing is.
2. Explain the major activities in marketing.
3. What are the functions of the marketing channels?
4. What are the objectives of promoting sales?
5. Are the packaging and brand name functions complementary? Discuss.
6. What are the public relations functions of a firm?
7. Explain the concept of after-sales service.
8. Explain the nature and purpose of promotion.
9. Describe and explain the devices used in promoting sales.
10. Discuss the methods of promoting sales, and their advantages and disadvantages.
11. How do loss leaders affect other products? Are all businesses capable of using loss leader pricing? Explain your answer.

Chapter 7 The Pricing of Goods

All profit-oriented firms, as well as non-profit organizations, establish prices for their goods or services. In order to set prices for goods and services, management must understand cost information and behaviour. *Cost* is the amount of money that a firm has spent in getting a product to its final usable stage. *Pricing* is the assignment by a firm of a numerical dollar value to a product or service.

7.1 Cost factors affecting the pricing of goods

The cost factors that affect the price of a manufactured product are:

- *cost of funds*: bank loans, leasing, cost of equipment
- *direct costs*: raw materials, labour
- *overhead costs*: energy, rates, packaging, storage, delivery, transport
- *administrative costs*: accounting, personnel, purchasing, market research, sales
- *promotional costs*: advertising, public relations, consultancy fees, publications, sales promotion.

These can broadly be classified into fixed costs and variable costs.

Fixed costs (FC) are the costs of readiness to produce the saleable goods. They are incurred by the firm even if the goods are not produced. They also include those costs that do not change with production volume for a particular period. Cost of funds and direct costs are fixed costs.

Variable costs (VC) are those costs which respond proportionately to changes in production activity within the cost range of operations. Overhead costs, administrative costs and promotional costs are variable costs.

When a firm knows the quantity of its product sold (Qs), its accounting profit (π) or loss (L) is calculated as follows:

$\pi = (P \times Qs) - (VC + FC)$
where P (price) x Qs is greater than (VC + FC)
L where (P x Qs) is less than (VC + FC).

The firm makes neither a profit nor a loss when $(P \times Qs) = (VC + FC)$.

7.2 Forms of market

The way prices are established depends on the market in which goods are traded. Economists describe several types of markets:

- perfectly competitive
- monopolistic competition
- monopoly
- oligopoly.

Perfectly competitive markets

In theory, a market is said to be perfectly competitive if the following conditions exist:

1. The goods traded are homogeneous and are thought to be so in the minds of buyers.
2. Market participants, whether buyers or sellers, cannot individually influence the market price of the products by their actions.
3. There is freedom of entry and exit.
4. Market participants have complete knowledge of price and costs.

Prices in perfectly competitive markets are determined by supply and demand. *Supply* is the total quantity of a product all suppliers are willing to sell at a particular selling price. *Demand* is the total quantity of a product all buyers are willing to purchase at a particular price. See Table 7.1 and Figure 7.1.

Looking at Figure 7.1, market equilibrium (ME) occurs where the curves intersect. At that price ($90), supply is sufficient to satisfy all demands (4,000 units) because suppliers and buyers agree on both price and quantity. This means that no single buyer or seller can influence the market. If a seller attempts to charge more than $90 per unit for the product, the purchaser will buy from someone else. A lower price than $90 makes no sense because individual suppliers can sell their entire supply at the market price in a perfectly competitive market. In a perfectly competitive market the demand curve for an individual supplier is a horizontal straight line at the selling price – see Figure 7.2.

Table 7.1
The supply and demand schedules for a hypothetical product that trades in a competitive market

Price per unit ($)	Quantity supplied (thousands of units)	Quantity demanded (thousands of units)
150	7	1
130	6	2
110	5	3
90	4	4
70	3	5
50	2	6
30	1	7

Notes

(a) At higher prices demand is small but supply is high.

(b) At lower prices demand is large but supply is small because fewer suppliers find it worth while to produce the product.

(c) As the price increases, the demand for the product decreases.

Figure 7.1
Supply and demand for a product

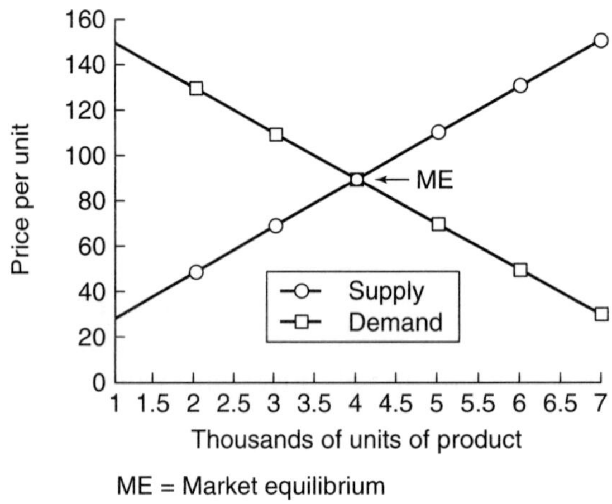

Figure 7.2
A supplier's selling price in a perfectly competitive market

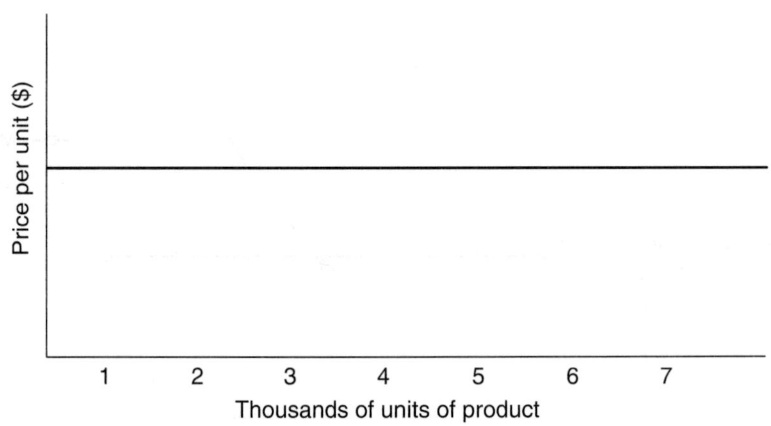

In a perfectly competitive market, an individual producer's marginal revenue is the same as its selling price. Associated with marginal revenue is marginal cost. *Marginal revenue* is the additional revenue that can be obtained from selling one more unit of a product. *Marginal cost* is the amount of cost increase made by a unit increase in output. What business strategy is now open to the individual producer? The sensible strategy is to produce at that level where marginal cost equals marginal revenue (price).

Table 7.2 shows the total and marginal cost data for a hypothetical producer of a product in a perfectly competitive market. Figure 7.3 shows the graphs of that data together with the $90 as marginal revenue.

Table 7.2 Schedule of production cost for a hypothetical producer

Units produced (thousands)	Total cost	Marginal cost
0	50	–
1	100	50
2	130	30
3	200	70
4	280	80
5	440	160
6	700	260
7	1,000	300

Marginal cost is the difference between any two levels of total production cost.

Figure 7.3 A perfectly competitive market

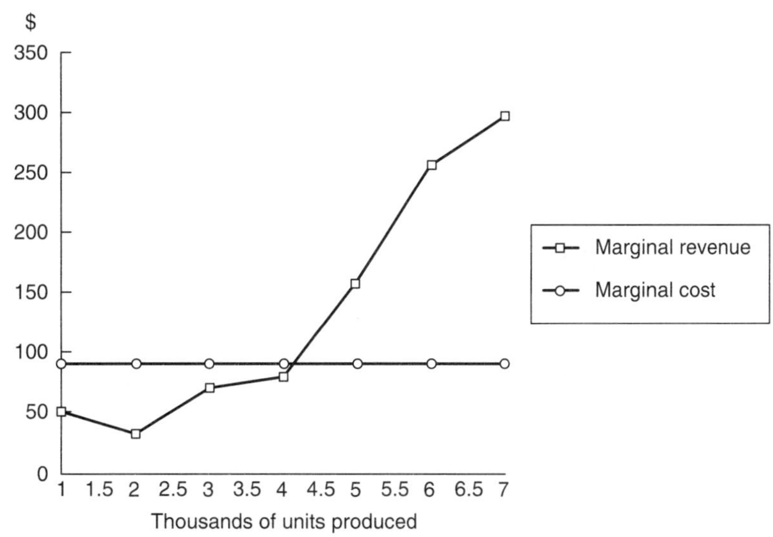

The marginal cost line crosses the $90 price line just above 4,000 units. At that quantity net profit or income is greatest (see Table 7.3).

Table 7.3 Schedule of revenue, cost and net income for a hypothetical producer

Tonnes produced (thousands)	Total revenue	Total cost	Net (loss) profit
0	0	50	(50)
1	90	100	(10)
2	180	130	50
3	270	200	70
4	360	280	80
5	450	440	10
6	540	700	(160)
7	630	1,000	(370)

Net income is greatest at production of 4,000 units.

The perfectly competitive market model shows aspects of economic theory which work well in aggregate terms. In the real world, individual producers modify it with specific pricing models.

Monopolistic competition

Monopolistic competition occurs when there are many sellers of similar but not identical products in the market. In such cases no single seller is able to exert influence over the market price of the products. Caribbean examples are gas service stations, village rum shops, village bread and fish sellers and fast food restaurants.

The solution to the product pricing decision rests on the same idea of maximizing net income that is achieved when marginal revenue equals costs.

Subtle differences exist between a perfectly competitive market model and the monopolistic competitive model. The differences lie in the shapes of the revenue and demand curves. For any individual producer in the monopolistic competitive model, its demand curve is downward-sloping. It takes that form because the firm differentiates its product from competing brands.

The demand for a product in monopolistic competition increases as the price declines. To increase unit sales the supplier must reduce prices.

Monopoly

A monopoly exists when a firm is the only producer of a product that is in demand. Examples of monopolies in the Caribbean are the electricity, gas and telephone services and the post office.

A monopoly usually sets reasonable prices since it is required by law to submit its production cost data to a regulatory body in order to obtain any further increase in prices. In the Caribbean, the telephone and electricity companies are made to do so whenever they ask for price increases.

Once the price has been set for a monopoly, the firm's production decision is the same as under monopolistic competition. A monopoly is usually able to maintain its prices at the highest possible level allowed by law. In such cases it only needs to decide how much to produce, just as in the case of the perfectly competitive market.

Oligopoly

An oligopoly market consists of several large suppliers which dominate a market and compete against each other. In the USA, the automobile and steel industries are examples. Caribbean examples are banks and soft drinks companies.

Because of its large size, any one of the firms can affect the market price of the product. As a result, the demand curve of one firm may be directly affected by the pricing decision of a seller's firm. For example, if one producer of soft drinks lowers its price, the demand for other producers' drinks will decline as buyers shift to the lower-price producer. This buyer's shift causes the demand curve for an oligopolistic firm to undergo sharp changes when going from one price to another. This can be illustrated by what is called a *kinked demand curve.*

There are various ways of determining prices in oligopolistic markets. One way is for an oligopolistic firm to establish a price; that is, for it to be a price leader. With this approach a price follower is confronted with a horizontal demand curve as in perfectly competitive markets. The problem for the price leader is to set prices at a level where profit is maximized.

7.3 The economist's approach to product pricing

For an economic analysis, it is crucial to estimate the demand for the products. Calculus is applied to the mathematical model to determine the price and optimum output level of the product. The solution to Example 7.1 below illustrates the solution process for a single product. It also clarifies the concept of optimality.

Example 7.1

A firm manufactures a single product. Assume its total cost function (TC) – that is, fixed costs plus variable costs – is as follows:

Total costs (TC) = 4,000 + 15x (see the Appendix on page 323 for derivation).

Assume that the expected relationship between price and output is as shown by the demand curve in the diagram below.

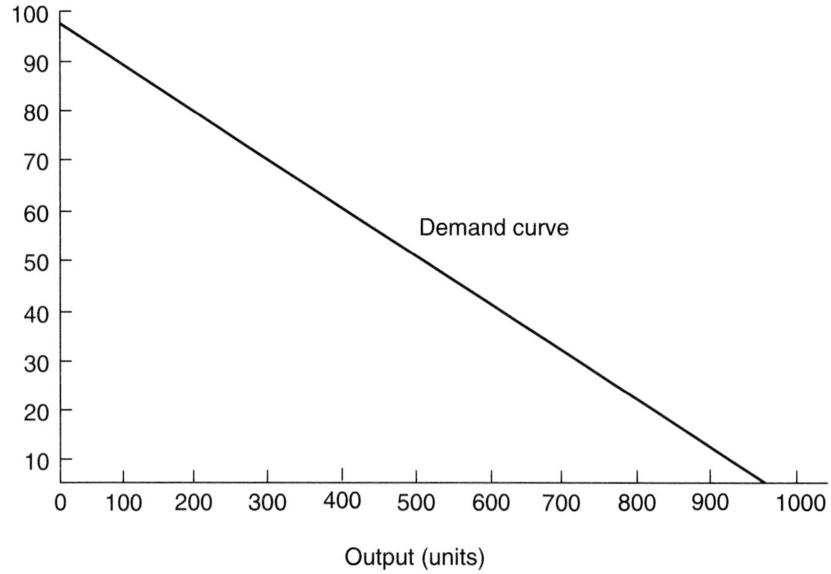

Required:

(a) The optimum output level (calculate).

(b) The selling price of the product.

(c) The firm's total cost and revenue respectively.

(d) The firm's profit.

(e) Show optimality test calculations to determine what happens if the output level as calculated in (a) is increased or decreased by one unit.

Solution:

(a) For each increase in output of 100 units the price falls by \$10. For each increase in output of one unit the attainable price falls by \$10/100 = \$0.1.

The price equation is SP = 100 – 0.1x

where

SP = selling price in dollars
x = output in units.

The total revenue (TR) accruing to the firm will be the product of the price per unit and the number of units to be produced and sold.

$TR = SPx = 100x - 0.1x^2$

Elementary calculus aids the solution process.

Marginal revenue

$$\frac{dTR}{dx} = 100 - 0.2x$$

$TC = 4{,}000 + 15x$

Marginal cost

$$\frac{dTC}{dx} = 15$$

The optimum output level is that value of x which equates these two expressions:

$$100 - 0.2x = 15$$
$$x = 425 \text{ units}$$

(b) The highest price at which the firm will be able to sell the optimum output is found by substituting for x in the selling price equations as follows:

$$SP = 100 - 0.1\ (x)$$
$$= 100 - 0.1\ (425)$$
$$SP = \$57.50$$

(c) $TC = \$(4{,}000 + 15(425))$
$= \$10{,}375$

$TR = 425 \text{ units} \times \$57.50$
$= \$24{,}438$ approx.

(d) $\text{Profit} = \$(24{,}438 - 10{,}375)$
$= \$14{,}063$

(e) If the firm produces one extra unit (426) it will incur additional costs of \$15. The firm will receive additional revenue of \$(100 – 0.2 (426)) = \$14.8. This will result in a loss of \$(15 – 14.8) = \$0.2. If 424 units are produced the firm will avoid costs of \$15 and lose revenue of \$(100 – 0.2(423)) = \$15.2. The firm will again make a loss of \$0.2. Note that any greater increases or decreases over 425 units will lead to greater reductions in profit.

Other product pricing methods are cost-plus mark-up, and the contribution approach.

Cost-plus mark-up pricing method

The pricing of a product is by no means a simple task. Business people usually use a cost-plus mark-up formula. The mark-up is an arbitrary mark-up percentage on cost. A procedure is shown in Table 7.4.

Table 7.4
How a cost-plus formula is used

	\$	\$
Direct costs:		
Labour		
Materials		
Depreciation		
Product overheads:		
Add x% on direct cost		
Total cost		
Profit mark-up		
Add y% on total cost		
Price:		

1 The direct costs of a product are calculated and to those costs is added an amount to recover production overheads.

2 A mark-up is also added to cover selling, administration, overheads and profit. That is designed to reflect what the decision maker regards as a reasonable level of profit.

The advantage of the cost-plus mark-up formula is that it is easy to apply. Disadvantages of the cost-plus mark-up formula are that the percentages are applied to historical cost data which are misleading, and the formula pays no regard to shifts in demand.

Contribution approach pricing model

This approach to pricing is different from the full cost pricing model. *Contribution* means the excess of revenue over variable costs for an identifiable activity. Contribution is usually expressed in per unit terms. The contribution approach when applied to cases where the traceability of costs to products can be determined quite easily shows the relationship between prices and costs that vary directly with sales. Fixed costs are not assigned to the cost objective directly under the contribution method but they are taken into account in determining the amount to be added to the variable costs to arrive at the price. Example 7.2 below shows how the contribution approach is used to calculate the price of a product.

Example 7.2

A firm makes standard mahogany rocking chairs. It sets its selling prices at variable costs plus 150 per cent of variable costs. The variable cost data for a standard mahogany chair are as follows:

Inputs	**Unit variable cost ($)**
Direct materials	70
Direct labour	60
Variable manufacturing overheads	80
Variable selling expenses	30
Variable administration overheads	10
	250

Required:

Calculate the selling price of a standard mahogany rocking chair.

Solution:

Selling price = \$250 + 1.50 x \$250

= \$625

7.4 Government intervention in the market

Caribbean governments interfere with the free workings of the price mechanism by using the following instruments:

- *taxation* which raises prices
- *subsidies* which lower prices
- *price controls* which dictate minimum and maximum prices.

They pursue such policies in order to achieve social ends. For example, the high taxes on liquor and tobacco are imposed by Caribbean governments to dissuade citizens from consuming too much alcohol and from smoking. Such habits are considered dangerous to health. Other justifications for higher taxes on products include saving foreign exchange by discouraging the consumption of imports, and encouraging economy in the use of a product.

The word *subsidy* means 'to support by grants of money'. Government subsidies can be applied at different economic levels. At the *micro-economic level*, government subsidies are paid to producers to increase the attractiveness of supplying a product, and to produce a social product. At the time of writing (1994), sugar is subsidized in Barbados.

At the *macro-economic level*, government subsidies are incentives to firms to establish themselves in a particular area or region. Such incentive subsidies can be classified as follows:

- subsidies related to the total costs and/or revenues of the firm, remission of tax profits, a low-cost loan or a grant
- subsidies related to the cost of capital inputs, for example buildings, equipment, plant
- subsidies related to labour costs
- the provision of factories for firms – these factories are sometimes provided below costs
- the provision of facilities that might benefit several firms, for example central training facilities.

All Caribbean governments offer incentives, which are stated in their investment-incentive laws, to firms or corporations from developed countries to establish firms in their countries.

There are two aspects to price controls: stockpiling and rationing. *Stockpiling* occurs with agricultural products, where governments guarantee farm incomes and pay farmers not to produce, for example in the USA and in the European Union. *Rationing* occurs when there is a shortage of goods, especially when there is a world war. To date Caribbean governments have not pursued policies either of rationing or of stockpiling.

7.5 Cartels

Cartels can emerge as a result of (a) large firms absorbing or taking over smaller firms, (b) firms amalgamating or joining together mutually to form bigger firms, and (c) firms cooperating with each other. These things are done by firms to obtain greater economies of scale or for price fixing.

In the USA, very large corporations which tend to dominate an entire economy are controlled by anti-trust legislation. In the United Kingdom the Department of Trade and Industry has the power to refer an organization to the Monopolies Commission when it is felt that a merger would present a monopolistic set of conditions – that is, pursue policies against the public interest. Cartels do not exist in the Caribbean nor in most developing countries.

7.6 Terms of sale

Cash sales, credit sales and hire purchase terms are associated with the selling price of a firm's product or service.

Cash sales

A cash sale is created when a person pays money directly to a firm's cashier for its product or service. A written receipt or a sales slip from an automatic cash register is proof that a sale was made. The advantages of a cash sale are that there is a stock movement – an item is sold for consumption purposes and it is replaced from stock – and the firm begins to earn money rewards from its cost sacrifices.

Credit

Credit is a facility extended by a vendor permitting another person (the *debtor*) to purchase goods or services without making immediate payment. A credit sale means that no cash is paid when the goods or services are handed over to a customer by someone who is authorized by the firm to do so.

In the Caribbean, interest rates range from 2 to 5 per cent of the total value of credit sales. The condition of credit is usually given for a period of ten days. Credit terms are usually written on invoices.

Advantages of credit sales from the buyer's point of view are (a) that money is not paid immediately and (b) that the buyer enjoys the use of the product or service for the period of the conditions.

Advantages of credit sales from the seller's point of view are (a) that it encourages customers to purchase goods on credit and (b) that it contributes to the firm's turnover.

A disadvantage to the seller is that in times of inflation the delayed payments as a result of credit sales mean that the currency loses some of its value, since its purchasing power at the end of a sale is dissimilar to its opening value. Also, credit sales inevitably lead to bad debts: customers who are incapable of paying for the goods or services because they are dishonest or bankrupt.

Hire purchase

Hire purchase is a practical and convenient source of short-term credit used for the purchase of equipment and household appliances. In the Caribbean, companies like Courts Caribbean Ltd and Cave Shepherd (Barbados) offer hire purchase agreements (see Chapter 17).

The business side of a hire purchase agreement is that a company hires the commodity to an intended purchaser, who usually pays an initial payment followed by a series of instalments until the commodity is paid for.

The advantages of hire purchase are that the person making the hire purchase (the *hiree*) has the use of the commodity, and obtains benefits from using the commodity without having to incur a large capital outlay. This is also a convenient way of acquiring ownership of a commodity.

A disadvantage of hire purchase is that it is an expensive form of credit. The interest element built into the hire purchase instalments is very high. Also, the goods do not become the property of the buyer until the last instalment is paid.

7.7 Cash and trade discounts

To encourage customers to pay the amount of money shown on their invoices before the end of the credit period, some firms offer a cash discount. To a seller a cash discount is called a *discount allowed*. To a customer it is called a *discount received*. In both cases the arithmetical calculations are similar in order to obtain the discount figure – see Example 7.3.

Example 7.3

Nevis Ltd sold goods to Roberts Ltd for $5,000 on 26 October 19XX.

The terms of credit were 2/10, N/30. Assume that Roberts Ltd received the invoice on 28 October, took advantage of the discount terms and paid for the credit sales by cheque.

Required:

Calculate (a) the discount taken and

(b) the value of the cheque sent to Nevis Ltd.

Solution:

Discount taken by Roberts Ltd
= 0.02 x $5,000
= $100

Value of cheque sent to Nevis Ltd
= $(5,000 – 100)
= $4,900

Many wholesalers and manufacturers publish catalogues in which their products are described together with listed retail prices. Those firms usually offer deductions from the list price to retailers or individual customers who buy large quantities of their goods. Those deductions in price are called *trade discounts*.

Example 7.4

In its catalogue Nevis Ltd advertises large pottery jars at a list price of $1,500 each (the price to retail customers).

The company offers a trade discount of 40 per cent.

Roberts Ltd, a retailer firm, bought 25 jars.

Required:

Calculate (a) the trade discount and

(b) the value of the cheque paid to Nevis Ltd.

Solution:

Amount of trade discount = List price x Rate of trade discount

List price – Amount of trade discount = Net price

Trade discount = 0.40 x $1,500 x 25

= $15,000

Value of cheque (net price) = $(1,500 x 25 – 15,000)

= $22,500

Value of the cheque paid to Nevis Ltd by Roberts Ltd was $22,500.

Trade discounts at times are altered. That policy enables a firm to adjust prices without re-issuing the catalogue or changing its list price. For example, suppose Nevis Ltd wants to continue advertising at the list price of $1,500 for each pottery jar but because of rising prices wants to reduce its discount to the dealer from $(1,500 x 0.40 = 600) to $(1,500 x 0.3 = 450) for each jar. It simply issues a new price list on which the trade discount is reduced from 40 to 30 per cent. The opposite of this example may also be applied.

There are differences between cash and trade discounts. *Cash discounts* are recorded in a firm's books. Discounts allowed are expenses and usually appear amongst the selling and distributing expenses. They decrease income. Discounts received are revenue and are added to a firm's gross profit as sundry income.

Trade discounts are not recorded in a firm's books. They are allowances off a list or retail price given to retailers by a manufacturer which represent their margin of profit. Trade discounts are used to calculate the net purchase price of goods sent to retailers.

7.8 Consumerism

Consumerism came about as a result of the bad side of marketing. It is based on the following premises:

1 That consumers should be given adequate, timely and meaningful information on the performance and quality of goods and services that a firm produces.

2 That consumers should not be charged extravagant prices for social goods.

3 That the performance and quality of a firm's product or service should meet certain standard specifications.

4 That consumers should be protected against the marketing of social goods which are hazardous to public health.

5 That consumers should be protected against fraudulent, deceitful or misleading information, advertising or labelling and should be given the facts needed to make sensible choices.

6 That consumers should be given the right whenever possible to choose from a variety of products and services at competitive prices, and have an assurance of satisfactory quality and service.

7 That a consumer or consumers' representation should be given the right to be heard and be assured that consumers' interest will receive consideration in the formation of government policy and fair treatment in its administrative tribunals.

7.9 Consumer protection groups and laws

Caribbean countries do not have many private consumer associations which look after consumers' interests on a daily basis. Nor do Caribbean countries have any established periodicals in which any wrongs done to consumers can be discussed, analysed or publicized. Guyana has a consumer association whose main function is to ensure that all complaints received from customers are investigated and remedial action taken against the wrongdoer. Trinidad & Tobago has consumer groups called The Housewives Association and Consumers Association. The functions of such bodies include education of the public via posters, brochures, community talks, demonstrations and discussions on health, nutrition, food adulteration and product hazards. Throughout the Caribbean region, consumers have the opportunity to seek redress through 'action line' programmes, which are run by both state-owned radio stations and private broadcasters.

Consumer protection is enacted through Caribbean laws. The specific laws of Jamaica which protect consumer interests and which are typical of those in other Caribbean countries are set out here with brief explanations.

The Food and Duty Act prohibits the sale of food which has poisonous or harmful substances in or on it.

The Food Storage and Prevention of Infestation Act ensures that manufacturers and distributors of food keep food free from the presence of rodents, insects, mites or fungi and free of conditions that involve an immediate or potential risk of damage to food.

The Public Health Act administered through the Ministry of Local Government, ensures the maintenance of sanitary conditions in shops and restaurants where articles of food and drink are manufactured, prepared for sale, stored, handled and sold.

The Trade Act is enforced by a price commission and seeks to protect the consumer by establishing fair prices, investigating profiteering and initiating prosecutions against bad vendors.

The Sale of Goods Act provides a framework within which the consumer can bring charges against a vendor in matters of sales of goods (see also Chapter 17).

The Hire Purchase Act sets out information which must be given to the prospective hirer in writing, including cash price, total hire purchase price and the amount of each instalment.

The Weights and Measures Act implemented through the Bureau of Standards, oversees the testing of weighing equipment used for trade.

The Ombudsman Act is administered by an ombudsman and a qualified staff – the consumer can ask the ombudsman to investigate and redress wrongs.

The Pharmacy Act is administered by a pharmacy council which:

- registers pharmacists
- regulates training
- ensures the maintenance of a proper standard of conduct by persons registered under the Act.

Key Points

- ➤ All profit-oriented firms as well as non-profit-making organizations establish prices for their goods or services.
- ➤ Pricing is the assignment of a numerical dollar value by a firm to a product or service.
- ➤ Prices in perfectly competitive markets are determined by supply and demand.
- ➤ In a perfectly competitive market the demand curve for an individual supplier is a horizontal straight line at the selling price.
- ➤ Marginal revenue is the additional revenue that can be obtained from selling one more unit of a product.
- ➤ Marginal cost is the amount of cost increase made by a unit increase in output.

- The perfectly competitive market model shows aspects of economic theory which work well in aggregate terms. In the real world, individual producers modify it with specific pricing models.
- Monopolistic competition occurs when there are many sellers of similar but not identical products in the market.
- Subtle differences exist between a perfectly competitive market model and the monopolistic competitive model. The differences lie in the shapes of the revenue and demand curves.
- The demand for a product in monopolistic competition increases as the price declines. To increase unit sales the supplier must reduce prices.
- A monopoly exists when a firm is the only producer of a product that is in demand.
- A monopoly usually sets reasonable prices since it is required by law to submit its production cost data to a regulatory body in order to obtain any further increase in prices.
- An oligopoly market consists of several large suppliers which dominate a market and compete against each other.
- There are various ways of determining prices in oligopolistic markets. One way is for an oligopolistic firm to establish a price – that is, for it to be a price leader.
- The economist's approach to pricing uses a mathematical model to determine the price and optimum output level of the product.
- Business people usually use a cost-plus mark-up formula to price goods.
- The contribution approach to pricing is different from the full cost pricing model. *Contributions* means the excess of revenue over variable costs for an identifiable activity.
- Fixed costs are not assigned to the cost objective directly under the contribution method but they are taken into account in determining the amount to be added to the variable costs to arrive at the price.
- Caribbean governments interfere with the free workings of the price mechanism using taxation, subsidies and price controls.
- At the micro-economic level, government subsidies are paid to producers to increase the attractiveness of supplying a product, or to produce a social product.

- At the macro-economic level, government subsidies are incentives to firms to establish themselves in a particular area or region.
- All Caribbean governments offer incentives, which are stated in their investment-incentive laws, to firms or corporations from developed countries to establish firms in their countries.
- There are two aspects to price controls: stockpiling and rationing.
- Cartels can emerge as a result of large firms absorbing or taking over smaller firms, firms amalgamating or joining together mutually to form bigger firms, and firms cooperating with each other.
- A cash sale is created when a person pays money directly to a firm's cashier for its product or service.
- Credit is a facility extended by a vendor permitting another person (the debtor) to purchase goods or services without making immediate payment.
- A credit sale means that no cash is paid when goods or services are handed over or rendered to a customer by someone who is authorized by the firm to do so.
- Hire purchase is a practical and convenient source of short-term credit used for the purchase of equipment and household appliances.
- A disadvantage of hire purchase is that it is an expensive form of credit. The interest element built into the hire purchase instalments is very high.
- To encourage customers to pay the amount of money shown on their invoices before the end of the credit period, some firms offer a cash discount.
- Trade discounts are used to calculate the net purchase price of goods sent to retailers.
- Consumerism came about as a result of the bad side of marketing.
- Consumer protection is enacted through Caribbean laws.

Questions

1 Describe the cost factors affecting the price of a manufactured product.

2 How is accounting profit or loss calculated?

3 What are the assumptions of perfectly competitive markets?

4 Someone asks you, 'What is monopolistic competition?' Explain in your own words what it is.

5 Write short notes on (a) monopoly (b) oligopoly.

6 When is a cash sale created? What are its advantages?

7 What are credit sales? Describe any advantages that buyers and sellers obtain from credit sales.

8 What is a hire purchase? What are its advantages and disadvantages?

9 Are there any differences between cash and trade discounts? Explain your answer.

10 List the premises on which consumerism is based.

11 Compare and contrast cost-based and demand-based pricing methods.

12 State the laws of your country that protect consumers' interests and compare them with the laws of Jamaica described on pages 131–32.

13 Discuss the role played by the ministry or government department in your country which looks after consumer affairs.

Chapter 8 Distribution

Distribution in a marketing sense means all the activities involved in the movement of goods or services from the producer to the supplier and to a convenient place where they can be seen and acquired by users. In fulfilling those activities, the distribution function incurs the following costs: delivery, depots, distributors, selling, sales promotion and advertising. Distribution is adequate when the product or service satisfies demand.

8.1 The distribution chain

The parties involved in the channels of distribution are manufacturers, wholesalers, retailers, facilitating agents and consumers.

- The *manufacturers* are the producers of the finished product which is made from raw materials or semi-finished components.
- *Wholesalers*, also called *middlemen*, sell the finished products to retailers or to institutions that require the products for re-sale.
- The *retailer* is also a middleman who does not produce the finished or semi-finished products but sells them to consumers.
- *Facilitating agents* are financial institutions or transportation firms which help manufacturers, wholesalers and retailers with the flow of the products in the distribution channel.

8.2 Outlets for distribution

The outlets for distribution are, for example, shops, department stores, mail order companies, telephone systems, auctions and vending machines.

Shops

Shops are owned by retailers who buy at one price from a manufacturer or wholesaler and sell at a higher price. Shops provide customers with a service. In the Caribbean, examples of shops are florists, pharmacists, newsagents, rum shops, ice-cream salesmen (with a mobile van), haberdashers.

Department stores

The department store is a large store which tries to control all aspects of its business in one place – it is *horizontally integrated*. It has many departments which sell lots of different kinds of household goods.

Mail order companies

This type of distribution is now called *direct response marketing*. This postal trade is obtained by advertisement in the press, direct mail, catalogues and mail drops.

Telephone systems

This is another kind of direct response marketing. A salesperson telephones prospective clients using numbers from a telephone directory. Space selling, for example for advertising in newspapers and magazines, is often done by telephone.

Auctions

An auction takes place in public. An authorized auctioneer uses the method of competitive bidding by prospective buyers to sell the principal goods. An auctioneer has physical control over the goods consigned to them. He or she arranges their display, conducts the auction, makes collection from buyers and remits the proceeds (less commission) to the principal.

In the Caribbean the types of goods sold by auction are old furniture, household items, government used vehicles and goods from bankrupt companies.

Vending machines

A vending machine is an automatic device which gives up a product or performs a service when the correct money (usually coins) is inserted into the machine. They usually sell soft drinks, coffee, tea, cigarettes and candy, or perform a service, for example washing clothes or playing records.

Vending machines are usually placed in areas where there is a large number of people, for example in office buildings, schools, universities, churches and entertainment centres.

Typical vending machines at the International Airport in The Bahamas

8.3 The importance of transport in marketing

Transportation is the means by which goods are moved from one place to another, for example by boat, bicycle, cart, plane, train or truck.

Transport is concerned with the temporary handling and storage of goods before their consumption. The sensible handling of transported goods influences the marketability of a firm's products. Transport of goods also involves inventory control, order size control and order processing, which in turn influences costs and pricing policies. If all factors are not carefully planned and considered, a transportation firm can incur added costs for businesses, whether they are operating in local, regional or international markets. By distributing goods to prospective users and providing a service (that is, accepting the risk) the transport function plays an important role in the marketing mix.

8.4 Forms of transport

In the Caribbean, goods are moved by land, air, sea and pipeline. On land goods may be moved on bicycles, on carts drawn by horses or donkeys, on trucks, by trains and vans via roads and highways, and by boat along river networks. Nearly all Caribbean export goods are carried to the airports or harbours by road.

The exception is crude oil, which is pumped from its source directly to tankers anchored in harbours or at sea. The oil pipeline is a special transportation method which was developed to overcome certain problems peculiar to a product. The crude oil from Aruba, Barbados, Curaçao, Trinidad & Tobago and Venezuela is piped directly from the source to oil tankers. Oil tankers also return the refined oil via pipelines.

Exports are also made by air. Air freighting is a growing industry. In nearly all Caribbean airports, there is a government corporation which deals with air freighted goods. Goods are carried by air when fast delivery is needed and the goods are not bulky or too heavy. Examples of Caribbean goods that are air freighted daily are: ceramics, fruits and flowers.

A group of packages going to one destination is often transported together in a container. *Containerization* makes sea and air freighting easier and is less costly. Material handling is easier and loading and turnaround times can be reduced. There is also less damage to goods and it makes sensible use of storage space. Examples of exports to other countries are aloes, bananas, bauxite, petroleum, spices, sugar and rum.

A substantial amount of Caribbean goods is transported by ships and boats between the islands as well as to the USA and European countries. Examples of exports by ships between Caribbean countries are bananas, plantains, potatoes, rum and sugar.

Containers being loaded on a ship in port

The advantages and disadvantages of the different forms of transport

The advantages of *land transport* are that it is a convenient way of getting bulky goods to customers, and it aids commercial expansion. The disadvantages are that it is expensive, and if the road network is poor, goods may be damaged.

The advantages of *air transport*:

1 It is a quick way of getting perishable goods or urgently required goods to the marketplace.

2 It enables new products to be distributed quickly to other regions and countries.

3 It allows buyers to carry a minimum of inventory or stock.

4 Sellers can therefore reduce or eliminate warehouse costs.

The disadvantages of air transport are that it is expensive, and it cannot easily handle heavy or bulky products.

Advantages of *sea transport* are that it is a good way of handling 'messy' products, for example oil or tar, and it is cheap in comparison with air rates. The disadvantages are that it delays information-gathering about a product, especially in foreign markets. It also means that the buying company must carry plenty of stock, which adds to the cost of the product.

8.5 The problems of distribution

A distribution system is made up of three elements:

1 A set of fixed facilities at which goods are produced or inventories stored.

2 A set of inventory goods.

3 A transportation network connecting the fixed facilities with each other and with customers and receiving points.

This network enables goods to pass from producing points to intermediate holding points and thence to re-sellers, processors or end users.

A manufacturing firm needs to minimize its inventory holdings and keep its transportation costs as low as possible. How can it do this?

1 It can create a traffic department which calculates the best rates and routes, and knows
   (a) what shipments are made from origin to destination
   (b) how often
   (c) under what conditions
   (d) by what routes and
   (e) with what degree of reliability.

2 It can analyse the needs and expectations of buyers at all distribution levels.

3 It can ask the middlemen at each distribution level to supply timely quantitative and qualitative data on the manufacturing firm's products.

4 It can employ a total logistic concept at the corporate level.

5 It can free transportation personnel from the idea of only carrying out a specific task or function.

Other problems of distribution include the following:

1 Delayed shipment because of improper labelling of goods.

2 Misdirection of goods.

3 Failure to comply with a custom authority regulation on exportation of goods.

4 Inadequate warehousing facilities – goods may not be adequately protected from the weather, or held in storage that is not secure.

5 Ineffective communication between sections of the distribution system.

6 Differences in opinion on how goods should be marketed and by whom.

7 Industrial unrest, for example disputes between the harbour or airport employers and employees which may lead to strikes and picketing.

8 Work-related problems. For example, since the introduction in some ports of cranes for the purpose of loading and off-loading cargo into and from ships in an economical way, management and workers in those ports have not changed their attitudes towards work. Workers still restrict their work activities, and Customs Officers restrict gantry cranes from working at their maximum capacity by using time-wasting documentary procedures and inspection techniques of a past period.

The minimization of some distribution problems

The first three of the problems listed above can be minimized by management educating the personnel responsible for a firm's exports in sensible, standardized documentation procedures. Problem 4 can be overcome by implementing proper warehousing methods: management can provide proper storage facilities, introduce policing methods, screen workers and dismiss workers for acts of pilferage. Problems 5 and 6 can be minimized by any of the following methods:

- proper channel design
- employment of democratic channel management, and
- employment of centrally controlled channel management.

If it is directly involved in problem 7, an exporting firm can make any of the following decisions:

- appeal to labour to change its position
- modify or abandon the policy that led to the unrest
- ask the government to help in settling the unrest
- cease its exporting activities.

Problem 8 can be remedied by selecting harbour or port management according to merit; by asking the labour unions to agree to the elimination of work preservation schemes; by asking labour to undertake training which will enable them to be 'all-rounders'; by asking customs to change those inspection techniques that are based on fiscal requirements as opposed to commercial requirements; and by linking computer networks and communication systems between the customs departments of different countries.

Key Points

- ➤ Distribution is adequate when the product or service satisfies demand.
- ➤ The parties involved in the channels of distribution are manufacturers, wholesalers, retailers, facilitating agents and consumers.
- ➤ Outlets for distribution are shops, department stores, mail order companies, telephone systems, auctions and vending machines.
- ➤ Transport is concerned with the temporary handling and storage of goods before their consumption.
- ➤ The transportation of goods is associated not only with handling but also with inventory control, order size control and order processing.

- In the Caribbean, goods are moved by land, air and sea.
- Air freighting is used by exporting firms when fast delivery of goods is needed and the goods are not too bulky or too heavy.
- Containerization makes air freighting easier and less costly.
- A substantial quantity of Caribbean goods are transported by ships and boats between the islands as well as to the USA and European countries.
- A distribution system is made up of three elements: (1) a set of fixed facilities at which goods are produced or inventories stored, (2) a set of inventory goods, and (3) a transportation network connecting the fixed facilities with each other and with customers and receiving points.

Questions

1. Write short notes on the distribution chain.
2. Describe the outlets for distribution.
3. Describe the forms of transport in the Caribbean.
4. What are the advantages and disadvantages of the different forms of transport?
5. Outline the problems of distribution and state how the problems can be solved or minimized.

A Note on Business Documents: Chapters 9–12

Business documents are official records by which a firm's economic affairs are conducted and recorded. They also reveal the basic uncertainties of a business. In some cases, business documents provide the means by which an accounting function records the economic transactions peculiar to that firm.

It is because of uncertainty, the role of money and the stewardship function which underlies economic action of managers that the need for business documents arises.

Business documents facilitate communication within and between firms. When they are used for transaction purposes, they help the management function, either now or in the future, to reconstruct seeming facts of reality. There is in fact a gap between what business documents recording monetary transactions claim to record, and observed reality.

Business transactions

The term *business transaction* means a 'transfer of goods or services from one person to another'. In the Caribbean, millions of transactions take place every day. Where a transaction involves the provision of goods and services in return for immediate cash payment, it is called a *cash transaction*. Where payment is delayed until a later date, it is called a *credit transaction*. There are two sides to all transactions: (a) goods or services are given up, and (b) cash payments are made for them. The time interval between (a) and (b) is called the *period of credit*. This is the time it takes for a firm to pay what it owes to another firm.

Business documents

Business documents used by Caribbean firms include inventory cards, purchase requisitions, requests for quotation, purchase orders, purchase invoices, shipping order forms, sales invoices, statements of account and debit and credit notes. Chapters 9–12 explain the need for these business documents, and describe why and how they originate in a firm.

Chapter 9 Processing Purchases of Goods

The purchasing of goods is an important function of a business. A firm purchases goods either for resale or as inputs into the making of other goods for resale. The goods that a firm does not sell are stored and are called *inventory*. Processing purchases requires verification and control by management over the ordering, receiving and payment for the goods.

9.1 Ordering the goods

In a small shop, the activities involved in the ordering of goods are done by the proprietor. In a large firm, the ordering operation is done by the purchasing department whose head is called a *purchasing officer*. The ordering function involves the following:

- the determination of the items to be purchased
- selecting a supplier
- placing the order.

9.2 The determination of purchases

The signal that goods are to be ordered in an on-going business is obtained from its inventory cards, which are kept and updated by an inventory clerk. The inventory card (Figure 9.1) is a record of each item that needs to be replenished. It has a minimum and a maximum stock level.

9.3 Starting the purchasing activity

To start the purchasing activity (see Figure 9.1) the stock department officer, after being informed by the stock clerk that the minimum stock has been reached, will prepare a purchase requisition asking the purchasing officer to order the specified number of doors.

A purchasing requisition shows the following information:

- who is making the request
- the number of units to be purchased
- when the units are required.

Figure 9.1
Inventory card

An inventory card provides a record of the stock of one item only. Here, the maximum stock is 20. The minimum stock is 5. On the date 10.4.19XX, the stock clerk will re-order fifteen 3' 8" x 6' 8" mahogany doors.

NO. 2				
Item				mahogany doors
Location: Rack 1	Bin 1			
Minimum: 5				Maximum: 20
Date 19XX	Quantity received	Unit cost $	Quantity sold	Balance
1.4	20	600		20
5.4			5	15
10.4			15	5

Figure 9.2 shows a purchase requisition form of the Samuels Company.

Figure 9.2
Purchase requisition

SAMUELS LTD		PURCHASE REQUISITION Requisition NO. R500
DATE NEEDED: 20.4.19XX		DATE REQUESTED: 10.4.19XX
Ship to: Stock room		
Requested by: A. Layne, Stock Clerk		
Quantity		Description
On hand	To order	3'8" x 6'8" mahogany doors
5	15	

9.4 Selecting the supplier

The purchasing officer obtains from trade catalogues a list of suppliers who sell the goods which the firm requires. The trade catalogue also shows pictures and gives details of the goods. From the list a supplier is selected who meets the firm's goals as to reliability in delivery dates, quality of goods, price and credit terms.

If the items requisitioned have not been ordered before, the purchasing officer will request prices from prospective suppliers via a formal letter, which is called a *request for quotation*. The letter informs the prospective supplier of the firm, and the agent asking for a quotation, what items and quantities are required and when the items are needed.

Figure 9.3 shows a request for a quotation from Samuels Ltd to Anthony Ltd, manufacturers of mahogany doors. In practice, these forms will be sent out to many different suppliers.

Figure 9.3 Request for quotation

Samuels Ltd 20 George Street ST VINCENT	**Request for a Quotation** THIS IS NOT AN ORDER
Anthony Ltd 201 Charlotte Street Port-of-Spain TRINIDAD	
Please quote us your terms and delivery charges on the item shown below.	RQ NO. 543 Date: 10.4.19XX Please reply by 15.4.19XX W. Samuel, Purchasing officer

Date needed: 20.4.19XX

Quantity	**Description**	**Quoted unit price**
15	3'8" x 6'8" mahogany doors	

TERMS:	FIRM: Anthony Ltd
DATE:	AGENT: M. Hewit

Figure 9.4 shows the same form sent back to Samuels Ltd with the requested data filled in by the sales agent of Anthony Ltd.

Figure 9.4 Request for quotation completed by sales agent

Samuels Ltd
20 George Street
ST VINCENT

Request for a Quotation
THIS IS NOT AN ORDER

Anthony Ltd
201 Charlotte Street
Port-of-Spain
TRINIDAD

Please quote us your terms and delivery charges on the item shown below.

RQ NO. 543
Date: 10.4.19XX
Please reply by 15.4.19XX
W. Samuel, Purchasing officer

Date needed: 20.4.19XX

Quantity	**Description**	**Quoted unit price**
15	3'8" x 6'8" mahogany doors	$605.00

TERMS: 2/10, N/30

FOB Port-of-Spain
FIRM: Anthony Ltd

DATE: 12.4.19XX

AGENT: M. Hewit

Notes

1 The credit terms of Anthony Ltd are 2/10, N/30. The expression 2/10 means that the prospective buyer can deduct 2 per cent of the amount stated on the bill if it is paid within ten days from the date of the bill. N means *net*, and N/30 means that if the buyer does not wish to take advantage of the cash discount, there is a 30-day limit in which to pay the amount stated on the bill. If the expression was N/EOM, that would mean that the net amount of the bill would have to be paid at the end of the month.

2 In addition to specifying credit terms (which can vary between firms), Anthony Ltd indicates that the goods will be shipped free on board (FOB) Trinidad by any means of transportation (aircraft, ship) at the shipping point. This means that the seller will deliver the goods to the carrier, but the buyer must bear the transportation costs whenever FOB shipping point is quoted. It is also possible for goods to be shipped FOB destination. This means that the *seller* will bear the transportation charges to whatever FOB destination is quoted.

Cash discounts are given to debtors to encourage prompt payment. Cash discounts applied to a purchase invoice are called *purchase discounts*.

A cash discount is different from a trade discount. A trade discount is a reduction in the catalogue price of an article, given by a wholesaler or manufacturer to a retailer, to enable the latter to make a profit and, because the latter bought in bulk, resulting in some savings.

9.5 Placing the order

A firm's order for goods is made via a *purchase order*, which is drawn up by a purchasing officer. It authorizes the supplier to send the goods specified on the form, and to charge the purchaser for the goods at the quoted price. The purchase order contains the following information:

- a figure which shows the quantity ordered
- a stock number for the item(s)
- a brief description of the item(s)
- the unit price
- the terms for paying the bill
- instructions for shipping the goods.

Figure 9.5 shows a purchase order of Samuels Ltd.

Figure 9.5
A purchase order

PURCHASE ORDER

PO 600
Req. No. 542

Samuels Ltd
20 George Street
ST VINCENT

Anthony Ltd
201 Charlotte Street
Port-of-Spain
TRINIDAD

DATE ISSUED	DATE NEEDED	TERMS
10.4.19XX	20.4.19XX	2/10, N/30

VIA CARIBBEAN AIRWAYS FOB PORT-OF-SPAIN

QUANTITY ORDERED	STOCK NO.	DESCRIPTION	UNIT PRICE
15	MD01	3'8"x 6'8"	

by W. Samuel
Purchasing Agent

The copies of a purchase order

The number of copies of a purchase order that are prepared by a firm's purchasing agent depends upon the size of the business and on its control system. The control aspect of purchases centres around the supplier, the requesting department, the purchasing department, the receiving department and the inventory department. Obviously, for Samuels Ltd, five copies of the purchase order will be prepared.

The top copy is sent to the supplier, Anthony Ltd, who will acknowledge receipt of the order. Copy 2 is forwarded to the requesting department to confirm that the goods are now on order. Copy 3 is sent to the purchasing department where it is filed. Copy 4 is sent to the receiving section. Copy 5 is sent to the inventory section where it is kept until the goods ordered actually arrive.

9.6 Receiving the goods

Copies 4 and 5 are linked up with accounting activities. When ordered, goods arrive at the receiving department, and the receiving clerks check the goods to determine whether any shortages, errors or damage have occurred in the shipment. The receiving clerk enters the count of the goods actually received on copy 4 of the purchase order. If any goods are damaged or missing, or they do not tally with their description on the purchase order, the receiving clerk holds the shipment and notifies the purchasing agent who can advise the receiving department either (a) to send back all of the goods, or (b) to send back the damaged goods, on receipt of which the shortfalls will be dispatched.

If there is nothing wrong with the goods, the receiving clerk initials the appropriate items in the approved section of copy 4. The goods are then sent along with copy 4 to the stockroom where the goods are checked before being placed into inventory. Copy 4 is used here for updating the inventory card(s). Copy 5 is also initialled by the receiving clerk and sent to the purchasing agent to inform him that the shipment has been received and accepted.

Figure 9.6 shows the purchase invoice of Samuels Ltd and Figure 9.7 is a flow chart of a purchasing system.

Figure 9.6
A purchase invoice

ANTHONY LTD
201 CHARLOTTE STREET
PORT-OF-SPAIN
TRINIDAD

Invoice No. 426

SOLD TO: Samuels Ltd
20 George Street
ST VINCENT

SHIP TO: Same

INVOICE DATE:

TERMS: 2/10, N/30

CUSTOMER ORDER NO.	**DATE**	**SHIPPED VIA**	**FOB**	**NO. OF CONTAINERS**
PO600	13.4.19XX	Caribbean Airways	Trinidad	
Quantity shipped	**Stock no.**	**Description:**	**Unit price:**	**Amount:**
15	MD101	mahogany doors	$605.00	$9,075.00

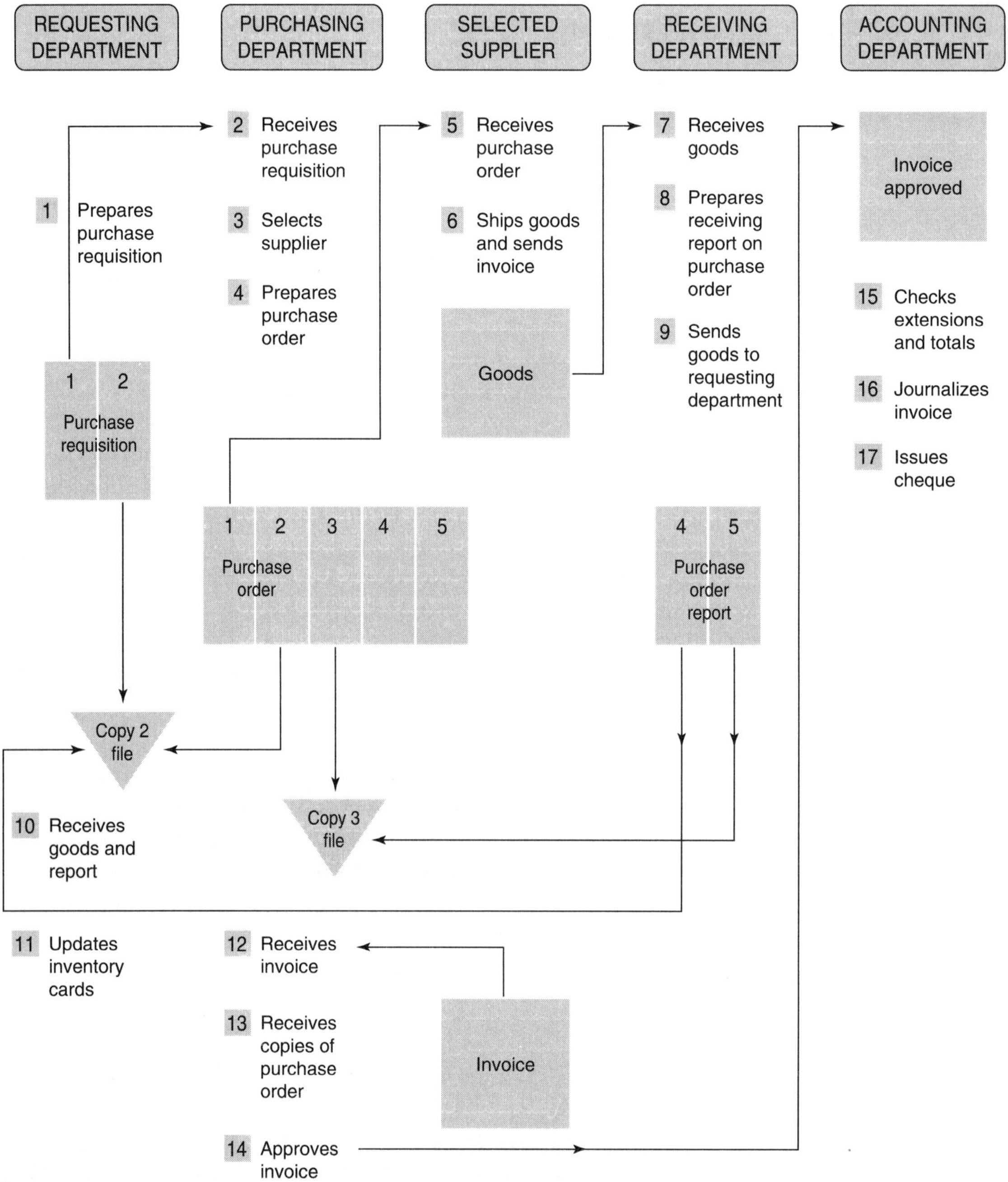

Figure 9.7
A flow chart of a purchasing system

Figure 10.3 on page 159 shows the sales invoice – note the similarities between Figures 9.6 and 10.3. To the purchasing firm a purchase invoice shows the items the company has bought. To the supplier company the sales invoice shows the items the company has sold.

9.7 Confirmation of the purchase order and the invoice

Copy 5 indicates to the purchasing agent that the ordered goods have been received in good condition. Now the agent awaits an invoice from the supplier. When the invoice is received, it shows the name and address of the seller and buyer, the invoice number and date, the terms, the buyer's purchase order number and date (for cross-reference), the method of shipment, the quantity, price and description of each item shipped.

Unlike the purchase order, an invoice contains a computation of the amount owed. Each amount shown in the amount column is called an *extension*. An extension is calculated by multiplying the unit price of an item by the number of units shipped.

9.8 Comparison of an invoice with the purchase order

When Samuels Ltd receives the invoice from Anthony Ltd it is compared with copy 5 of the purchase order to verify that it has been billed only for the goods actually received as previously ordered. If there are any discrepancies between the purchase order and the invoice, the supplier is notified. If the invoice is correct, the purchasing department stamps the invoice with an official stamp. The invoice is then forwarded to the accounting department. There, it is re-checked for arithmetical accuracy, journalized and approved for payment. Copy 5 is then entered in numerical sequence in the purchasing department's file of completed purchase orders.

9.9 The purchase invoices and accounting

Figure 9.8 shows in diagrammatical form the accounting treatment of a firm's purchase invoices in relation to its purchase book, purchase ledger, general ledger and cash book.

Figure 9.8 Accounting treatment of a firm's purchase invoice

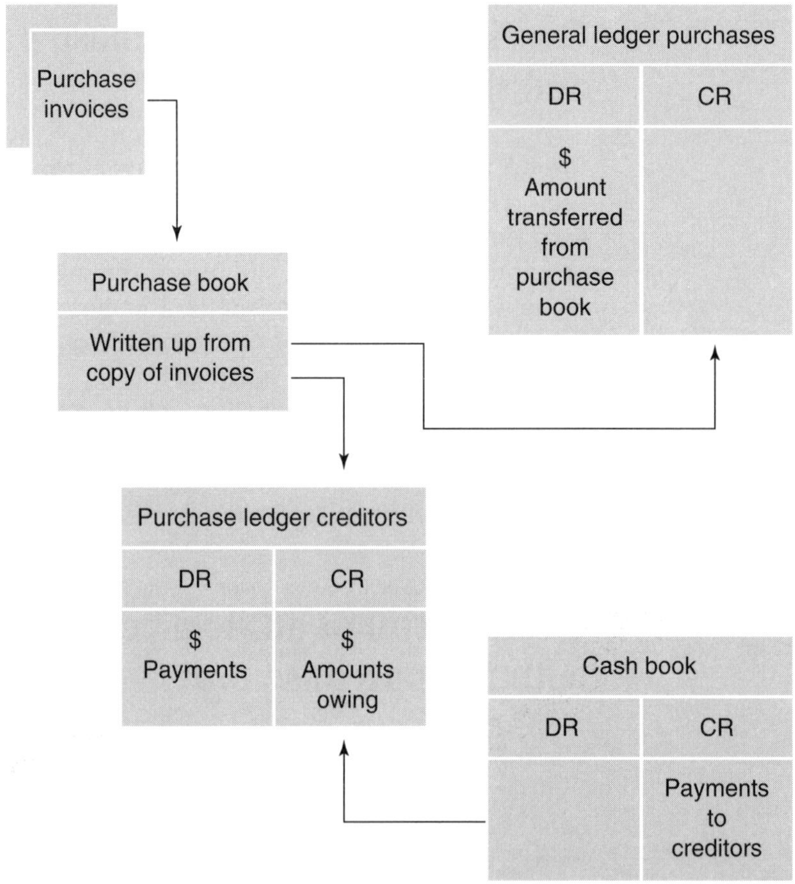

Key Points

- The goods that a firm does not sell are stored and are called *inventory*.
- In a large firm the ordering operation is done by the purchasing department whose head is called a *purchasing officer*.
- The signal that goods are to be ordered in an on-going business is obtained from its inventory cards, which are kept and updated by an inventory clerk.
- An inventory card has a minimum and a maximum stock level.
- A purchasing requisition shows who is making the request, the number of units to be purchased, and when the units are required.
- The purchasing officer obtains from trade catalogues a list of suppliers who sell the goods that the firm requires.

- Cash discounts are given to debtors to encourage prompt payment. Cash discounts applied to purchase invoices are called *purchase discounts*.
- A purchase order authorizes the supplier to send the goods specified on the form, and to charge the purchaser for the goods at the quoted price.
- The number of copies of a purchase order that are prepared by a firm's purchasing agent depends upon the size of the business and on its control system.
- When ordered goods arrive at the receiving department, the receiving clerks check the goods to determine whether any shortages, errors or damage have occurred in the shipment.
- Unlike the purchase order, an invoice contains a computation of the amount owed.
- An *extension* is calculated by multiplying the unit price of an item by the number of units shipped.
- If there are any discrepancies between the purchase order and the invoice, the supplier is notified.

Questions

1. Why is there a need for business documents?
2. What is meant by a *cash payment*, a *credit transaction*, a *period of credit*?
3. Briefly outline the procedures in processing the purchasing of goods for a merchandising firm.
4. What information does a purchasing requisition show?
5. How does a firm go about selecting a supplier of goods?
6. What information does a request for a quotation show?
7. What are credit terms? What are cash discounts? What does FOB mean?
8. Outline the flow of the copies of a purchase order.
9. Draw a flow chart of a purchasing system.
10. Show the accounting treatment of the money flows resulting from a firm's purchase invoices.

Chapter 10 Processing Sales on Credit

Processing credit sales in a firm involves the following activities: (a) a system for the control of credit sales, (b) receiving and approving the orders, (c) preparing a shipping order, (d) securing credit approval, (e) packing and shipping the goods, (f) billing the customers, and (g) preparation of the sales invoice.

10.1 The control of credit sales

A firm ensures that a customer's order is properly handled and promptly approved or disapproved, that the goods are dispatched from the stock, and that the customer is accurately billed for the goods. It does this by placing responsible people in charge of the sales, inventory and accounting departments respectively.

10.2 Approving orders

Orders for goods reach a firm's sales department in different ways, for example by telephone, telex, sales staff, letters and, of course, by purchase order forms. A firm that processes a large number of orders received in so many ways standardizes that procedure so that it can deal with them quickly and efficiently. Sales clerks enter each order on the firm's shipping order form.

In a medium to large firm, the control aspect of credit sales normally requires that seven copies be made of the shipping order form.

Figure 10.1 shows a shipping order form prepared from the purchase order submitted to Anthony Ltd by Samuels Ltd (see Chapter 9). The shipping order is a facsimile of a purchase order, but the sales clerk verifies the accuracy of the credit terms, stock numbers and unit prices on the purchase order.

When the sales clerks complete a shipping order, they attach copy 1 of the shipping order to the purchase order and place it in the unshipped order file. Copy 1 is a control copy which is kept in the sales department as a record that the order was received.

Samuels Ltd
20 George Street
ST VINCENT

SHIPPING ORDER
No. SO 511

DATE: 12.4.19XX

SOLD TO: Anthony Ltd
201 Charlotte Street
Port-of-Spain
TRINIDAD

SHIP TO: Same

FOB	Ship via:	PO Number 600	PO Date
Port-of-Spain	Caribbean Airways	Terms: 2.10, N/30	10.4.19XX Date needed: 20.4.19XX

QUANTITY	**STOCK NO.**	**DESCRIPTION**	**UNIT PRICE $**	**QUANTITY SHIPPED**
15	MD01	3'8" x 6'8"	605.00	
15		TOTAL		15

Figure 10.1
A shipping order

10.3 Securing credit approval

A firm's credit department determines whether or not a customer is likely to pay the bill when it falls due. Assuming that a customer has a good credit rating, the credit clerk will send copy 2 to the customer to acknowledge that the order has been received and is being processed.

At this stage the clerk signs all other copies. The clerk's signature indicates to others who will make further decisions on the copies that the customer's credit has been checked and approved. Copy 3 is filed and the other copies are sent to the stock department.

10.4 Packing and shipping of goods

When copy 4 arrives in the stockroom, a clerk assembles the specified items and packs them in boxes or containers. Each item is ticked off on copy 4, which is enclosed with the contents of the boxes or containers. Copy 5, the control copy, is filed. From it the inventory cards can be updated.

The stock clerk's duties are completed at this stage. Copies 6 and 7 are sent to the sales department.

10.5 Billing for the goods

In the sales department, copies 6 and 7 are compared with the control copy 1 in order to verify the correctness of the items shipped. On copies 6 and 7 arithmetical calculations are performed by a sales clerk who multiplies each quantity shipped by the unit price, enters the result in the amount column and totals it. Copy 6 is now placed in an order shipped file. Copy 7 is sent to the accounting department. Copy 7 is a key document – it provides the data for the preparation of the sales invoice.

10.6 Preparing the sales invoice

The sales invoice looks like a completed copy of the shipping order. It shows how much a customer owes a business for goods or services.

At least three copies of a sales invoice are prepared in the billing section of an accounting department. Copy 1 is sent to the customer, copy 2 is kept in the accounting department as a source document for journalizing the sales transactions, and copy 3 goes to the sales department where it is used for analysing sales revenue. Figure 10.2 is a flow chart of a sales system, and Figure 10.3 shows the invoice from Anthony Ltd to Samuels Ltd.

10.7 Sales invoices and accounting

Figure 10.4 shows the links between a firm's sales invoices, sales book, general sales ledger, sales ledger (debtors) and the cash book.

Figure 10.2
Flow chart of a sales system

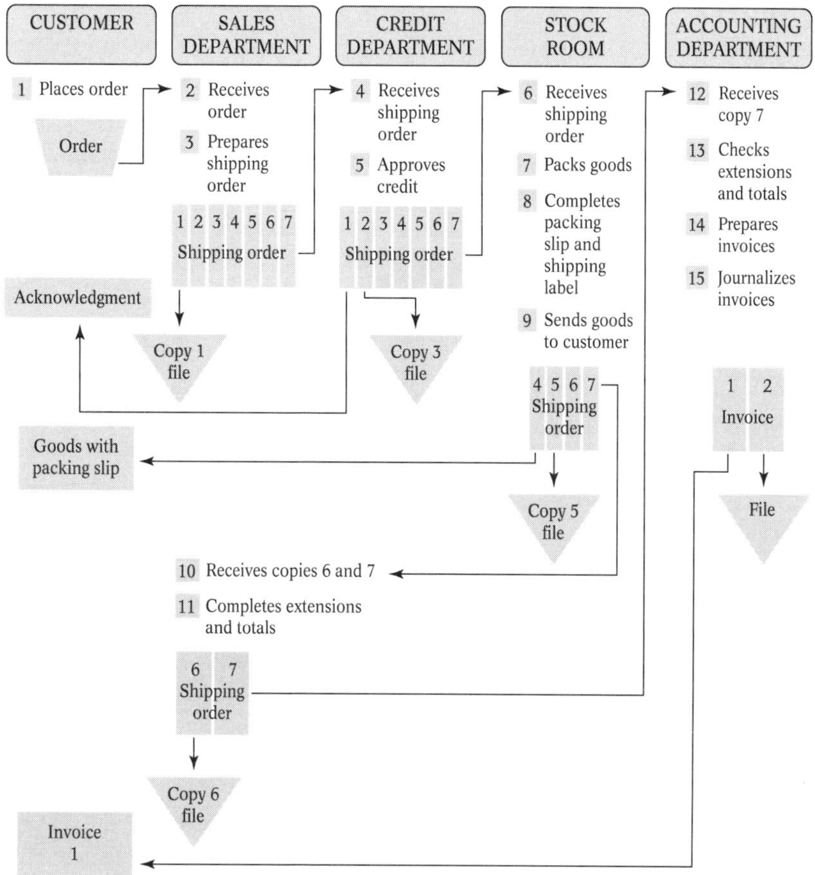

Figure 10.3
A sales invoice

Anthony Ltd **201 Charlotte Street** **Port-of-Spain** **TRINIDAD**				**Invoice No.** 426
SOLD TO: Samuels Ltd, 20 George Street, ST VINCENT **SHIP TO:** Same				**Invoice date:** 20.4.19XX **Terms:** 2/10, N/30
Purchase order No. 600	**Date** 13.4.19XX	**Shipped via** Caribbean Airways	**FOB** Trinidad	**No. of Containers** 1
Quantity	**Stock no.**	**Description**	**Unit price $**	**Amount $**
15	MD01	Mahogany doors	605	9,075.00
			Total	9,075.00

Figure 10.4 Accounting treatment of a firm's sales invoices

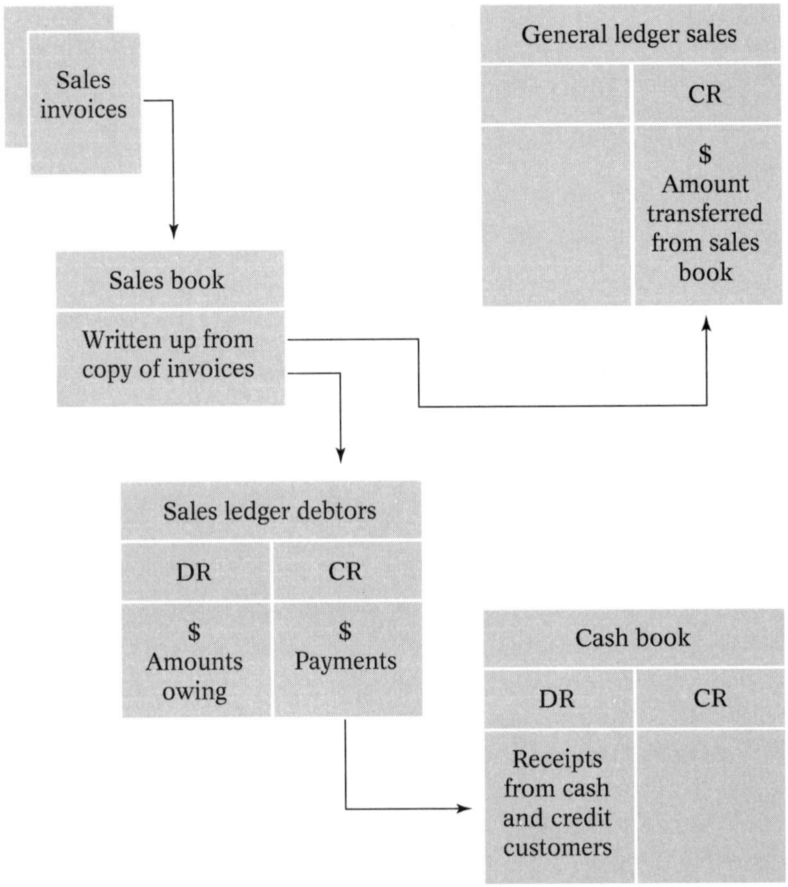

10.8 Credit and debit notes

A credit note is created if the goods shipped are found to be faulty, or if a supplier has overcharged a customer on a sales invoice.

Let us assume that the purchasing agent of Samuels Ltd notifies Anthony Ltd that two mahogany doors were received in a damaged condition, and that they are being sent back. When the doors are returned, Anthony Ltd will issue a credit note to Samuels Ltd for $1,210. The credit note acknowledges that the amount owed by

Samuels Ltd on the invoice should be reduced by the dollar amount of the doors returned. The accounting treatment of Samuels Ltd is to credit the purchaser's account or purchase returns account with the dollar amount of the goods returned.

A debit note from the supplier of goods can also inform the debtor of an increase in the amount owed to a creditor. Let us assume that the accounting department of Anthony Ltd notifies Samuels Ltd that the total cost of the mahogany doors is $9,220 and not $9,075. Anthony Ltd will then issue a debit note to Samuels Ltd. The accounting treatment of Anthony Ltd will be to credit the sales account and debit the Samuels Ltd account with the amount of the increase.

In general, three copies each of a credit or debit note are issued for the particular case. Copy 1 goes to the customer. Copy 2 goes to the seller's accounting department as a source document for crediting/debiting the customer's account, and copy 3 is filed by the sales department.

After the dollar amount of a credit or debit note has been recorded in the supplier's books and in the customer's books, their records of how much is owed should tally.

10.9 Statement of account

A statement of account originates from the supplying firm. It is a follow-up to an invoice, and is sent to firms or customers who owe for credit sales. The statement is issued from the accounting department, prepared from the data found in the customer's accounts.

A statement of account may be sent to all customers at the end of each month, or may be sent out on a cycle plan. The firm that is owed money for goods sends such statements to debtor customers so that account balances can be verified. The statement reminds debtors that a settlement is due.

A statement of account can be prepared either as a non-descriptive statement or as a descriptive statement. A *non-descriptive statement of account* shows the debtor's balance due at the end of a month. This type of statement is used by professional people, for example doctors, dentists, accountants. Most merchandising businesses use a *descriptive statement*, which lists the customer's transactions during a particular month. Figure 10.5 shows the statement used by Anthony Ltd.

Anthony Ltd 201 Charlotte Street Port-of-Spain TRINIDAD				
Account no. 365720				
Samuels Ltd 20 George Street ST VINCENT				
Month ending 27 April 19XX				
				Balance forward: Nil
DATE	**REFERENCE**	**DESCRIPTION**	**ORDER NO.**	**AMOUNT**
27 April				
Current	Over 30 days	Over 60 days	Over 90 days	Over 120 days
			Balance	

Anthony Ltd 201 Charlotte Street Port-of-Spain TRINIDAD		
Account no. 365720		
Month ending 27 April 19XX		
Balance forwarded		Nil
Date	Reference	Amount
29 April 19XX		
Please check (✓) invoices paid. Please detach and return this stub with your payment		
Balance		

Figure 10.5
Statement of account

10.10 VAT and the sales invoice

A sales invoice can also show where value added tax (VAT) is in operation, (a) by VAT registration number and (b) by a statement of the VAT charge for the supply of goods described on the invoice.

VAT is a way of obtaining revenue for a government by taxing each process that adds value so that those people who eventually obtain the benefit of the product pay a tax in proportion to the consumption enjoyed.

VAT is a European device – to date Trinidad & Tobago, Granada and Jamaica are the only Caribbean countries that have introduced VAT legislation. An advantage of VAT is that it spreads taxation over a wider range of consumer products. A disadvantage is that it requires many businesses to keep VAT records.

The example below shows how VAT is calculated on a sale that includes a discount.

Example 10.1

Samuels Ltd sells the following items to Wash Ltd of 30 Perm Road, St Vincent:

Two 3' 8" x 6' 8" mahogany doors at $750 each
Six copper hinges at $10 each
Twelve 2" copper screws at $5 each

Other relevant data:

Delivery charge $25
VAT rate 10%
Terms: Cash discount of 5% if paid within 10 days

Sales invoice No. 905
Sale date 5.8.19XX
VAT registration no. 256

Required:
Prepare the sales invoice and show the VAT.

Solution:
See Figure 10.6.

Figure 10.6 Sales invoice showing the calculation of VAT on a sale that includes discount

Sales invoice no. 905 — 5.8.19XX

TO: Wash Ltd
30 Perm Road
St Vincent

FROM: Samuels Ltd
20 George St
St Vincent

VAT reg. no. 256

Quantity	Description and price	Amount excl. VAT	VAT rate %	VAT net $
2	3'8" x 6'8" mahogany doors at $750 each	1,500.00		
6	Copper hinges at $10 each	60.00		
12	2" copper screws at $5 each	60.00		
	Delivery charge	1,620.00	10	153.90*
		25.00	10	2.50
		1,645.00		156.40
	VAT	156.40		
	TOTAL	$1,801.40		

*$(1,620 x 0.10 – (0.05 x 162)) = $153.90

Key Points

- Processing credit sales in a firm involves the following activities:

  (a) a system for the control of credit sales
  (b) receiving and approving the orders
  (c) preparing a shipping order
  (d) securing credit approval
  (e) packing and shipping the goods
  (f) billing the customers
  (g) preparation of the sales invoice.
- Orders for goods reach a firm's sales department by telephone, telex, salesmen, letters and purchase order forms.
- The shipping order is a facsimile of a purchase order.
- A firm's credit department determines whether or not a customer is likely to pay the bill when it falls due.
- An invoice shows how much a customer owes.
- A credit note is created if the goods shipped are found to be faulty, or if a supplier has overcharged a customer.
- A credit note acknowledges that the amount owed by a debtor should be reduced by the amount shown on the note.
- A debit note also originates from the supplier of goods. It informs the debtor of an increase in the amount owed to a creditor.
- After the dollar amount of a credit or debit note has been recorded in the supplier's books and in the customer's books, their records of how much is owed should tally.
- A statement of account originates from the supplying firm. The statement is issued from the accounting department. It is prepared from the data found in the customer's accounts.
- A statement of account can be prepared either as a non-descriptive statement or as a descriptive statement.
- VAT is a way of obtaining revenue for a government by taxing each process that adds value so that those people who eventually obtain the benefit of the product pay a tax in proportion to the consumption enjoyed.

Questions

1. List the activities involved in processing credit sales.
2. Why do firms standardize the receipt of orders?
3. When are the stock clerk's duties completed in processing sales on credit?

4 What is a sales invoice? What information does it contain?

5 Draw a flow chart of a sales system.

6 Show the accounting treatment of the money flows resulting from a firm's sales invoices.

7 Explain the concept of value added tax (VAT).

8 A furniture maker purchased the following items:

	Basic purchase price
	$
Wood	7,000
Stationery	500
Machinery	5,000

He paid $800 for accountancy services. The VAT was 10 per cent.

(a) What are his total purchases?
(b) What was the total VAT?
(c) What was his total invoice payable?

9 Assume that the same furniture maker recorded the following credit sales ledger entries for a particular week:

Day	**Credit sales**
	$
1	2,000
2	2,500
3	4,000
4	5,000

Returned goods were valued at $500.

Calculate
(a) his total credit sales
(b) the VAT charges
(c) the money owed to him.

10 Reconsider the problems in questions 8 and 9. Assume no bad debts. Calculate the amount due to the tax department.

Chapter 11 Business Instruments

Business instruments are documents or things sanctioned by custom or authorized by the laws of a country to facilitate money payments between individuals and firms. In the Caribbean the business instruments which facilitate everyday internal business transactions are legal tender, tenders for work activity, and cheques.

11.1 Legal tender

Legal tender means those forms of money that are accepted by law in settlement of a debt. One clause of the Barbados Currency Act 1965 states that currency shall be legal tender in the island for payment of any amount. Another clause states that coins, if the coins have not been illegally dealt with, shall be legal tender to an amount not exceeding $10 in the case of coins of denominations of not less than 25 cents, and not exceeding $2 in the case of coins of a lower denomination. The other Caribbean islands have similar currency Acts.

11.2 A tender for work activity

A tender is an advertised notice in the local or foreign press made by a large firm, by a government or by one of its corporations or departments, requesting interested firms to tender – that is, to submit a bid price for doing the advertised job.

Examples of tenders for various work activities are operation of a canteen, provision of laundry services, repairs and redecoration of government buildings, the manufacture of police uniforms, provision of security services, or road development projects. The advertised tender notice generally contains the following information:

1 The nature of work to be done and the commencement date.

2 The address of the authority awarding the contract.

3 The duration of the tender contract.

4 How the tender is to be sent.

5 Where the tender dossier can be obtained, the amount of deposit money to be paid for it, how the dossier will be sent or where it can be inspected if it relates to a foreign tender.

6 The closing date, time of submission of tender and date when the tender will be opened in public.

7 Regulations as to the sum of money, or approved securities or accredited insurance which must be put up as surety by the contractee if contract is awarded.

8 Warning as to what will be done if contractee owes money to national insurance or revenue departments of governments.

9 Warning that the authority will not bind itself to accept the lowest or any tender.

10 A note drawing attention to the labour clauses of the Public Contracts Act and stating where such an Act can be obtained.

Figure 11.1 Tender for a cleaning service

Figure 11.1 shows a typical tender notice.

1. Tenders are invited for the provision of cleaning services at the General Post Office complex at Cheapside, St. Michael, for the period 1 April 1991 to 31 March 1993.

2. The services required are:

(a) the daily cleaning of all areas of the Post Office and the Administration Building except the vaults;

(b) a thorough weekly cleaning of the Sorting Office, Parcel Processing and Delivery areas (basement) and vaults;

(c) 2(a) will be performed between 5 p.m. and 9 p.m. and 2(b) will be done during working hours at a time to be agreed between the contractor and Postmaster General;

(d) the total area to be cleaned is approximately 6,800 sq. metres.

Itemised details of the services to be provided are set out at Appendix 1 – Detail of Tender which must be obtained from the Postmaster General, and tenders must be based on those details. It is not necessary therefore for tenderers to submit their own separate details.

3. The successful tenderer will be required to enter into a contract in a form approved by the Solicitor General or other Legal Officer in the Public Service nominated by him, and must provide a surety for the due performance of the Contract. This surety must be:

(a) by way of a deposit with the Treasury of a sum of money or approved securities to the value of not less than 10 per cent of the contract price; or

(b) by way of a bank or accredited insurance company whose liability shall not be less than 10 per cent of the contract price. The cost of obtaining such a surety shall be the responsibility of the contractor who need not specifically make arrangements for sureties unless and until his tender has been accepted; or

(c) by way of satisfactory personal sureties.

4. TENDERERS SHOULD BE AWARE THAT THE LABOUR CLAUSES (PUBLIC CONTRACTS) ACT, CAP. 349, SHALL IN SO FAR AS IS APPLICABLE TO THE SUBJECT OF THE TENDER, APPLY TO ANY CONTRACT MADE IN RESPECT OF THE TENDER. FULL DETAILS OF THE CONDITIONS OF THE ACT, CAP. 349, MAY BE OBTAINED FROM THE CHIEF LABOUR OFFICER, LABOUR OFFICE, NATIONAL INSURANCE BUILDING, FAIRCHILD STREET, BRIDGETOWN.

5. Tenderers should contact the Postmaster General at telephone 426-3424 for an appointment to visit the General Post Office Complex to ascertain the extent of the work to be done. Forms of Tender and Detail of Tender are obtainable from the Postmaster General.

6. Tenders on the appropriate Form of Tender together with Detail of Tender (Appendix 1) must be submitted in sealed envelopes marked 'TENDER FOR THE PROVISION OF CLEANING SERVICES AT THE GENERAL POST OFFICE COMPLEX, CHEAPSIDE, ST. MICHAEL' and addressed to the Chairman, Tenders Committee, c/o Central Purchasing Department, Holborn Circle, Fontabelle, St. Michael, to reach him not later than 4.30 p.m. on Wednesday, 20 March 1991. Tenders received after this time and date will not be considered.

7. Tenderers must delete either 'agree' or 'do not agree' at paragraph 4 of the Form of Tender. Failure to do so will render their tenders ineligible for consideration.

8. Tenders must be accompanied by certificates from the Director, National Insurance Scheme, and the Commissioner of Inland Revenue indicating whether or not there are any outstanding payments due to those authorities by the tenderers.

9. Tenderers who are indebted to those authorities will only by considered for award of contract if they agree to a percentage of the payment resulting from the award of contract being deducted from each payment in order to satisfy the indebtedness to those authorities. The percentage to be deducted should be agreed on by the tenderers and those authorities.

10. No tender will be considered unless it complies with the conditions set out in this notice.

11. The Government does not bind itself to accept the lowest or any tender.

11.3 Cheques

A cheque is a bill of exchange (see page 174) drawn on a banker and is payable on demand. It can be open, crossed, specially crossed, an 'A/c payee only' cheque or a 'Not negotiable' cheque (Figures 11.2–11.5).

An *open cheque* is one that is not crossed. It can be cashed at the bank to which it is addressed by anyone who presents it and claims to be the payee. Such a cheque must be endorsed – that is, signed on the back by the person cashing the cheque.

A cheque with two lines drawn across its face with or without the words 'and company' is said to be *crossed*. A crossed cheque will only be cashed if its presenter is known to the cashier as the drawer/customer. It is usually cleared into a bank account, although a crossed cheque does not have to go into the account of the person named on the cheque. The person named on the cheque can endorse it with '(pay name of person)'. The bank will obey instructions.

Where a cheque has the name of a bank filled in on the face, it is said to be *specially crossed*. Such a cheque is usually cleared into the account of the payee, but only at the bank named in the crossed section on the face of the cheque.

A cheque crossed *'A/c payee'* means that the drawer wishes to restrict the cheque. If an unauthorized person collects the money the bank is liable to the true owner.

Where a cheque is crossed *'Not negotiable'*, it does not have the power of a negotiable instrument. For example, if a person takes a 'Not negotiable' cheque from a transferor, it is taken subject to any defects in title of the transferor. The transferee must ensure that the transferor really owns the cheque. A 'Not negotiable' crossing does not prevent the transfer of a cheque.

Figure 11.2 An open cheque

Figure 11.3
A generally crossed cheque

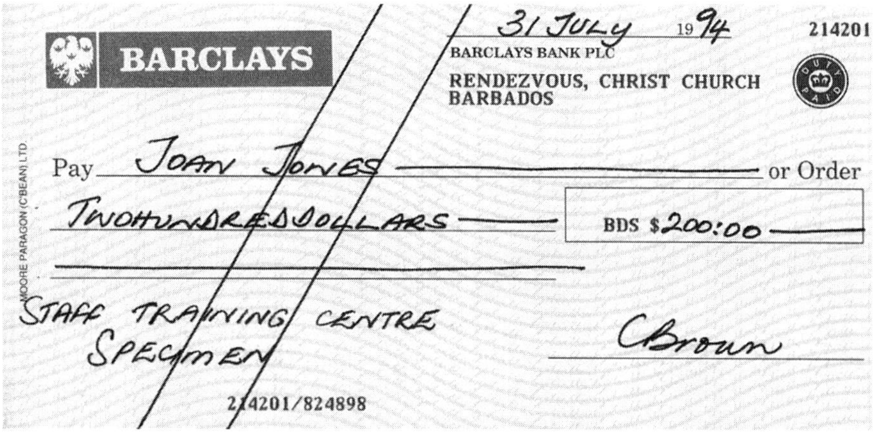

Figure 11.4
Another type of crossed cheque

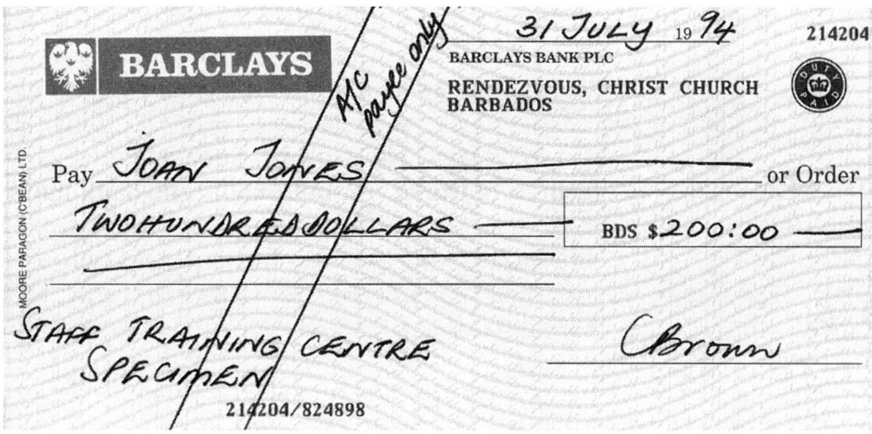

Figure 11.5
The person to whom this cheque has been made out has endorsed it so that it can be paid into another person's account

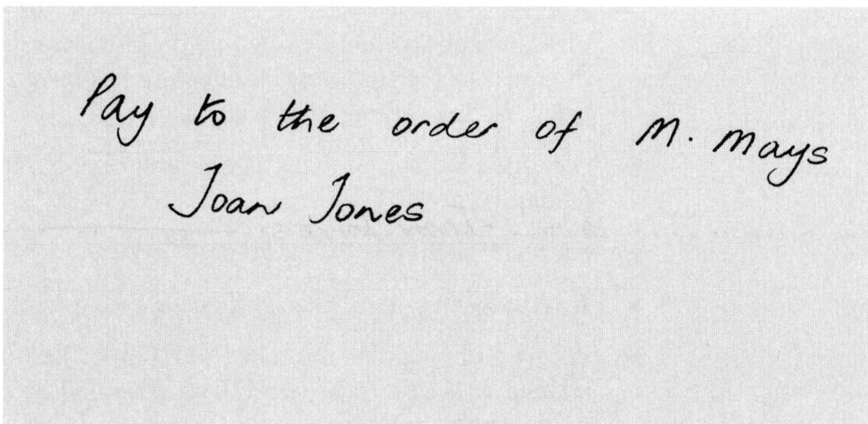

Advantages of paying by cheque

A cheque can be used to withdraw money from a current account. It may be used to instruct the paying banker to pay in cash, or to transfer a specified sum of money to the account of some other customer.

Paying by cheque eliminates the need for counting and checking legal tender. A cheque can be made safe by crossing it. If such a cheque is stolen it is impossible for the thief to cash it. A cancelled cheque acts as a receipt. An issued and cashed cheque is proof that money was paid for an obligation rendered. Many Caribbean banks return cancelled cheques together with bank statements to their customers as proof that their obligations were fulfilled.

A cheque can be post-dated and handed to the payee to make claims for payments as they become due. It can be stopped: if a drawer is dissatisfied with a purchase, the drawer can take it back to the supplier and if still dissatisfied can stop the payment. A cheque is negotiable – that is, it can be passed from person to person, provided it is endorsed. Payment by cheque delays the time of actual payment and thus provides a period of credit.

Dishonoured cheques

Where a cheque is presented for payment and the drawer does not have the funds to cover it in his or her current or deposit account, the bank usually dishonours the cheque. Dishonoured cheques are returned to the customer by the bank marked 'Refer to drawer'. It is illegal to issue a cheque that will be dishonoured.

Key Points

- Legal tender means those forms of money that are accepted by law in settlement of a debt.
- A tender for work activity is an advertised notice made by a large firm, by a government or by one of its corporations or departments, in the local or foreign press, requesting interested firms to submit a bid price for doing the advertised job.
- A cheque is a bill of exchange drawn on a banker, payable on demand.
- An open cheque is one that is not crossed.
- A crossed cheque is usually cleared into a bank account.
- Where a cheque has the name of a bank filled in on the face of the cheque, it is said to be specially crossed. Only the named bank may process that cheque.

- A cheque crossed 'A/c payee' means that the drawer wishes to restrict the cheque.
- Where a cheque is crossed 'Not negotiable', it does not have the power of a negotiable instrument.
- It is illegal to issue a cheque that will be dishonoured.

Questions

1. What do you understand by the term *business instruments*?
2. List the details included in an advertised tender for work activity.
3. Discuss the many forms that a cheque can take.
4. What are the advantages of paying by cheque?

Chapter 12 Business Documents Used in Settling Overseas Payments

Caribbean countries trade with one another and with other countries outside the region, for example Canada, the USA, the United Kingdom, France, Germany, Japan and South American countries.

The Caribbean banks facilitate the payment for import and export trade between Caribbean and foreign firms. Customers of Caribbean affiliated banks are able to effect payments to overseas firms simply by the book-keeping transactions made with their holding banks. Caribbean affiliates, for example Barclays, Canadian Imperial and the Royal banks, have accounts with their holding banks in the world's capitals, and the holding banks have accounts with their affiliates in Caribbean countries.

The payment of goods or services by Caribbean importers to foreign exporters can be made via its banking service by telegraphic money order, by bank draft, by bills of exchange and through documentary credits.

12.1 Telegraphic money order

The quickest way of sending money abroad is by telegraphic money order. Let us assume that Samuels Ltd has an account with Barclays Bank in St Vincent and notifies the bank that it wishes to pay Anthony Ltd, which has an account with the National Commercial Bank (NCB) in Trinidad & Tobago, by a telegraphic money order.

This method of payment requires that Samuels Ltd completes an application form which shows the following: name and address of the beneficiary; whether the beneficiary is to be informed that the payment should be picked up from the overseas bank; and whether the bank's service charges are to be paid by the firm initiating the payment or to be deducted from the amount to be paid.

Assume that Barclays' service charge amounts to $150 and that Samuels Ltd agrees to pay the charge. Barclays will now send an authenticated cable or telex message to NCB to pay Anthony Ltd $9,075 and to be paid $150 for its service charges. Samuels' total bill is now $9,225. The accounting treatment of Barclays would be to debit Samuels' account with $9,225 and credit NCB's account with $9,075 and with interest charges of $150.

12.2 Bank draft

A bank draft is a cheque drawn by a bank on itself. It enables business people to pay foreign firms to whom they are indebted. It is a cheque which has the backing of a bank.

If Samuels Ltd has a good credit rating with Barclays and wishes to pay its debt by a banker's draft, Barclays will readily send a bank draft to Anthony Ltd via airmail. This method is cheaper than the telegraphic money order. The CARICOM traveller's cheque is a special type of banker's draft.

Two examples of a bank draft in different currencies

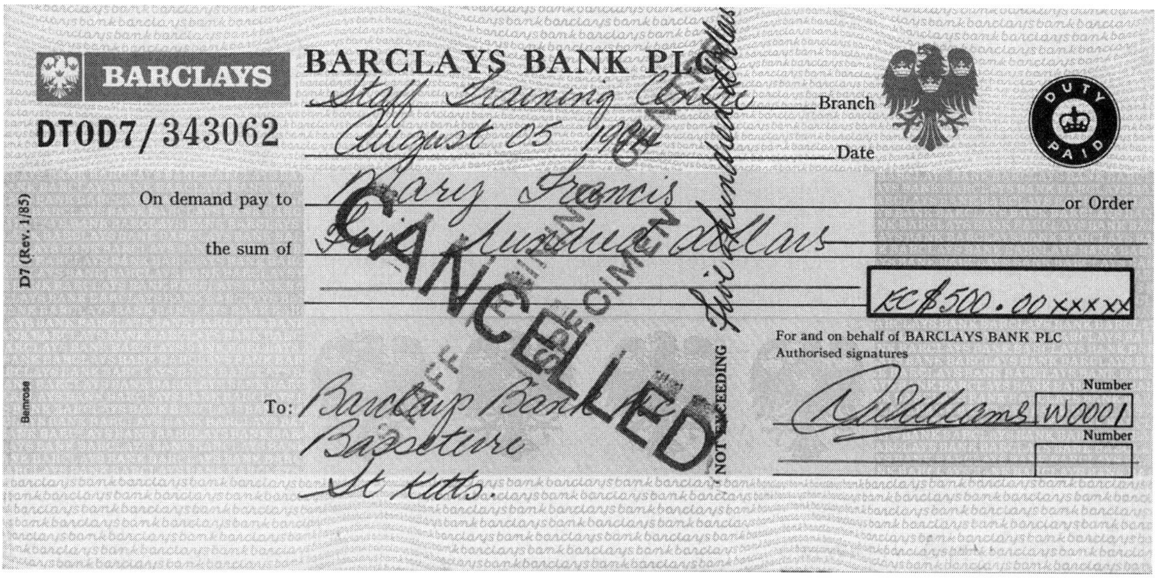

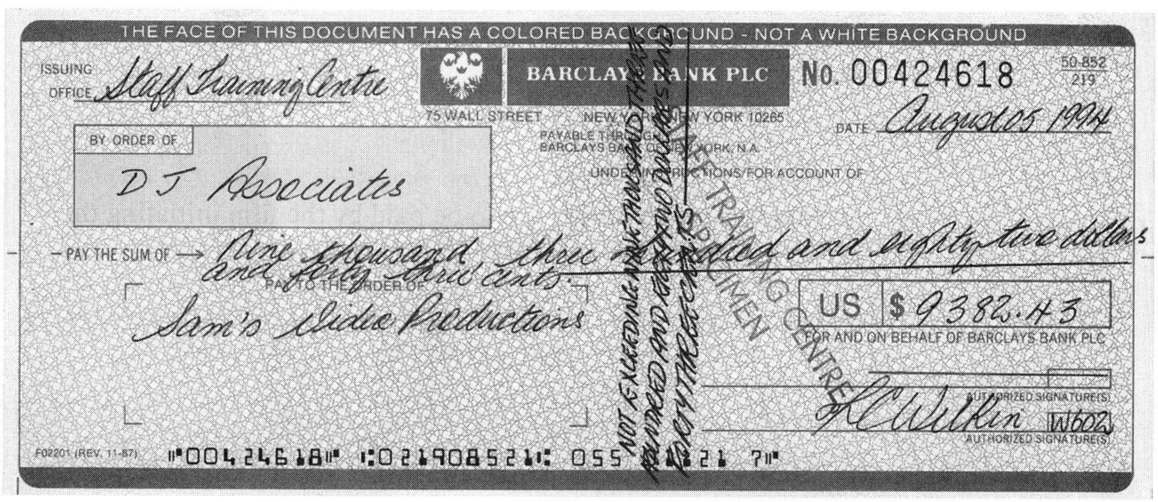

12.3 Bill of exchange

A bill of exchange is a commercial negotiable document. *Negotiable* means the power to confer upon a holder in due course a title free from equities. *Free from equities* means free from the possibility of a counter-claim for which a previous owner might be liable.

A bill of exchange is defined as 'an unconditional order in writing, addressed by one person to another, signed by the person giving it, requiring the person to whom it is addressed to pay on demand or at a fixed or determinable future time a sum certain in money to, or to the order of, a specified person or to bearer'. Figure 12.1 shows a specimen bill of exchange made out by Samuels Ltd to Anthony Ltd.

Figure 12.1
A specimen bill of exchange

Kingstown
ST VINCENT
25 April 19XX

Three months after date pay W. Layne, c/o National Commercial Bank, Port-of-Spain, Trinidad, the sum of TT$9,225.00.

To:	Anthony Ltd	**SIGNED:**	W. Samuel, Director
	201 Charlotte Street	for	Samuels Ltd
	Port-of-Spain		20 George Street
	TRINIDAD		ST VINCENT

Notes

1 Three months is the determinable future date.
2 W. Layne is the bearer or payee.
3 TT$9,225 is the certain sum of money.
4 Anthony Ltd is the drawee – that is, the person to whom the bill of exchange is addressed.
5 W. Samuel is the drawer – that is, the person giving the bill of exchange.
6 There are three parties to a bill:
   (a) the drawer, the person who draws the bill, who is generally a creditor of the drawee
   (b) the drawee, the person who is to pay the money
   (c) the payee, the person who is to receive the money (who is often the same person as the drawer).

Types of bills of exchange

A bill of exchange may be of two types: a sight bill or a usance bill. A *sight bill* is payable on presentation. A *usance bill* is payable at a number of days or months after sight or date.

A bill that is payable, for example 90 days after sight, is payable 90 days after the date of acceptance – that is, after it is sighted by the drawee. For example, a 90-day bill which is sighted on 20 January would be payable on 20 April. The calculations are as follows:

11 days left in January
28 days in February
31 days in March
20 days in April

<u>90 days</u>

The bill would be payable on 19 April if it was a leap year. A bill that is payable 90 days after date is payable 90 days from the date of the bill.

The exporting of goods is a risky business, and a bill of exchange contains pitfalls. To guard against the falsification of goods, an exporter firm can ask an importer to instruct its bank to open a documentary credit (see page 177) in the exporter's favour.

12.4 Promissory note

A promissory note is defined as 'an unconditional promise in writing made by one person to another, signed by the maker, engaging to pay on demand, or at a fixed or determinable future time, a sum certain in money to, or to the order of, a specified person or to bearer'.

Promissory notes are rarely used in domestic trade. They are more common in international trade in respect of long-term contracts for capital goods where the buyer may issue the notes as legal instruments which can be used to claim the instalment of the contract price.

The parties to a promissory note are: (a) the *promisor*, the party who makes the promise and signs the note and (b) the *promisee*, the party to whom the promise is made. Figures 12.2–12.4 are different forms of promissory note.

Figure 12.2
Promissory note showing two parties, the promissor and the payee

Kingstown
ST VINCENT

25 April 19XX

Three months after date I promise to pay Anthony Ltd on order, the sum of TT$9,225 for value received.

W. Samuel

Figure 12.3
A joint promissory note

Kingstown
ST VINCENT

25 April 19XX

On demand we promise to pay to Anthony Ltd, the sum of TT$9,225 for value received.

Mr W. Samuel
Mrs J. Samuel

Figure 12.4
Joint and several promissory notes

Kingstown
ST VINCENT

25 April 19XX

Three months after date we jointly and severally promise to pay to the order of Anthony Ltd, the sum of TT$9,225 for value received.

Mr W. Samuel
Mrs J. Samuel
Mr W. J. Samuel, Jr

12.5 Documentary credit

A documentary credit is a business document addressed by an importer's bank to an exporter's bank undertaking to pay, accept or negotiate a bill drawn on an importer against authentic shipping documents. It guarantees that an exporter will be paid for goods once they have been shipped and stipulated conditions of the documentary credit fulfilled. This means that the bill of lading (see below) must be clean.

The banks only handle documents, so an importer must ensure that the goods are of the quality expected by stipulating that the shipping documents include a certificate of quality or certificate of analysis. Those documents are certificates issued by a business organization in the exporter's country which is nominated by an importer to inspect or test the goods and certify their quality or content. Figure 12.5 shows an application and agreement for documentary credit.

12.6 Bill of lading

A bill of lading is 'a receipt for goods placed on board a vessel or aircraft, signed by the person who contracts to carry them'. It contains written conditions on which the goods are to be carried for a specified freight. It is a document of ownership to the goods.

A person who presents a bill of lading to a ship owner or to someone acting as the ship owner's agent is given the goods. The ship owner or agent must, of course, act in good faith. The bill of lading often makes the goods deliverable to order. It does not possess full negotiability. The bill of lading is issued in sets of signed negotiable originals and unsigned non-negotiable copies. The originals will be required by the consignee in order to retain control of the goods. Unsigned copies are kept by the consignor, or by brokers if the shipment of the goods was handled by them. Figure 12.6 shows a bill of lading.

Consignor and consignee

A *consignor* is a merchant who sends goods to a *consignee*. The goods are sent with a pro-forma invoice which notifies the agent that goods of a stated value have been dispatched. If the consignee cannot sell the goods, they are returned to the consignor without incurring any liability. If the goods are sold the consignee sends an account sales to the consignor.

Figure 12.5
A documentary credit

BARCLAYS **APPLICATION FOR DOCUMENTARY CREDIT**

date

TO

Barclays Bank PLC		branch
accreditor	accreditor's reference	branch reference
beneficiary(ies)		
to be advised through/established with		

Please open on my */our behalf your revocable */irrevocable credit by (a) airmail/cable with *brief/full details at

rate, in favour of the above named beneficiary(ies) for *up to/about

say

available against his */their drafts drawn on yourselves or your correspondents at sight

for per cent of the (b) invoice value and accompanied by the following documents

Signed INVOICES (c) marked Import Licence No.

Full set of clean on board blank endorsed Shipping Company's BILLS of LADING, marked notify:-

Short Form Bills of Lading *are/are not acceptable

*INSURANCE will be arranged by me/us and I/we engage on demand to place in your hands duly endorsed in blank a Policy or Certificate of Insurance approved by you.

*INSURANCE Policy or Certificate (in duplicate) endorsed in blank for the invoice value of the goods plus covering Marine and War Risks (d)

OTHER DOCUMENTS

covering the following GOODS (e)

To be shipped from To

not later than

Partshipments* permitted/prohibited Transhipments *permitted/prohibited

This credit to be available for negotiation or payment aboard until inclusive

FURTHER INSTRUCTIONS

Subject to Uniform Customs and Practice for Documentary Credits (1983 Revision.) I.C.C. Brochure 400

NOTES: * Delete as appropriate: all deletions and alterations to be initialled.
a) unless otherwise stated sent by airmail.
b) Insert C.I.F., C. & F., F. O. B. etc as required
c) Number must be quoted when Import Licence is required.
d) Insert other risks and/or clauses required, e.g. SR & CC Warehouse to Warehouse, etc.
e) Brief description only.

CRE 201
(BARBADOS 09/91)

CONTINUED OVERLEAF

Figure 12.6 A bill of lading

B.L. No.

Shipper

BILL OF LADING – COMBINED TRANSPORT OR PORT TO PORT SHIPMENT

Consignee

THE GEEST LINE

WINDWARD TERMINAL
P.O. BOX 20, BARRY
SOUTH GLAM. CF6 8XE
TEL: BARRY (0446) 700333
TELEX: 498359
FAX: (0446) 700623
FAX: (0446) 748401 (FREIGHT OFFICE)

Notify Party

Pre-carriage by | Place of Receipt

Ocean Vessel | Voy. No. | Port of Loading

Port of Discharge | Place of Delivery

Container No.	Seal No. Marks & Nos.	No. of containers or P'kgs.	Kind of Packages, Description of Goods	Gross Weight	Measurements

THE ABOVE PARTICULARS PROVIDED BY THE MERCHANT

TOTAL NUMBER OF CONTAINERS OR PACKAGES (IN WORDS)

Goods of a dangerous or damaging nature must not be tendered to the carrier for receipt or loading unless written notice of their nature and the address of the shipper have been previously given to the carrier, the carrier has expressly agreed to carry those goods, and the nature of the goods is distinctly marked on the outside of each package. A special order giving consent to carriage of the goods must also be obtained from the carrier.

RECEIVED the goods in apparent good order and condition as specified above unless otherwise stated to be carried by GEEST LINE from the place of receipt or port of loading as applicable to the port of discharge or place of delivery as applicable if this bill is used as a combined transport bill or from the port of loading to the port of discharge if this bill is used as a port to port bill.

Weight, measure, marks, numbers, quantity, contents, value unknown to the carrier.

One of the original bills of lading must be surrendered duly endorsed in exchange for the goods or delivery order.

It is agreed that Geest Line and its agents are not responsible for notification of arrival of the goods at port of discharge or place of delivery.

THE CONTRACT CONTAINED IN OR EVIDENCED BY THIS BILL OF LADING AND ALL PERFORMANCE AND CARRIAGE OF OR IN RESPECT OF THE GOODS IS SUBJECT TO ALL THE TERMS AND CONDITIONS ON THE FACE AND ON THE REVERSE HEREOF. ATTENTION IS DRAWN IN PARTICULAR TO THE CONDITIONS ON THE REVERSE HEREOF.

In accepting this bill of lading the merchant expressly accepts and agrees to all its stipulations, exceptions, terms and conditions on the face and on the reverse whether written, printed, stamped or otherwise incorporated as if they were all signed by the merchant.

IN WITNESS whereof (2) original bills of lading have been issued on behalf of GEEST LINE, one of which being accomplished the others to stand void.

BILLS OF LADING MARKED COPY ARE NON-NEGOTIABLE. SHIPMENT SUBJECT TO ALL TERMS AND CONDITIONS PRINTED ON FACE AND REVERSE OF THE ORIGINAL SIGNED BILL OF LADING.

FREIGHT PAYABLE AT | DATED | per pro GEEST INDUSTRIES LTD. by:

FOR CONDITIONS OF CARRIAGE SEE OVERLEAF | AT

For the Manager
THE GEEST LINE

NUMBER OF ORIGINAL BILLS:

An account sales shows the details of sales, expenses incurred and the commission due. It is usually accompanied by a remittance for the balance.

A consignee also can be a *del credere* agent – that is, one who guarantees the consignor against bad debts. For this an extra commission called a *del credere commission* is paid.

If a consignment of goods is sent on cost, insurance and freight (CIF) terms, the consignor pays the insurance and freight. The consignee usually pays the duty and handling charges and claims for them in the account sales.

12.7 Import licences

Import licences are issued by the Department of Trade of each Caribbean country to firms or individuals who wish to import goods. Not all kinds of goods are allowed to enter Caribbean countries. Some import licences are issued for specific purposes. These specific licences specify what kind and volume of goods should be imported. In general, import licensing helps Caribbean governments to control imports.

The control aspect of import licensing runs counter to the notion of free trade. The data compiled for the various categories of imports from import licences help in the calculation of each country's balance of trade.

Key Points

- The Caribbean banks facilitate the payment for trade between Caribbean importers and exporters and foreign importers and exporters.
- The payment for goods or services by Caribbean importers to foreign exporters can be done via its banking service by telegraphic money order, bank draft, bill of exchange and documentary credits.
- A bank draft is a cheque drawn by a bank on itself.
- A bill of exchange is a commercial negotiable document.
- A bill of exchange may be a sight bill or a usance bill.
- The exporting of goods is a risky business.
- The parties of a promissory note are (a) the promisor, the party who makes the promise and signs the note and (b) the promisee, the party to whom the promise is made.

- A documentary credit guarantees that an exporter will be paid for goods once they have been shipped and stipulated conditions of the documentary credit fulfilled.
- A bill of lading contains written conditions on which the goods are to be carried for a specified freight.
- A bill of lading often makes the goods deliverable to order. It does not possess full negotiability.
- A consignor is a merchant who sends goods to a consignee.
- An account sales shows the details of sales, expenses incurred and the commission due. It is usually accompanied by a remittance for the balance.
- Import licences are issued by the Department of Trade of each Caribbean country, to firms or individuals who wish to import goods.
- The control aspects of import licensing run counter to the notion of free trade.
- The data compiled for the various categories of imports from import licences help in the calculation of each country's balance of trade.

Questions

1. Explain and name the bank facilities that are available to Caribbean importer firms for settling debts to foreign firms.
2. Draw up a bill of exchange and explain its components.
3. Name the parties to a promissory note.
4. What is a documentary credit?
5. 'A bill of lading is an unimportant document.' Discuss.
6. Explain the purpose of an account sales.

Chapter 13 The Nature of Management

The concept of management emerged as a result of people's adaptation to a hierarchical way of life. A firm has a hierarchy and a 'pecking order'. As shown in Chapter 4, a firm is made up of functional, interrelated parts which need to be supervised in order to obtain beneficial results. Management can thus be defined as 'a process by managers of bringing together resources, both human and physical, to manufacture a social product or to accomplish a service on a continuous basis'. That process also involves aspects of control and regulation.

13.1 An overview of management

Management comprises those people who collectively and individually discharge the process of getting things done in an organization. Management is vested in a board of directors, which delegates many of its responsibilities. The extent of such delegation depends on the size of the company and the complexity of its operations. The board appoints one of its members as managing director. This official is subject to the general direction of the board and is responsible for the operation of the organization. In turn, the managing director delegates many of his or her duties while retaining overall responsibility for policies and their directions. Delegation is usually on functional lines, so that departmental heads are placed in charge of the natural divisions of the business, for example production, administration and selling. Figure 13.1 shows the hierarchical structure of such a system.

Figure 13.1 Hierarchical structure of management

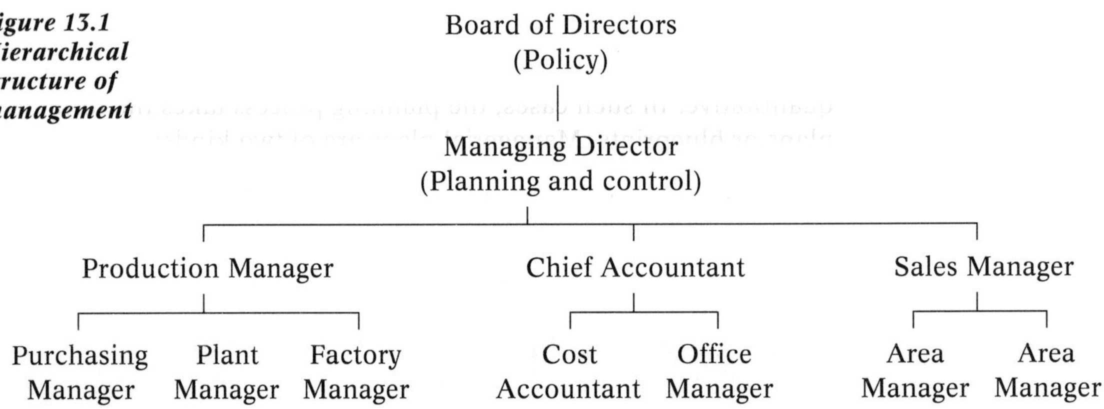

The chart shows the chain of command and the direct lines of delegation and responsibility. For example, the Production Manager is responsible to the Managing Director for all matters within his or her sphere of influence.

13.2 An outline of delegation

Delegation is a process whereby a manager transfers part of his or her function to a subordinate so that the subordinate has the authority to perform or supervise a task. The responsibility for the task is not delegated. A manager who delegates is sharing the workload. Further, the delegator should (a) set clear objectives and indicate to the subordinate the standard of performance expected, (b) define the level and limits of authority delegated, and (c) establish a control system to monitor results.

Delegation enables decisions to be taken down the hierarchy and speeds up communication. It aids development in the sense that delegatees learn how to participate in management by making economic decisions, and to accept the consequences of their choices.

13.3 Managerial activity

Managerial activity comprises certain characteristics, which are described below.

Planning

Managerial planning is a process in which management's mental abilities and capacities are brought to bear on an abstract or real-world phenomenon which has an effect on the firm, for the purpose of understanding its nature and finding solutions for current or future implementation in the firm. Managerial planning, observations and analysis are generally written down and can be either qualitative or quantitative. In such cases, the planning process takes the form of plans or blueprints. Managerial plans are of two kinds:

1 Repeat factor plans, for example regulations pertaining to work practices and product sequencing.

2 Dynamic plans, for example budget information.

What is the purpose of a firm's plan? It is to facilitate the accomplishment of its objectives. Planning is necessary because a firm exists in an uncertain environment where the rate of change is continuous. The imperatives of technology, the complexities, nuances, competitiveness and the power of the unions within firms make managerial planning a necessity.

Planning provides a clear focus on the objectives of a firm. It leads to an evaluation of the most economical method of organizing a firm's activities and provides a framework for control. Planning involves the following:

- the awareness of an opportunity
- establishing and determining suitable objectives
- premising or forecasting, ie making assumptions about the future
- developing alternative courses of action
- evaluating the alternative courses of action
- selecting the most sensible alternative
- formulating derivative plans
- quantifying plans in terms of budgets.

Control

Control has many meanings but it is an inescapable feature of all organizations. From the point of view of the firm, it means the regulation and monitoring of activities for directing, regulating and coordinating production and other business activities for the purpose of achieving profitable objectives. This means that the management function uses predictive models in order to exercise control. The establishment of a control system requires the following:

- the establishment of standards
- performance measurement
- the correction of deviations from plans.

Further, in order for a control system to function sensibly, the following must be highlighted by management:

1 The action, or information conveying the desired action, must be communicated.

2 Control should reflect the plans it is designed to follow.

3 Control should be flexible, allowing for changes to take place in the planning process, and for unforeseen events.

4 Control should be economical.

5 Control should indicate corrective action.

6 Deviations from plans should be monitored promptly.

7 Control should be understandable.

8 Control should be forward looking.

Coordination

A dictionary definition of *coordination* is 'arranging so as to work punctually and harmoniously'. From a management perspective, it means the maintenance of a working harmony between all the departments of a firm during a budget period.

A *budget* results from the bargaining procedures and agreements between top management and department heads of estimated work activities, revenues and cost requirements for their respective units. A budget is a dynamic instrument, a statement of expected results expressed in numerical terms. The budgets that make up the plan are usually expressed in financial terms, in work hours, production units and machine hours. A budget forces a firm's management to make in advance a numerical compilation of expected cash flows, expenses and revenues. It is the budget's adjustment to economic reality in a budgeted or subsequent period through managerial action which ensures the adequate coordination between a firm's departments.

Motivation

As explained above, a firm's budget is a systemic factor. It is an ever-present factor in the life of economic agents. It is manipulative. This means that management can adjust or re-adjust a budget constraint whenever it strays from what is planned. The adjustment is done by way of variance analysis, which places blame or praise on managers who in turn blame or praise the employees under their control. Obviously, the budget affects human behaviour.

There are two aspects of motivation, psychological and managerial. The psychological view of motivation means that the mind moves or directs a person's behaviour towards the minimization or reduction of tension which can arise from external or internal factors. The managerial function of motivation means that managers, via budget adjustments, can influence employees' job performances by way of incentives. *Incentives* are things given to employees in order to make them more productive, for example increased pay, participation in the budget activity, job security and satisfaction, self-actualization, advancement, achievement, recognition and growth in the job, and good working conditions.

Other forms of incentive are not linked to the budget, for example bonus and commission schemes, share option schemes which provide employees with the right to apply for shares at a given price, quota schemes for sales people under which financial rewards are given depending on the amount by which the quota is surpassed, or profit-sharing schemes under which a part of the profits is distributed each year to employees either in cash or in the form of the company's shares.

13.4 Teamwork in an organization

The nature and layout of a factory forces employees to work in groups or teams. This is obvious where production is integrated, for example in sugar, cement and car assembly plants. Road construction and road repair work are also good examples in the Caribbean.

Teamwork is designed to encourage production at rates above a minimum standard. The units produced or work done by workers in excess of a given management standard are regarded as time saved by the team, and each member of the team is paid a bonus for time saved in addition to the basic wage. The bonus is an *incentive*. The purpose of an incentive scheme is to induce employees to increase their work efforts and to earn a higher wage or salary. From the firm's viewpoint, an incentive scheme reduces the unit cost of goods.

In general, a group bonus scheme contributes to cooperation among workers. It also contributes to reductions in accidents, absenteeism, spoilage and waste at the workplace. A team effort and its successful outcome leads to the boosting of a group's morale.

13.5 Management responsibility

The word *responsibility* means 'an ability to discharge an obligation'. A firm's management has responsibility to its employees, to its customers, the environment, and to the firm itself.

Responsibility to employees means that management should provide good working conditions and must ensure that sensible interpersonal relations exist at the workplace. Management's responsibility extends also to employees' education and to the provision of sickness and retirement benefits.

Responsibility to customers means that management should provide sensible, timely, dependable and adequate services or quality social products at reasonable prices. Management also has a responsibility to conduct research, in order to improve a service or product, and to pass on cheaper-quality products to customers.

Responsibility to the environment means that management should obey the laws, traditions and customs of the locality and accept the commercial practices of the various trades and markets in which it operates. In this sphere too, responsibility implies that management should develop policies that avoid employee exploitation, pollution and the destruction of the physical environment, and should pursue policies that harmonize with a country's economic and social policies.

Management responsibility to the firm means that it must safeguard its assets. Further, the financial objectives which are related to capital structures, working capital decisions, cash forecasting, investment of surplus funds, credit policies, the raising of short-term and long-term finance, capital budgeting and acquisition and mergers, must be profit-oriented decisions.

13.6 Communication

Communication is an act of conveying signals which helps towards the understanding, doing and fulfilment of an objective. People communicate by gestures and sounds, or language. In a firm, communication through the media of verbal language and report writing is vital. Both in the firm and in the environment generally, social interaction and work direction are made possible by the use of language.

Important information is supplied every day to the large firm, so formal communication of important pieces of information is necessary. The prerequisites for formal communication are sensing, recording and storage. Formal communication ensures that an important piece of information is not distorted when it is distributed internally within the firm. Internal communication means that an edited version of an important piece of information is transferred from one segment of a firm to another. This transfer of information is usually by circulars, newsletters and reports.

Formal communication reduces uncertainty. It ensures that bad or good economic decisions resulting from formal internal communication can be traced directly to a firm's economic agents, and blame or praise allocated accordingly. In short, formal internal communications lead to decision analysis.

For a high standard of communication to be achieved in a large firm, (a) the contents of the information must be clear and unambiguous, (b) the correct selection of information must be passed to each department, (c) the information must be communicated to arrive at its destination in time to be useful and (d) the communicated information must be genuine.

Internal communication can also originate from a firm's employees. This kind of communication can occur as a result of employees' participation in a firm's budget or by suggestion schemes, where employees outline a firm's direction on how, for example, a work practice should be done.

13.7 The business report

A business report is a document (looseleaf or bound) which generally contains typed information of some aspect of a business, for example marketing, production or sales projections. There are two kinds of report: general and special. A *general report* contains information about, for example, the firm's goals and objectives, outlined in broad detail. *Special reports* contain information on the production of a new product or a firm's plans for the future, outlined in specific detail.

The purpose of a business report is to convey relevant information to a recipient. Special reports convey information relating to special terms of reference defined by either the sender or the recipient. A business report is an alternative form of information transmission to verbal communication. It provides tangible evidence that information has been collected and transmitted. Business reports enable continual reference to be made to the information they contain.

A business report:

- should have a concise descriptive title
- should include the names of the people and department(s) to whom the report is addressed, dates to which the report refers, date of compilation and name of sender
- should be in the form best suited to the recipient
- should be timely
- should be logically arranged and contain all relevant information.

13.8 Leadership styles

Leadership style is the way in which management gets its employees to perform their work duties. Employees' work performances can be induced via authoritarian, democratic, laissez-faire or laissez-passer styles of management.

An *authoritarian* or *structured management style* has the following features:

1. Employees are told what to do and how to carry out work duties.
2. The power to make technical decisions, for example whether to make or not to make a product or to close a department, is management's sole responsibility.
3. Only management controls, rewards and punishes.

An authoritarian management style only considers economic needs. It does not consider motivation. It enforces authority. It adheres strictly to a defined hierarchy of posts and to a system of rules governing the rights and duties of post holders. It is impersonal in its interpersonal relations. An authoritarian style of management operates as a closed system. Its problems and successes are analysed and dealt with by reference to its internal system, and no consideration is given to the impact of the external environment.

A *democratic management style* involves participation. Participation is a process of joint decision making by two or more parties in which the decisions have future effects on those making them. Characteristics of a democratic management style are employees' participation in decision making and control, and delegation. A democratic management style also provides for (a) employees' representation at board level, (b) joint consultation through work councils, and (c) participation through collective bargaining, in work levels and in the budget process.

The advocates of democratic leadership styles believe that involving employees in a firm's decisions will stimulate and encourage them to identify with the firm's goals and to increase their productivity. However, a firm that practises a democratic style of leadership experiences conflict during which compromised agreements are reached between interest groups as to the distribution of inducements, followed by periods of apparent calm during which agreements are implemented.

The terms *laissez-faire* or *laissez-passer* were used by a group of 18th-century French political economists known as the *physiocrats*. (The Greek work *physis* means 'nature'.) The physiocrats believed in a spontaneous, unartificial and natural commercial system. *Laissez-faire* means 'let people produce' or 'let them get on with the job'. *Laissez-passer* means 'let people move around as they please'.

Laissez-faire suggests individualism. It is amoral. It advocates a great deal of freedom for capitalists to seek profits in a market free of encumbrances and restrictions. Adam Smith's economic legacy of the market as 'an invisible hand' that channels egotistic drives into the most socially useful activities is the core of the laissez-faire notion.

What are the merits and demerits of laissez-faire? In many ways it created the massive industrialization that took place in Britain, France and the USA in the 18th century. (It did not create a similar industrialization in the Caribbean in that same period.) It spread the notion that only rich people save, are inventive and can manage. It was responsible directly for the growth of the trade union movement in those countries.

The demerits of the laissez-faire notion were highlighted by Lewis and by Keynes. W. A. Lewis objected to the laissez-faire system on the following grounds:

1 Within this system, income is not fairly distributed but is distributed in accordance with the scarcity of the resources the individual possesses.

2 It gives no protection to employees.

3 It is unstable.

4 It cannot keep control of foreign trade.

5 It cannot cope with major change without being too slow, and cruel.

J. M. Keynes stated:

> 'Let us clear from the ground the metaphysical or general principles upon which, from time to time, laissez-faire has been founded. It is not true that individuals possess a prescriptive "natural right" in their economic activities. There is no compact conferring perpetual rights on those who have or those who acquire. The world is not so governed from above that private and social interest should always coincide. It is not so managed here below that in practice they do coincide. It is not a correct deduction from the principles of economics that enlightened self-interest always operates in the public interest.'
>
> Quoted in D. E. Moggridge, *Maynard Keynes: An Economist's Biography*, 1992

Is laissez-faire a management tool in the Caribbean? The Caribbean governments regulate conditions of employment and intervene in many ways in the economies of their countries. The answer is no.

What kinds of leadership styles are practised in Caribbean firms? To answer that question sensibly requires investigation. One might expect that in those Caribbean countries where Catholicism is dominant, an authoritarian leadership style would be evident. In those Caribbean countries where Protestantism is dominant there is some sort of democratic leadership style.

What are the benefits obtained from the authoritarian and democratic styles of leadership? European evidence suggests that participative styles of leadership are associated with higher-producing work groups and that an authoritarian style of leadership leads to higher productivity in repetitive work. That evidence needs to be tested in a Caribbean setting.

Key Points

- ➤ The concept of management emerged as a result of people's adaptation to a hierarchical way of life.
- ➤ Management can be defined as a process by managers of bringing together resources, both human and physical, to manufacture a social

product or to accomplish a service on a continuous basis. That process also involves aspects of control and regulation.

- Management comprises those people who collectively and individually discharge the process of getting things done in an organization.
- Management is vested in a board of directors. The board delegates many of its responsibilities. The extent of such delegation depends upon the size of the company and the complexity of its operations.
- Delegation is a process whereby a manager transfers part of his or her function to a subordinate so that the subordinate has the authority to perform or supervise a task. The responsibility for the task is not delegated.
- Delegation enables decisions to be taken down the hierarchy.
- Managerial planning, observation and analysis are generally written down and can be either qualitative or quantitative.
- Managerial plans are of two kinds: (a) repeat factor plans, for example regulations pertaining to work practices and product sequencing, and (b) dynamic plans, for example budget information.
- Planning is necessary because firms exist in an uncertain environment where the rate of change is continuous.
- Planning provides a clear focus on the objectives of a firm.
- Planning leads to an evaluation of the most economical method of organizing a firm's activities and provides a framework for control.
- Control is the regulation and monitoring of activities for directing, regulating and coordinating production and other business activities for the purpose of achieving profitable objectives.
- Coordination is the maintenance of a working harmony between all the departments of a firm during a budget period.
- A budget results from the bargaining procedures and agreements between top management and departmental heads of estimated work activities, revenues and cost requirements for their respective units.
- A budget is a dynamic instrument, a statement of expected results expressed in numerical terms.
- It is a budget's adjustment to economic reality in a budgeted or subsequent period through managerial action which ensures the adequate coordination between a firm's departments.

- The managerial function of motivation means that managers, via budget adjustments, can influence employees' job performances by way of incentives.
- A firm's management has responsibility to its employees, customers, environment and to the firm itself.
- Responsibility to employees means that management should provide good working conditions and must ensure that sensible interpersonal relations exist at the workplace.
- Responsibility to customers means that management should provide sensible, timely, dependable and adequate services or quality social products at reasonable prices.
- Responsibility to environment means that management should obey the laws, traditions and customs of the locality and accept the commercial practices of the various trades and markets in which it operates.
- Management's responsibility to the firm means that it must safeguard its assets.
- Communication is an act of conveying signals which helps towards the understanding, doing and fulfilment of an objective.
- The prerequisites for formal communication are sensing, recording and storage.
- Internal communication means that an edited version of an important piece of information is transferred from one segment of a firm to another.
- Formal communication reduces uncertainty.
- The purpose of a business report is to convey relevant information to a recipient.
- A business report is an alternative form of information transmission to verbal communication.
- Employees' work performances can be induced via authoritarian, democratic, laissez-faire or laissez-passer styles of management.
- An authoritarian management style only considers economic needs. It does not consider motivation.
- A democratic management style involves participation.
- The advocates of democratic leadership styles believe that involving employees in a firm's decisions will stimulate and encourage them to identify with the firm's goals and to increase their productivity.

- A firm that practises a democratic style of leadership experiences conflict during which compromised agreements are reached between interest groups as to the distribution of inducements, followed by periods of apparent calm during which agreements are implemented.
- Laissez-faire suggests individualism. It is amoral. It advocates a great deal of freedom for capitalists to seek profits in a market free of encumbrances.
- The laissez-faire doctrine in many ways created the massive industrialization that took place in Britain, France and the USA in the 18th century. (It did not create a similar industrialization in the Caribbean in that same period.)
- European evidence suggests that participative styles of leadership are associated with higher-producing work groups and that an authoritarian style of leadership leads to higher productivity in repetitive work. That evidence needs to be tested in a Caribbean setting.

Questions

1. What do you understand by the term *delegation*? Use an organization chart to show the lines of delegation and responsibility.
2. Outline the aspects of managerial responsibility.
3. 'Planning is a waste of time in a firm.' Discuss.
4. Outline the characteristics of managerial responsibility.
5. What is communication? Is it of importance in the firm?
6. What are the purposes of a business report?
7. What features should a business report possess?
8. Explain and contrast the authoritarian and the democratic styles of management.
9. Explain the term *laissez-faire*. What are the merits and demerits of laissez-faire?

Chapter 14 The Role of Government

The classical economists of the 18th century believed in a laissez-faire economic system. They believed that the economic affairs of the society were best guided by the decisions of private individuals. The role of government was to provide defence and security. Today government has a much expanded role. It must provide social services, stabilize the economy, regulate some areas of business activity, and try to achieve a more equitable distribution of income.

In less developed economies like those in the Caribbean, governments must also try to stimulate growth and development in the economy. The private sector in the Caribbean is very weak and the government may have to take on some of those activities that are normally undertaken by the private sector in developed countries (see page 205).

14.1 The responsibilities of government

Governments in the Caribbean have a number of responsibilities to undertake to maintain the level of economic welfare of the country. For example:

1 They must decide on the allocation of expenditure between private goods and social goods. To do this they tax individuals in the society, which reduces their ability to spend on private goods. The revenue received by the government is used to provide social goods like health, education, defence and the protection of the general welfare of the citizens (see pages 196–99).

2 They must use economic policy to try to stabilize the economy. Government must try to reduce the level of unemployment, keep down the rate of inflation and maintain a good balance of payments position. It uses monetary and fiscal policy to stabilize the economy (see Chapter 5). Fiscal policy is the use of the government expenditure and taxes to achieve these goals.

3 The achievement of a more equitable distribution of income should be one of the goals of government. In any society there are individuals with a very high income and individuals with a low income. The operation of the free market economy tends to increase these differences in income. The government tries to reduce these differences by redistributing income from the rich to the poor. This is done by taxing the rich at a higher rate than the poor.

4 Making profits is the main motive of businesses. If left to themselves, businesses will engage in all types of practices to increase their profits. The government must undertake certain types of regulatory practices to protect the consumer from excessively high prices, unsafe goods and fraudulent practices by businesses (see pages 201–204).

5 In the Caribbean, governments must also try to encourage growth and development in the economy to try to eradicate poverty.

14.2 The provision of social goods

Social goods are goods from which it is difficult or impossible to exclude individuals from enjoying the benefits or where one person's enjoyment of the benefits does not reduce the benefits to all other consumers. For example, it is difficult to exclude any individual from the national security provided by the defence force. In this case we say that the *exclusion principle* cannot be applied. In the case of private goods like food and clothing, one perons's consumption of the goods precludes anyone else from enjoying the benefits. On the other hand, the use of a bridge by one individual does not reduce the benefits of the bridge to other people. The price mechanism does not work to provide social goods efficiently. They have to be provided by the government.

Merit goods like education and health services which are socially desirable cannot be provided in sufficient quantities by the free market. These are also provided by the government.

One of the most important social goods provided by the government is *security*. This is done by passing laws in parliament to protect the rights of the individual. The police force and the courts of law enforce these laws. The laws of the country determine which actions are illegal. They also specify penalties – fines and imprisonment – for breaking the laws. By enforcing the laws the police protect the citizens of a country from wrongful acts like robbery, house breaking, murder and unlawful destruction of property.

The defence force also provides security. It defends the country from foreign enemies, and prevents small groups of dissatisfied citizens from overthrowing the government. The Coast Guard prevents smuggling of drugs, weapons and other illegal goods, the Fire Service protects homes and businesses against damage by fire, and the Prison Service keeps criminals away from the rest of the society.

At the regional level, most Caribbean countries participate in the *Regional Security System*, which is a cooperative effort between the

A Grenadian policeman and two Jamaican soldiers co-operating as part of a peace-keeping force in Grenada

Caribbean countries to provide collective security for the region. They cooperate in such areas as the fight against drug trafficking, responding to natural disasters, and giving assistance to any country in the region in times of civil unrest. For example, countries worked together to repair damage following hurricanes Gilbert and Hugo, to restore public order in Grenada after the killing of the Prime Minister in 1983, and to return Trinidad & Tobago to a state of normality following Abu Bakr's attempted coup in 1990.

Social security and social welfare

In the Caribbean, social security is provided by the National Insurance Schemes (or Social Security Scheme in some countries). The employers deduct the national insurance contributions from each worker's income. This is added to the employer's contribution and paid in to the National Insurance Scheme (NIS). The worker's contribution is usually about 5 per cent. A maximum contribution is usually determined by the government. In Barbados, for example, that maximum is about $3,050 per year. The employer's contribution is also about 5 per cent, but some countries require the employer to pay more. The main aim is to provide financial support to the elderly members of the society by providing retirement benefits, and other benefits to less fortunate members of the society, for example:

Unemployment benefits paid to workers who are temporarily unemployed.

Sickness benefits paid when the worker loses income due to illness.

Disability benefits paid when an individual is unable to work due to a serious injury.

Maternity benefits paid to mothers when they have a child.

Widow's benefits paid to the wife when her husband dies – this benefit is paid until she dies or re-marries.

Invalidity benefit paid when illness results in the person becoming a permanent invalid.

Social welfare payments are paid to people who are not covered by the National Insurance Schemes. The benefits are paid to old age pensioners and orphans. Other payments are made to people who lose their houses in fires or in natural disasters like hurricanes and floods.

Other social services

A government may provide a variety of other social services. Some are provided free, while for others a fee has to be paid. For example:

Education All of the Caribbean countries provide free primary education. Most also provide free secondary education, and Barbados provides free or partly free university education.

Health services Governments in the Caribbean provide hospitals and health clinics. They also provide inoculations against diseases like smallpox, measles and dengue fever, and sanitary inspectors to ensure that the environment is kept clean so as to prevent the spread of diseases.

Water and sanitation services Running water is provided by the government. To make the water safe, it is usually treated with chlorine to kill some of the bacteria. The government also provides garbage collection services in the towns and sometimes also in the rural areas.

Infrastructure Infrastructure – roads, bridges, airports and seaports, for example – is necessary for the development of the country. These facilities are provided by the government because they cannot efficiently be provided by the private sector. In Barbados and Jamaica, some public transport is provided by the government. However, transport is provided privately in the other Caribbean countries.

Social services are provided through the *government budget* which is presented annually in the House of Parliament. This is a statement of the revenue and expenditure plans of the government during the coming year. The budget spells out in detail what items the government is going to spend its money on, and the sources from which the government is going to get its revenue.

Government expenditure can be divided into two categories: current expenditure and capital expenditure. *Current expenditure* is spending on goods and services that are used up within the year under consideration. These include wages and salaries, stationery and office supplies, food items, interest on loans, and servicing and repair of capital equipment. *Capital expenditure* is spending on infrastructure, capital equipment and government buildings.

Government revenue comes from a variety of sources. These are taxes, licences, fees charged by the government (hospital fees, airport service charges, etc), the sale or lease of government assets, and grants (gifts) from foreign governments. Revenue from taxes, licences and fees is called *current revenue.*

The government has a current deficit if current expenditure is greater than current revenue. It has a surplus if current revenue is greater than current expenditure. If total expenditure exceeds total revenue, the government has an overall deficit. This has to be financed by local and foreign borrowing. In the Caribbean, governments do a lot of foreign borrowing to finance capital projects.

14.3 Taxation

Taxes are compulsory levies made by the government on private individuals and organizations. They are imposed for various reasons:

1 *To raise revenue.* Governments need revenue to provide social goods, and taxation is one way of raising revenue.

2 *To redistribute income.* If people with higher incomes are taxed at a higher rate, this has the effect of distributing income more equally. This may reduce the level of saving and increase spending if people with a lower income spend more of their income.

3 *To protect local industries by taxing imported goods.* This has the effect of making them more expensive than local goods, so protecting local goods from foreign competition. This form of taxation tends to increase the level of domestic economic activity since domestic production of the protected goods is stimulated. However, it encourages inefficient production and may be bad for the economy as

a whole, as consumers are required to pay higher prices for the goods so produced.

4 *To discourage the consumption and hence the production of goods like alcohol and cigarettes.*

Taxes can be classified in a number of ways. The most common is to describe them as direct and indirect taxes. *Direct taxes* are levied directly on the person who pays the tax. For example:

Personal income tax – a tax paid on individual income. It is usually deducted when the worker's salary is paid, so it is sometimes called 'pay-as-you-earn' tax (PAYE). The tax rate increases as the income increases. As an individual's income increases, he or she moves into a higher tax bracket.

Corporate/business income tax – income tax paid by business firms.

Levies – these are imposed on individual incomes, for example the health levy and the transport levy in Barbados, and the social services levy in St Kitts-Nevis.

Wealth taxes – these are based on the wealth of the individual. They include house and land tax and inheritance tax.

Capital gains tax – this is a tax on the gains from the sale of an asset. For example, if a real estate agent buys a house for $100,000 and then sells it for $110,000 without making any improvements, he or she has made a capital gain of $10,000 and must pay tax on that amount.

An increase in the level of direct taxes reduces the level of economic activity in a country. It reduces the amount of money people have to spend and hence reduces the level of economic activity.

Indirect taxes are taxes on goods and services. These taxes are paid by the seller of the goods or service but the tax is passed on to the consumer in the form of higher prices. The consumer pays the tax indirectly to the government through the seller. Examples of indirect taxes:

Customs duty – sometimes called a *tariff*. It is paid on imported goods and services. It can either be an *ad valorem tax* (the tax is a percentage of the value of the goods) or a specific tax (a specific amount of tax is paid on each unit of the goods, say $5 per gallon or $2 per tonne). Such taxes have the effect of protecting the production of local goods from foreign competition.

Excise tax – tax on local production, for example excise taxes are imposed on the production of local rum and cigarettes.

Consumption tax – tax paid on the purchase of commodities used for consumption purposes.

Sales tax – this is a tax paid on the sale of commodities to the final consumer. It is different from consumption tax because it is imposed at the point of sale and is added to the price displayed for the commodity. The restaurant tax paid in most of the Caribbean islands is an example.

Value added tax (VAT) – this is a tax imposed on the value added at each stage of production and distribution. For example, if a dairy sells milk valued at $100 to an ice-cream manufacturer, the manufacturer will have to pay VAT on $100. Now if the manufacturer produces ice-cream valued at $150 he has added $50 ($150 – $100) in value and will have to pay VAT on $50. In the Caribbean, this tax is imposed in Grenada and Trinidad & Tobago.

Indirect taxes have the effect of increasing the prices of the goods on which they are levied. They may therefore be a source of inflation. *Inflation* is a continuous rise in the general level of prices.

Indirect taxes are usually levied at the same rate for all individuals, so they take up a higher proportion of the poorer people's income than that of richer people. Thus they are said to be *regressive taxes.* Income taxes take up a higher proportion of income as income increases, so they are called *progressive taxes.* If a tax takes up an equal proportion of the incomes of both rich and poor it is called a *proportional tax.*

14.4 The regulatory role of government

Another important role of the government is its regulatory role, which is to protect consumers from unscrupulous practices by businesses and to influence business activity. The main areas of consumer protection are health and safety standards, the sale of goods, hire purchase agreements and the regulation of monopolies.

Health and safety standards

The government has to make sure that the goods which are provided for sale meet certain standards for health and safety. For example, inspectors from the Ministry of Health inspect meat products offered for sale and also inspect restaurants and food processing plants. Technical inspectors test electrical goods to ensure that they are safe. This helps to ensure that businesses provide products that meet the health and safety standards of the country.

Price controls

The government may impose a ceiling on the prices of certain essential commodities to make them available to consumers at reasonable prices. Items that are usually subject to price controls are medicines, meat, fish, rice, sugar, powdered milk and salt fish.

Consumer protection agencies

Consumer protection agencies are usually private organizations which serve as watchdogs to protect consumers from the unscrupulous practices of businesses, and provide consumers with information about products that are offered for sale. The government may endorse the work of these agencies and sometimes provides legal monetary support for their activities.

The sale of goods

All Caribbean countries have laws that protect the consumer from being cheated by businesses. These laws deal with the following:

1 Goods must satisfy the purpose for which they are intended (they must be of a merchantable quality). For example, a refrigerator must be able to make ice and keep food cold.

2 If goods are sold by sample, the entire order must correspond with the sample. For example, if a sample of paper towels is made of two-ply paper, then the entire order must be the same.

3 If the goods are sold by description then the goods must fit the description. If you order a certain type of vacuum cleaner, then you cannot be given an inferior substitute or be forced to purchase a more expensive one.

4 Weights and measures used in the sale of commodities must be accurate. Inspectors travel around checking the accuracy of scales used by shopkeepers, fish vendors and vegetable vendors, for example.

5 Goods must carry an accurate description of contents, for example 100 per cent cotton or 14 carat gold. Firms can be prosecuted for false labelling.

6 Advertising must not be misleading or make false claims about what a product can do. For example, a product should not be advertised as a cure for AIDS, since no such cure currently exists.

7 Guarantees on mechanical and electrical equipment should be honoured.

Hire purchase agreements

Many consumers buy expensive goods on hire purchase. They make a down-payment and pay off the balance in instalments. The law protects the rights of the consumer and specifies the conditions under which the firm can take back (repossess) the goods. This ensures that the firm does not repossess goods if the consumer misses a single payment.

Regulation of monopolies

A monopoly is a firm which is the only seller of a product or service. In Caribbean countries the telephone company is a monopoly, and so is the electricity company. Monopolies can use their power to extract higher prices from the consumer because there is no alternative source. Governments have to regulate the price charged by these monopolies. In order to increase their prices, regulated monopolies must apply to the government for an increase. There is usually a hearing to determine if the price increase is justified. The regulation of monopolies may reduce the profitability of such firms and hence reduce the availability of internally generated funds for expansion.

Influencing business activity

Governments also use their regulatory power to influence business activities in the country. They may use legislation, regulations, taxes and subsidies to affect the business activity.

Legislation The government can pass legislation to facilitate economic activity. For example, most Caribbean countries have legislation giving incentives for the development of the hotel industry and the manufacturing sector. The Hotel Aid Act in most Caribbean countries is an example of this type of legislation.

Regulations The regulations for the operation of business can also be used to affect the level of business activity. For example, in order to establish a business a variety of procedures have to be gone through. The government can encourage the establishment of both domestic and foreign businesses by simplifying the procedures for getting licences, duty-free concessions, tax holidays and registering the business. When the business is operational, regulations should be reduced to the minimum consistent with the good conduct of businesses.

Taxation (fiscal incentives to industry) These are tax concessions given to manufacturing firms to make them more profitable and expand their output. These fiscal incentives include duty-free importation of raw materials, tax holidays and investment tax credit.

Infant industry protection This is another use of taxation to influence business activity. Many small firms in the Caribbean need protection from more established foreign competition. After a few years the small firms grow and become more efficient – they learn by doing. The protection can then be removed. Protection is provided by tariffs, quotas (limits on the import of commodities) and an outright ban on imports. In many cases the infant industries do not 'grow up' and the protection remains in place for many years.

Subsidies Monetary incentives are concessions given to firms to reduce their costs and to enable them to produce more. These include subsidies (grants), government guarantee of loans, and lower interest rates for certain types of investment.

Provision of factory space Special allocations of space in industrial estates are another form of subsidy. This reduces the cost of setting up a business, since the firm does not have to build its own factory, and the rent of the space is nominal.

These activities are supported by the government's overall management of the economy to promote economic stability and encourage investment. Governments undertake economic planning to encourage economic growth and development.

14.5 Agencies promoting economic growth and development

One of the roles of government is to provide the right climate for business in the country to grow. If the business sector grows, the entire country grows. Some of the agencies that governments use to assist businesses in the Caribbean are:

1 Export promotion – the government offers export promotion assistance through the export promotion corporations in the various countries. They provide information on export opportunities in different countries of the world. The Commercial section in many of the countries' embassies helps by providing information and marketing assistance in the foreign countries. For example, the Tourist Board marketing offices are usually located in the embassies.

2 Export credit insurance is provided through the central banks. This insurance guarantees that exporters will be paid even if their foreign clients are unable to pay.

3 Assistance in training is given in the form of scholarships in technical fields. Technical schools have also been established to train

people in skills like mechanical and electrical engineering, refrigeration and construction.

4 Foreign experts are sometimes brought in temporarily by the government to do technical work and to train local workers. These are usually provided through international development agencies like the United States Agency for International Development (USAID), the Canadian International Development Agency (CIDA) and the British Development Division (BDD).

5 The Industrial Development Corporations in the various countries have programmes in place to encourage foreign firms to set up in the country. Some industries require more investment funds than are available locally. Others need foreign technology. Foreign firms are encouraged to set up in these industries.

6 The agricultural sector benefits from government assistance in a number of ways, for example extension services provided by the agricultural department, subsidized planting material and seeds, research services and regional institutions like the Caribbean Agricultural Research and Development Institute (CARDI) and the Windward Islands Banana Growers Association (WINBAN).

7 Sometimes governments need to help ailing industries by nationalizing them to provide the capital necessary for the proper functioning of the business.

In the Caribbean the private sector is very weak and has a history of mainly buying and selling. Such firms will generally not invest in risky manufacturing enterprises which require a lot of capital. In this case it may be necessary for the government either to undertake the investment itself or to guarantee the loans to these firms. If the firm cannot repay the loan, the government will have to repay it. The governments have also established Development Banks and Development Corporations which give loans for the establishment of new risky industries which would not normally be financed by the commercial banks.

Key Points

- The main responsibilities of all governments are the provision of social goods, stabilization of the economy, the achievement of an equitable distribution of income and regulation of businesses. In the Caribbean, governments also try to encourage economic development.
- The government determines the allocation between social and private goods by taxing individuals and organizations and using the proceeds to provide social goods. This is done through the annual budget.
- Social goods are those for which the exclusion principle cannot be applied, or the benefits of one individual do not reduce the benefits to another individual. The government also provides merit goods like education and health.
- Taxation is the government imposition of compulsory levies on people or organizations. Taxes can be direct or indirect.
- Direct taxes are imposed directly on an individual or organization. They include taxes on income and wealth. The PAYE tax is the most common direct tax.
- Indirect taxes are paid by the seller of a commodity and are passed on to the consumer in the form of higher prices, for example import duties, consumption tax and excise tax.
- The regulatory function can be divided into four aspects: maintaining health and safety standards, regulating business practices with respect to the sale of goods, regulating hire purchase agreements, and regulating monopolies.
- To encourage growth and development, governments help businesses in a number of ways, for example by giving fiscal and monetary incentives, protecting infant industries, promoting exports and offering training and technical assistance.

Questions

1 Discuss the main responsibilities of government. Are there special responsibilities that governments in the Caribbean need to undertake?

2 (a) What is a *budget*?

(b) What is a *fiscal deficit*?

(c) Distinguish between *current expenditure* and *capital expenditure*.

3 Explain what is meant by *social goods*, and give examples. How do governments provide social goods?

4 What are some of the social services provided by the government in your country? Try to determine whether they are merit goods or social goods. Give reasons for your conclusion.

5 What is *taxation*? Explain the purposes of taxation.

6 Distinguish between *direct* and *indirect* taxes. Give examples of both types of tax in your country.

7 Explain what is meant by *regressive* and *progressive* taxes. Give examples of each type.

8 Explain the ways in which the government tries to protect the consumer.

9 What do you understand by *infant industry protection*? Can you identify any of these industries in your country?

10 (a) Identify five types of service that governments provide to the private sector.

(b) Explain how two of these types of service work in your territory.

(c) Select *one* of the services you have named in (a) and give three reasons why the government of your country, as opposed to the private sector, provides that service.

(CXC June 1987)

A Note on Contracts: Chapters 15–17

The next three chapters focus on the legal principles governing business activities. Many of these legal principles were originally derived from Britain. Through the process of colonization, the laws and legal system of Britain were transplanted to the countries of the Commonwealth Caribbean.

Except for St Lucia, the legal system of each of these countries is generally described as the *common law system*. The common law originally applied to all British citizens, and was brought to the Caribbean by the colonists when they settled here. The term also applies to a system of law in which the legal principles are established by judges in individual cases. This body of law is largely unwritten. In assessing new cases, judges often refer to previous decisions, to ensure that their own decisions are consistent over time. These legal principles are established by the courts and not by the legislature, so they are described as 'judge-made laws'. The St Lucian legal system is different from that of its neighbours in that part of its law was derived from Britain, and part from France. It therefore has a system of mixed legal traditions.

However, not all laws are established by judges. Most of our laws are now made by the legislature. These laws are written laws. They are different from judge-made laws in that they are enacted by the legislature, and are described as *statute laws*, or simply *legislation*. Sometimes judges also have to interpret the laws enacted by the legislature.

In the following three chapters you will be introduced to legal principles that apply both to judge-made laws and to statute laws.

Chapter 15 Agreements Leading to Contracts

Every second of the day, someone, somewhere, enters into agreement involving a contract. When a person selects an item in a supermarket and pays the cashier, a contract comes into being between the purchaser and the owner of the supermarket. Contracts could even come into existence between students. If you agreed either verbally or in writing to exchange your school lunch with another student for cash every day for five days, an agreement in the nature of a contract could arise, provided that certain conditions are satisfied. (These conditions will be clarified later.)

In time, you will engage in activities involving very complex contractual agreements, for example the purchase of items on hire purchase, the hiring of a gardener, the renting of a house, the purchase of a house or car, the purchase of the services of a doctor or lawyer, the employment of a builder to construct a house. These are all activities that involve some kind of agreement between two or more parties to do or to refrain from doing a particular act or acts. If these agreements are to be meaningful, then they must be binding on both parties and capable of being enforced.

It is the same in the world of business. Depending on the nature of its operations, a business may have to hire workers, order raw materials to manufacture its products, sell goods and services, advertise and market its products, buy land and borrow money to expand its operations. All of these activities are conducted on the basis of agreements of one kind or another. Consider how uncertain life would be if businesses did not have reasonable guarantees that agreements would be honoured between those who entered into them. If agreements could not be honoured or enforced, economic activity would come to a standstill. It would be impossible to plan for the future. Contracts are the life-blood of business and social activity. Without the device of the contract, business would not survive.

But not all agreements are necessarily contracts in the legal sense. How then do we determine when a real contract exists?

15.1 What is a contract?

Consider the following definition which has been selected from *The Oxford Companion of Law*:

> 'A contract is an agreement between two or more persons intended to create a legal obligation between them and to be legally enforceable.'

The idea of 'legal obligation' imports the notion that the agreement is one that the law recognizes and will enforce.

Agreement is, perhaps, the single most important component of a contract, but in order for a contract to be legally enforceable, a number of other important elements must exist.

> 'It must be an agreement freely entered into between two or more parties who have the legal capacity to enter into the agreement. The agreement must also be backed by good and valid consideration and one which is made for a lawful purpose in a form required by law.'

This means that a valid contract requires five elements:

- agreement
- consideration
- capacity
- a lawful purpose
- a form approved by law.

In this chapter each of these elements will be considered in turn.

It is important to bear in mind that contracts may be created in a wide variety of circumstances. For example, they may arise from face-to-face conversations, by an exchange of letters, by telephone conversations, through the exchange of telegrams, and now by exchange of telexes and faxed messages. Special forms are used in most business transactions – see Chapter 17.

15.2 Agreement

A contractual agreement arises when one party (normally described as the *offeror*) makes an offer to another party, and that other party (described as the *offeree*) decides to accept the offer.

The basic idea involved in the notion of agreement could be expressed in more technical language. Each party makes a promise to accept the other's terms. The exchange of promises produces agreement and this is analysed in terms of offer and acceptance. This may be illustrated in a practical way:

The offer:	Clement says to Healey, 'I'll pay you $50,000 for your car.'
Acceptance:	Healey replies, 'I agree.'
Agreement:	Clement makes an offer and Healey accepts the offer.

In effect, when the two parties reached agreement, their minds were at one with each other. Their agreement means that they have exchanged promises with each other. They regard their agreement as binding their promises. In every contract there must be an offer and an acceptance.

However, no agreement is enforceable unless the parties intend to be bound by the agreement. In other words, they must intend that their agreement produces a legal relationship such that if one party defaults, the agreement could be enforced by a court, and the defaulting party made to compensate the other party.

Intention to create legal relations

Not all agreements, however, give rise to legal relationships. An invitation by a friend to dinner is a social gesture and is not a binding agreement. Likewise, if two parties agree to take a walk together, or one party extends hospitality to another, no one can seriously contend that these forms of agreement produce contracts.

So too agreements between husbands and wives, parents and children are not normally enforceable at law. These agreements are said to be made for domestic reasons, in good faith and not intended to be rigid and binding. If these agreements were made enforceable they could well produce discord in the family.

Of course, evidence could be presented that the parties to a marriage did intend to create a legal relationship. For example, the parties to a marriage and even a union other than a marriage could agree on their respective shares to a property they have acquired or improved. Such an agreement is likely to be enforced if it is proved.

Another category of agreements which the courts are unwilling to enforce are agreements between trade unions and employers. Such agreements, known as *collective agreements*, are said to be undertakings that are binding in honour only. Parliament can, however, pass laws to enforce collective agreements if it wishes.

It is possible too for parties to enter into an agreement and say that the agreement is not to be binding in law. Once such intention is clear, the agreement will not be enforced by the courts.

Not all offers necessarily lead to a contract. Indeed, in some cases protracted negotiations take place before an agreement exists.

Distinction between invitation to negotiate, and offer

A distinction must be made between an invitation to negotiate, and an offer. Consider the following conversation between two parties, Reginald and Brian. Up to the point when Reginald says 'Agreed', the parties are merely negotiating.

Reginald:	'Would you like to buy my bicycle?'
Brian:	'How much do you want for it?'
Reginald:	'Look, you're my special friend. I'll give it to you for $50.'
Brian:	'Really? At that price I might as well go to the store and buy a new one. Your bike is five years old. I'll give you $20.'
Reginald:	'Agreed! Accepted!'

Brian's offer of $20 is a good example of a counter-offer. Indeed, the contract was agreed on the basis of the counter-offer.

Other examples of invitations to treat may be cited. A circular or catalogue advertising goods for sale is no more than an attempt to invite people to make offers. Nor does the display of items in a shop window or in a self-service shop amount to an offer by those businesses to a customer to sell – the display is merely an invitation to the customer to buy.

Auctions are particularly interesting. Does the auctioneer offer goods for sale? What the auctioneer does is to call for bids from the people at the auction. The call for bids is an invitation to treat. It is when the auctioneer's hammer falls that he agrees to a bid. At that point a contract comes into being.

It is critically important that both parties are aware that an offer has been made. For this reason, an offer should be clear, definite and easily ascertainable. If the offer is vague or indefinite, then should the parties seek to enforce their rights the court would be unable to determine what the parties really intended. Acceptance of an offer cannot take place if the party making the offer does not communicate it to the other party. Until the party to whom the offer has been made (the *offeree*) is aware of the offer and its terms, he or she cannot accept it. Hence the rule: 'The offeror must communicate an offer to the offeree before the offeree can accept or reject the offer.'

Acceptance

Some of the principles that apply to an offer also apply to an acceptance. So, for example, acceptance could only come from the party to whom the offer was made. If the offer is directed to a group of people, or to the public at large, then it may be accepted by any member of the group or public who is aware of the offer.

Acceptance must be absolute. There can be no acceptance if new conditions are attached. If a party adds new conditions then it may be said that a counter-offer has been made. Consider the following scenario based on the actual facts of a case.

Anthony v. *Timothy*

6th June 1991	Timothy writes to Anthony as follows: 'I am willing to sell my estate to you for $7,000.'
8th June 1991	Anthony replies by letter: 'Your offer is excessive. I am willing to pay $4,000.'
27th June 1991	Timothy replies, 'Your offer is disappointing. I cannot accept it.'
29th June 1991	Anthony then writes: 'I have decided to accept your original price of $7,000.'

In this case, the court said that Anthony's letter of 8th June was a rejection of Timothy's offer. Anthony could no longer revive the contract by simply changing his mind. Anthony's offer on 29th June was a counter-offer. So no contract existed. Negotiations would have to begin all over again.

The point was made that acceptance must be communicated to the offeror. Does silence mean acceptance? Not at all! An offeror will not be allowed to impose an agreement by proclaiming that silence means consent. Contracts come into existence by agreement.

However, sometimes acceptance may not have to be communicated. An offeror could prescribe a mode of acceptance. Consider the very famous case which established this rule. A manufacturer offered by advertisements a health product to the general public as a prevention and cure for 'flu. When a member of the public sued the manufacturer because the product did not live up to the claims made for it, the manufacturer argued that the claimant had not communicated acceptance of the offer before using the product, and that no contract had come into existence. The court did not accept the manufacturer's argument. It said that the terms of the offer indicated that once a person bought the health product, the contract would come into effect. So the manufacturer had prescribed a mode of acceptance which the claimant accepted by mere purchase of the health product. Therefore the claimant did not have to notify the manufacturer that the offer had been accepted.

A common practice, particularly relating to the purchase of land, is to agree to the purchase *subject to contract*. This means that the parties agree to the general details of their contract but wish to make sure that all is well before they complete the agreement and give it legal effect. When parties agree 'subject to contract' or some similar term, they are not obligating themselves to each other. This device is common and useful especially when a house or land is being purchased.

Modes of communication

It should by now be clear that a contract can be verbal or in writing. Modern methods of communication mean that contracts may be entered into in a matter of seconds. If negotiations between the parties take place through the post, or by telexes or telegrams, how does one know when there is acceptance of an offer?

Where the contractual negotiations are conducted by an exchange of letters, acceptance of an offer could, in theory, occur in one of the following situations:

- the letter of acceptance is put into the post
- the letter of acceptance reaches the address of the offeror, or

- the offeror actually sees and reads the letter of acceptance.

Attractive arguments could be presented for each of these possibilities. But in fact the courts have decided that a contract conducted through the post is concluded at the moment when the offeree posts the letter of acceptance, even though the letter never reaches the offeror. What if the offeree changes his mind? Could he recall his acceptance by telephone, telegram or by fax? What do you think?

Termination of offers

People often change their minds, and a party negotiating a contract may decide to withdraw an offer made to the other party.

The circumstances leading to termination can vary. An offer could simply be withdrawn, it could be terminated by an indirect revocation, it could lapse because a condition stated by the offeror for the continuation of the contract did not materialize, or it may be affected by the death of one of the parties.

Revocation or withdrawal of an offer may take place and be effective any time before its acceptance by the other party. This applies even though the offeror states that the offeree must give a response by a certain date. To be effective, however, the revocation must be communicated to the offeree.

If a business is conducting negotiations for a contract through the post or by telex or fax it has to be careful. It was noted above that acceptance is valid on the date of posting the letter. A different rule applies in the case of a revocation of an offer. The revocation takes effect when the offeree receives the letter, or cable or telex. It must be clear too that the offeror knows that the offeree – that is, the other party – is aware of the revocation. Consider these facts:

Jamaica Foods Ltd v. *St Lucia Natural Products Ltd*

24th May 1991 Jamaica Foods Ltd posted a letter to St Lucia Natural Products offering them 5,000 boxes of ackees.

10th June 1991 Jamaica Foods Ltd posted another letter to St Lucia Natural Products, cancelling the offer.

12th June 1991 St Lucia Natural Products Ltd faxed their acceptance and confirmed it in a letter posted on 14th June 1991.

20th June 1991 The letter of revocation from Jamaica Foods Ltd, posted on 10th June 1991, reached St Lucia Natural Products Ltd.

Faced with these facts, a court would give judgment in favour of St Lucia Natural Products Ltd, because the revocation of the offer was received by St Lucia Natural Products Ltd after the company had accepted the offer.

An indirect notice to the offeree could lead to the revocation of an offer. For example, Jennifer offers to sell her wardrobe to Claudette for $500. She adds that the offer is open for three days. On the next day Jennifer meets Yasmin and in the presence of Linette offers her the wardrobe for $400. Yasmin promptly accepts. Linette then meets Claudette and mentions that Jennifer has sold the wardrobe to Yasmin. If Claudette contests Jennifer's action it is unlikely that she will succeed. By selling the wardrobe to Yasmin, Jennifer displayed an intention to revoke her offer. In any event, Claudette could not deny that she had knowledge of Jennifer's change of mind since Linette, a witness to the proceedings, told her so.

Offers can also be revoked by lapse of time. If an offer states that it is open until a specific time, the offer lapses at the expiration of the specified time. If the offeror fails to indicate the duration of the offer, then the offer lapses after a reasonable time has passed. Surely an offer cannot remain open for all time. What is reasonable will depend on the facts.

Likewise, just like an acceptance, an offer may not be absolute. It could be conditional on some event. So if the condition is not satisfied or does not come to fruition then the offer lapses.

What if the offeror or offeree dies or becomes insane? There is much uncertainty here. Surely the offeree cannot accept the offer if he or she has had notice of the offeror's death? Much may, however, depend on the stage of the contract and the personality of the contractor. If the offer does not have to do with the personality of the offeror and the promise could be satisfied from the offeror's estate or company, then it seems logical that unless the offeree is notified, death would not automatically cancel the offer. On the other hand, if it is the offeree who dies before the offer is accepted, then the offer is not capable of being accepted. Death frustrates the exchange of promises.

In the case of the mentally ill, problems of capacity are presented (see page 222).

15.3 Consideration

Essentially, contracts are agreements or bargains between two parties, and each of the parties receives something in return for the promise made by the other. Each party enters into an agreement on the basis that something will be done by or received from the other party. The exchange of promises is an agreement that the party accepting the offer promises to do something for the offeree. The 'something' that is received by the offeree is described as *consideration*. This element is essential to all contracts made in our legal system (and in other systems based on the European and American systems). However, consideration is not necessary for *contracts under seal*. These are contracts in which the parties put their agreement into writing, on paper or parchment, sign the agreement, affix a seal and deliver the contract. In technical terms, the instrument used is described as a *deed*. Originally the purpose of the seal was to prove that the document was genuine.

To illustrate the idea of consideration, look at this example:

Stetson v. *Douglas*

Stetson: (offeror) 'I have a job available to cover the roof of my house.'

Douglas: (offeree) 'I'm willing to do it for you. It's a small house. I'll do it for $1,000.'

Stetson: '$1,000? For a small house? C'mon. Putting on the roof of that house is about $700.'

Douglas: 'OK. I'll accept $700.'

In this example, Stetson has received a promise or undertaking by Douglas to cover the roof of his house. So Stetson will receive a benefit – that is, a finished roof – by paying Douglas for his labour. For his promise to complete the roof of Stetson's house, Douglas too will receive a benefit: $700. Each party to the contract will receive some benefit or interest for the exchange of their promises. In this instance, the benefit that each party receives is the *consideration*.

Consideration could be a detriment

Consideration imparts the idea that no one should be compelled or required to part with or give away goods or services without getting some kind of compensation in return. But not all contracts necessarily yield a benefit. Some contracts may bring some disadvantage or detriment to the offeree. Consider the following exchange between Amos and Ronald. Amos is heavily in debt and needs money urgently, and Ronald knows this.

Ronald: 'Are you interested in selling your gold watch?'

Amos: 'Bet I am! These days I need money badly! My

watch is gold-plated and was bought for over $5,000. It's a Rolex, made in Switzerland, not Hong Kong, you know! It's less than a year old.'

Ronald: 'How much do you want for it?'

Amos: 'Make an offer, man.'

Ronald: 'Look, it's a lovely watch. How about $200?'

Amos: '$200? You're crazy! Look, I need cash. Take it for $500.'

Ronald: 'Agreed! Let's settle now! Here's your cash.'

Amos has legally agreed to suffer an economic detriment; he has parted with a watch costing $5,000 for the paltry sum of $500. Amos also receives a legal benefit. By virtue of the contract, he has become legally entitled to receive $500, a sum he may not have had before. It is this benefit which constitutes the consideration arising from his promise to sell.

From the above, the following definition of consideration reproduced from the fifth edition of *Black's Law Dictionary* should prove useful:

> 'The inducement to a contract. The cause, nature, price, or impelling influence which induces a contracting party to enter into a contract. The reason or material cause underlying the formation of a contract. Some right, interest, profit or benefit accruing to one party, or some forbearance, detriment, loss or responsibility, given, suffered or undertaken by the other.'

So though consideration can take many forms, it must always be remembered that in every case consideration must be something done by the offeree as a result of a promise made by the offeror. The offeror must get something in return for a promise. Otherwise the promise is merely gratuitous, a mere favour and without legal benefit. The important point to bear in mind is that *a contract is legally enforceable only if the promises are supported by consideration.*

Consideration must move from the offeree

The requirement of consideration has other implications. If two parties enter into a contract for the benefit of a third person, the third person cannot enforce the contract because that person did not provide any consideration. Suppose Martha and Desmona make an agreement to the effect that Desmona will sew a dress for Martha and Martha will pay Valencia $100. If Martha defaults, Valencia cannot maintain an action against Martha because Martha was not a party to the contract and did not give any consideration for the benefit negotiated on her behalf. This rule has proved inconvenient in several cases. Some countries with a legal system that is dissimilar to most of those of the English-speaking Commonwealth Caribbean have attempted to get around the difficulty by allowing third parties to claim the benefit of a contract. Interestingly, the rule does not apply in St Lucia. There, a specific law provides that 'a party to a contract may stipulate for the benefit of a third person, when such benefit is the condition of a contract which he makes himself, or of a gift which he makes to another'. If the third party has signified agreement, the party who made the contract for the third party's benefit cannot revoke it.

Adequacy of consideration

Parties are usually free to contract on whatever terms they wish. Thus it may be perfectly possible for a contract to be overwhelmingly in favour of one of the parties. Put differently, a party may not have received a fair, just and proper compensation for a promise. However, the law is not really concerned with what value parties to a contract receive for their bargain. The reason is simple. The courts take the view that a sane person is entitled to make any contract, even though he or she ends up with what some might think is a bad bargain. Then, too, it is not always easy to determine the value that parties attach to a bargain. Some things are important to some people and not to others. The courts therefore are primarily concerned with the presence or absence of consideration and not whether the consideration is adequate or fair or just. Courts will only interfere if there is error, fraud or some form of gross misconduct.

Take the following example of an error.

10th March 1991	Rene writes a letter to Wade offering to sell his computer to Wade for $2,000.
20th March 1991	Wade replies by fax and declines to accept the offer and makes a counter-offer of $1,000.
21st March 1991	Rene replies by telegram. He rejects Wade's offer and makes a counter-offer to sell the computer for $1,500. However, in sending the telegram, the wireless office quotes a price of $150.
22nd March 1991	Wade replies by fax as follows: 'I am delighted to accept your offer to sell the computer for $150. A cheque is in the post.'

Clearly, Wade could not compel Rene to keep his promise to sell the computer because of the obvious error. It would take a lot to believe that Rene, after offering his computer for sale for $2,000, would accept $150.

Other simple rules apply. Since consideration is something of value that a party receives for a promise, it cannot be something which that party received in the past, before the contract was made. If a party has received a benefit in the past, and an offer is being made on the basis of that past benefit, then nothing is being received in respect of the present promise. The consideration is really a past consideration. For all practical purposes, it is no consideration at all. Usually, the consideration for any contract is something which the offeree or promisee will pay or provide or give, either at the very moment the contract is made (*present consideration*) or in the future (*future consideration*).

There are, however, some exceptions. Examine carefully the following facts:

> Bertha is an employee of Design Fabrics (Barbados) Ltd. The owners of the company always praised Bertha for her work and on several occasions promised her a special reward. After a very successful year, Design Fabrics (Barbados) Ltd wrote to Bertha as follows: 'In consideration of your services as the Implementation Manager in working our fabric designs, the Board of Directors have agreed to give you a 20% share in the profits of our designs.' Bertha replies, 'I am pleased to accept your offer.'

Clearly, Bertha is being rewarded for past services, and there is no consideration to support it. Could the agreement be enforced? The answer is yes. The courts have reasoned that Bertha's services were given at the request of her employers and that given the company's praises and promise of a special reward, both parties must have understood that at some point in time Bertha's services would be remunerated by further payment. Obviously too, if such an offer was made in advance – that is, before Bertha accepted her present employment – it would also have been legally enforceable.

Just as past consideration is no consideration, a promisee cannot offer as consideration something which the law or another agreement imposed on the promisee. Neither valuable consideration nor a benefit would accrue in this situation.

15.4 Capacity

In the next few years, you will celebrate your 18th birthday. When that milestone is reached, in the eyes of the law of most, if not all, Commonwealth Caribbean countries, you will no longer be a minor or an infant but an adult. This means that you will be able to enjoy all the contractual rights and liabilities that other adults enjoy. In more technical language, once you have become an adult you acquire *full* legal capacity to make a contract and be bound by its terms.

Why is a minor restricted when people below the age of majority have been known to handle the shopping for their families in supermarkets and other places? In general, it is felt that minors – that is, people who are under 18 years of age, or any other legal age of majority – are immature and inexperienced and may not fully understand the consequences which flow from contractual agreements. Given too their continued dependence on their parents, minors may not be able to bear the financial responsibilities and other obligations that arise from contractual agreements.

Another class of people who may have legal restrictions similar to minors are the inebriated (drunk) and the insane. What if such people enter into contractual agreements?

Contracts made by minors

The general rule is that a minor does not have the legal capacity to make a contract. If a minor contracts to acquire an interest in some matter that imposes substantial obligations, then the contract is valid and binding upon that minor unless he or she repudiates it during minority or within a reasonable time after the age of majority. Once the contract is affirmed by the minor, then the other party cannot refuse to perform the terms of the contract.

The law, however, does make certain contracts enforceable against minors. The most important of these are described as 'contracts for necessaries'. By these contracts minors are obliged to pay for necessaries that are supplied to them. This is really a rule of common sense. If such contracts were not enforceable against minors, no one would be willing to sell or supply them with food and services. Moreover, to deny minors access to necessaries would place them at a severe disadvantage. They might starve!

Necessaries include not only food, clothing and lodging, but also the costs of education and instruction in an art or trade. Even legal advice could be treated as a 'necessary'. To succeed in a claim against a minor it must be proven that the 'necessaries' are consistent with the minor's style of living and that the goods and/or services are actually suited to the circumstances of the minor.

Likewise, if the minor enters into a contract of employment or apprenticeship, that contract would be enforceable against the minor, if the contract is beneficial to the minor. Consider this unusual but actual case.

> *Roberts* v. *Gray*
>
> Gray, a minor, wanted to become a professional billiard player. He made a contract with Roberts, a professional player, to go on a world tour together and to play matches against each other. Roberts spent considerable time, energy and money on the arrangements. Gray changed his mind about the tour and repudiated the contract. Roberts took Gray to court and the court agreed with Roberts. The court said that playing billiards with a professional was valuable education for a minor who wanted to make a career as a professional player.

These rules really emphasize that people below the age of majority must be very careful when seeking to enter into contractual agreements.

Sometimes, Parliament enacts legislation to give contractual rights to people under the age of majority. A good example is the Barbados legislation governing cooperatives. Under the Cooperative Societies Act No. 23 of 1990, a person who has attained the age of 16 years may become a member of a cooperative, exercising most of the contractual rights given to adults. The material provision states that a member who is under the age of 18 years could enter into a contract with the cooperative of which he or she is a member, and with respect to the contract the minor is *sui juris*. This phrase, *sui juris*, simply means that minors have the capacity to manage their own affairs in respect of their membership of the cooperative. To put it differently, minors are under no legal disability and do not have to rely on a guardian or parent to act for them.

Contracts made by inebriated (drunk) and insane people

Curiously, many of the rules that apply to minors also apply to insane and to inebriated people.

If a person is insane and has been hospitalized in a psychiatric institution for treatment, such a person cannot be held bound by a contract. On the other hand, if the person suffers from mental disorders from time to time, then the situation is slightly different. Sometimes, that person may be in good mental health; on other occasions, he or she may be ill. The most important question is whether at the time the person made the contract he or she was so ill that they could not reasonably be said to have understood the nature of the contract that had been entered into. Obviously this is a matter of fact.

If the contract is one for necessaries, then the mentally ill person would be bound. However, if the contract is for a non-necessary item then the rule is different. In this instance, if the mentally ill person can show that he or she was so ill that they did not know or could not appreciate their own actions, and the other party knew this condition, then when the mentally ill person recovers, he or she has the option of either repudiating the contract or accepting it.

In general, the capacity of a drunk person to contract is much the same as a person who is mentally ill. The lesson is to avoid contracting with people when they are drunk.

15.5 Lawful purpose

No contract would be enforceable if it offends what may be described as the public good or public morals. Such contracts could also be illegal, because they often entail the commission of a criminal act. This applies irrespective of whether the contract is one between private individuals or business houses. Listed below are some contracts which are regarded as illegal.

A contract to commit a crime, a civil wrong or a fraud on a third party

A contract to commit a crime, such as to rob, assault, murder or obtain goods by false pretences, or to circulate obscene pictures, is illegal. Such contracts involve offences prohibited under criminal law. Likewise a contract to commit a civil wrong is unenforceable. Examples are agreements to slander a third party, to damage the property of another, to impersonate another, to breach someone's copyright over a musical item, and to fake physical injuries in order to claim monetary damages against an insurance company.

A very important rule is that *no party will be allowed to benefit from a crime which that party committed or in which that party was involved*. So if, for example, a man intentionally killed his wife, he would not be allowed to claim under her will. No court will allow a person to recover the fruits of a crime.

Contracts that are sexually immoral

This category of contracts is held to be contrary to good public morals. For example, a contract by a landlord to lease a house for use as a brothel would be declared illegal. So too would a contract to pay a party for sexual favours.

Contracts that interfere with the course of justice

No court will enforce a contract that interferes with the administration or dispensation of justice. For example, an agreement by a witness to a case not to give evidence in that case would not be enforced. Similarly an agreement to prevent the prosecution of a party who committed a criminal act would be of no effect.

Contracts that corrupt public affairs

A good example of such a contract is an attempt to buy or sell a public office or to influence the appointment of a person to a particular post or office. Consider these facts:

Ronald: 'If you get me the appointment as the Manager of the Government Store, I'll reward you.'

Bertrand: 'What would you give me?'

Ronald: 'I'll give you $5,000 and appoint anybody you recommend for employment in the store.'

If Ronald got the appointment and did not keep his side of the bargain, Bertrand would not succeed in enforcing the agreement against Ronald. Indeed, both would face criminal charges. Such contracts deny fair competition for offices and, in the words of one writer, would 'diminish the respectability, responsibility and purity of public offices'.

Contracts prejudicial to the state

Another class of contract that would not be enforced is a contract that is prejudicial to the state in its relations with other countries. A contract with a resident of an enemy country during wartime is said to be contrary to the interests of that country. Indeed, if the contract existed before the outbreak of hostilities, the contract is then terminated instantly. The rights that accrued between the parties before the war nevertheless remain enforceable. Whether the parties to the contract could eventually claim their respective rights is a different matter.

A contract that disturbs the good relations between a state and a foreign country is also unenforceable. The rules for this class of contract are less clear because relations between countries tend to change dramatically. Sometimes it is difficult to tell when a country is a friend or foe.

A contract to defraud the state of revenue

The state relies heavily on revenue in the form of taxes, consumption duties, licences, sale of items, and fines. Thus if parties to a contract enter into an agreement that directly or indirectly defrauds the state of revenue to which it is entitled, such a contract would not be enforced. For example, if a contract of employment was so designed as to permit an employee to avoid paying taxes in a way that the tax law did not approve, such a contract would be illegal.

Contracts in restraint of trade

Another class of contracts which the courts could declare unenforceable are contracts in restraint of trade, so-called because they restrict the liberty of a party to the contract from carrying on a trade, business or profession with such persons or businesses as that person chooses, when and where he or she likes.

Some restraints are imposed by legislation enacted by Parliament. Others are imposed by agreement. Restraints by agreement vary but include the following:

- restraints accepted by employees restricting their liberty to practise or trade in the same business as their employer after they leave the employment
- restraints upon a trader restricting the trader to ordering supplies from a specified supplier
- restraints agreed by associations of manufacturers, traders or merchants, to regulate prices and output
- restraints by employees regarding the terms and conditions of their employment
- restraints imposed by buyers of produce and business upon sellers, to minimize or prevent the sellers from competing with the buyer on the same market, in the same goods or business activities.

What is the legal status of these contracts? Generally, contracts in restraint of trade are treated as unenforceable. However, the courts may enforce an agreement if it is seen to be reasonable and necessary from the point of view of the parties and it is in the interest of the community.

The rules vary according to the parties to the contract. For example, the rules relating to an agreement concerning the sale of a business are not the same as those relating to agreements between employees and employers. The latter form of agreement is, perhaps, more interesting.

It may seem odd that people should be prevented or restricted from practising their trade or profession as they would like after they are no longer in the employment of their employers. Consider this case. Thomas Devlin decides to sell his video business. If Thomas plans to move directly across the street and open up a new store, then it is very possible that many of the people who supported the old video business would decide to patronize his new business. That could be disastrous for the purchaser of the old business. Thus to avoid this problem the parties could agree that Thomas may not open a competing store within a specified distance of the old business for a period of, say, five years.

Consider too the case of an employee who enjoys an executive position with a large company and who acquires information about the company's new products, trade secrets, and new research findings. If that employee resigns and joins a competitor, then the competitor could benefit from the new information made available to it by the employee. It therefore seems fair and reasonable for the company to protect itself by contracting with the employee that, on resignation, the confidential information is not made available to the competitor.

Contracts of this type are common in very large companies, especially in highly commercialized countries, but they are not totally unknown in the Caribbean. As time goes by and our economies become more complex, we may see more of them.

15.6 Form of contracts

A contract may be verbal, in writing, by deed, or even implied by conduct. Such contracts are described as *simple* or *informal* contracts. On the other hand, some contracts must be done in a special way or take a special form. These contracts are described as *formal contracts* or *specialty contracts,* and are usually known as *deeds*. They must be in writing, signed, and have a seal affixed to the written document. The main reason for such written contracts is to prevent fraud by one or both parties to the contract. The following contracts are required to be in writing:

- bills of exchange
- cheques and promissory notes
- contracts of marine insurance
- transfer of shares in registered companies
- assignment of copyrights
- hire purchase contracts
- contracts assigning debts

There are two other types of contract which need not have all their terms in writing but which must be evidenced in some written form. These are *contracts for the sale of land* and *contracts of guarantee.* A contract of guarantee is one in which a person agrees to be responsible for the obligations of another if that other person fails to honour his or her obligations. The person providing the guarantee is referred to as the *guarantor.*

Identifying the elements of a simple contract

So far, we have considered all the essentials of a legally binding contract. Figure 15.1 is an example of a simple contract, which contains the five essential elements.

Figure 15.1 Example of a written contract

THIS AGREEMENT, made the 28th day of June 1991, **BETWEEN** Jonathan Busboy, twenty years of age, Teacher of 22D Meat Street, St Munster, Anybody Land (hereinafter referred to as "the Seller") **AND** Brotherton Brawling, thirty years of age, Carpenter of 388A Juris Street, Courtown, St Justice, Anybody Land (hereinafter referred to as "the Buyer").

WITNESSETH, that the Seller, in consideration of the agreement hereinafter set out, agrees to and with the Buyer to sell to the Buyer, a Peugeot 1908 GT1 motor car, Engine Number AZX 333333, Chassis Number CDCB 278945, the said car being owned and licensed in the name of the Seller.
In consideration of which the Buyer agrees to pay to the Seller the sum of Eighty Thousand Dollars ($80,000).

In Witness

____

Jonathan Busboy

____

Brotherton Brawling

____

Date

Notes

The various elements may be identified as follows:

1 *Agreement*

(a) *The offer*: Brotherton Brawling offers to buy the car for $80,000.

(b) *The acceptance*:	Jonathan Busboy accepts the offer and agrees to sell his car for $80,000.
2 *Consideration*	(a) Brotherton Brawling receives the car for his promise to pay $80,000 for it. (b) Jonathan Busboy receives $80,000 for his promise to sell the car.
3 *Capacity*	Both parties are over the age of majority. (Contracts do not usually include the ages of the parties.)
4 *Lawful purpose*	The buying and selling of cars between private individuals is fully recognized by the law. The purpose of the contract is, therefore, lawful.
5 *Form approved by law*	No particular form is required by the law for this type of contract. But, given the nature of the contract, the parties have sensibly decided that it is best to put the contract in writing.

Key Points

- Except in a few cases, the law allows parties to contract on whatever terms they wish.
- A contract is an agreement between two or more parties enforceable by law. For a contract to exist there must be (a) agreement resulting from offer and acceptance, (b) an intention to create a legal relationship, (c) consideration, (d) capacity and (e) a lawful purpose to the contract.
- Contracts do not arise from agreements that are purely domestic or social in character, for example agreements between husbands and wives, parents and children. However, if the parties intend an agreement to be binding and there is evidence to that effect, the courts could enforce it.
- All simple contracts must have consideration. Simply stated, consideration is the reason or cause underlying the exchange of promises. Some simple rules to remember:

  (a) Consideration must be real or sufficient but need not be adequate – that is, it need not have the same value or benefit for both sides.

  (b) Consideration must move from the offeree. Only a party who has given something could enforce a promise made to him or her.

  (c) Consideration is not required in the cases of contracts made under seal.

- Capacity refers to the legal ability or right to enter into contracts and to enforce such contracts.
- In general, minors or infants, being under the age of majority, are not liable for contracts made by them. However, in the interest of the minor, a contract for necessaries can be enforced against the minor. Necessaries include food, shelter, clothing, employment, education and even legal representation. All other contracts made by infants may be enforced if the minor asserts the contract.
- Most of the rules applying to minors also apply to mental patients and to people who are drunk.
- In the course of hostilities, enemy aliens are allowed neither to make nor to enforce contracts.
- Unless statute so provides, collective bargaining agreements – that is, agreements made by unions and employers to govern pay and conditions of employment – are not legally enforceable.
- Contracts in restraint of trade restricting the right of a party to carry on a business, trade or profession some time in the future are unenforceable. The main types are:
  - (a) an agreement restricting a trader to ordering supplies from a particular supplier
  - (b) a contract in which the seller of a business agrees that he or she will not compete with the buyer
  - (c) a contract restricting an employee from working when, where and with whom he or she wishes
  - (d) a contract between traders, businessmen, etc to control the price of goods or the output of goods and services.
- Contracts may be created verbally or in writing, or may be inferred from conduct.
- Some contracts must be in the form of a deed, eg mortgages, a contract to convey land.
- Some contracts must be in writing, eg contracts for the sale of land, cheques, promissory notes, bills of exchange.
- Some contracts must be evidenced by some form of writing. The most important is the contract of guarantee, a contract in which a party agrees to pay the loan of another should that other person default on the loan payment.

Questions

1 Consider *offer* and *acceptance* in the following situations:

(a) buying a carton of fruit juice from a vending machine

(b) parking in a car park that allows entry by automatic tickets

(c) buying a roti from a restaurant

(d) taking a ride on a bus or in a taxi

(e) seeing an advertisement for a calculator in a display window for $10 and on reaching the cashier the price is quoted at $100.

2 Mrs Laforce, a teacher at Adella's school, asked Adella to help her to interview certain people during the summer holidays. She promised to pay $5 for each person Adella interviewed. Adella worked hard throughout the holidays and interviewed 200 people. Mrs Laforce failed to pay her the money. Advise Adella as to her claim against Mrs Laforce.

3 State whether the following statements are *true* or *false*, and explain the reasons for your choice:

(a) All contracts must have consideration.

(b) Contracts for the sale of land must always be in writing.

(c) In the case of contracts conducted through the post, an acceptance is effective once the letter reaches the offeror.

4 Bernard, acting on his own free will, trimmed the bush around Joshua's house. When Joshua saw what Bernard had done he was so pleased that he promised to pay him $50 for his work. Could Bernard enforce Joshua's promise?

5 Would you advise that all important contracts be written even though the law may not require it? Why?

6 Claire, a minor, purchased a diamond ring. When she turned 18, Claire returned the ring to the seller saying: 'I no longer need the ring. May I have my money back?' The seller refused. If Claire sued, would she succeed?

7 Ashton was declared insane by a court which also appointed a guardian for him. While detained at a psychiatric hospital, Ashton got away and entered into an agreement to purchase some clothes from Bongo Clothing. Could Bongo Clothing enforce the agreement?

8 Megarry entered into a contract to supply Butterman, on a monthly basis, with certain drugs which only pharmacists are allowed to sell. After the first month's delivery, Megarry asked Butterman for payment. Butterman refused. Could Megarry enforce the agreement?

9 Make a list of some agreements you have entered into. Identify which of these are contracts and explain why you think so.

10 Examine newspapers, mail-order catalogues, advertising leaflets, etc and identify

(a) invitations to treat and (b) offers. In the case of the offers, how may acceptance be (i) communicated (ii) revoked?

11 Write short notes explaining the following types of contract:

(a) bills of exchange

(b) cheques

(c) promissory notes

(d) contracts of marine insurance

(e) contracts assigning debts

(f) contracts transferring shares in a company.

Chapter 16 Discharge and Breach of Contract

Once the parties to a contract have performed their promises then the contract is said to be *discharged*. But this may not always happen. Disputes may arise over the interpretation of the contract or the manner in which a party performed an obligation under the contract. A party may refuse to carry out his or her side of the contract. Alternatively, a party may deliberately put him or herself in a position where they are unable to perform obligations. In some instances, it may not have been possible for one or both of the parties to perform their obligations because of events outside the control of the parties.

There are four ways in which a contract may come to an end and the parties be discharged from their obligations. These are:

- performance
- agreement
- frustration
- breach.

16.1 Performance

It is a basic rule that the parties to a contract must carry out precisely what they have agreed under their contract. If the contract is to be performed by the payment of a sum of money, then once the sum is paid, the contract is discharged. However, where one of the parties does something slightly different or even slightly less than what was agreed, then that party may not be able to claim the full benefit of the contract (because that party would benefit at the expense of the other). To avoid this hardship, certain exceptions to the basic rule were developed.

Exceptions

The first exception may be described as *the doctrine of substantial performance*. This means that if a party to a contract has substantially carried out the obligations under the contract, the party could recover for the work that was done. If the party has done the work badly, then the other could counter-claim for faulty workmanship or performance. Consider this example:

> *Murphy Desnoes* v. *Albertha Grant*
>
> Murphy Desnoes, a joiner, agreed to build for Albertha Grant a bookcase, a wardrobe and kitchen cupboards for $4,500. The contract price was inclusive of materials. On completion, Albertha paid Murphy $3,000, identified several defects, complained about poor workmanship and refused to pay the balance.

If Murphy sued, a court is likely to say that the contract was substantially performed and that Murphy should be paid the outstanding balance of $1,500, less the cost of the defects.

The second exception to the basic rule relates to *partial performance.* Consider again the facts of *Murphy Desnoes* v. *Albertha Grant.* If Murphy had only built the wardrobe then the contract would only have been partially performed. In that instance and provided that Albertha willingly accepted the benefit of the completed wardrobe, then a court could order that Murphy be paid for the benefit of the wardrobe. Of course, the parties do not have to go to court. They can settle the matter amicably.

The third exception to the basic rule is brought into play *when one party prevents the other from performing his or her side of the contract.* Consider these facts, which are based on an actual case.

> *Planché* v. *Colburn* (1831)
>
> Planché agreed to write a book on 'Costume and Ancient Armour for the Juvenile Library', a series published by Colburn. It was agreed that Planché would be paid £100. Planché collected material and wrote part of the book, but the defendants abandoned the project. Further negotiations fell through. The court awarded Planché 50 guineas as reasonable remuneration for the work done.

The principle which may be derived from this example is that a party who is prevented from performing his side of the bargain by the other party can recover for the part of the work that has been completed.

The fourth exception arises in respect of the so-called *divisible contracts.* These contracts involve payments in stages. A good example is a contract to build a house. Usually, but not always, a contract to build a house makes provision for the payment to be made in stages. For example, payments may be made on completion of:

(a) foundation, walls, and floor slab

(b) construction of all internal and external walls with a ring beam

(c) all roof work inclusive of installation of doors

(d) internal and external plastering

(e) installation of all windows, hanging of doors and fixing of ironmongery

(f) bedroom cupboards, kitchen cabinets, installation of sanitary ware, floor finishes, internal and external decorations, drainage works

(g) removal of all debris from the site and installation of public utility services.

A breach of contract at any of these stages may entitle the contractor to payment for the stage that was completed when the breach occurred. If the breach was caused by the house owner, it may be possible for the contractor to sue on the entire contract. On the other hand, if the breach was induced by the contractor and the house owner had to incur additional expense as a result, then the contractor could be liable to meet the new costs of the house owner. Liability depends on the particular circumstances at the time of the breach.

16.2 Agreement

A contract can be brought to an end by the agreement of the parties. There are three main ways in which this could be done.

1 In their original contract the parties may have agreed that the contract should end on a certain date or on the occurrence of a particular event. Alternatively, the parties may have agreed that one or both parties could terminate the contract by giving notice. Contracts of employment are usually drawn up in this way.

2 A contract can be discharged by the parties if they enter into a new contract. The new contract discharges the old contract, as long as it satisfies all the requirements of a valid contract. If the parties have not performed their obligations under the original contract, there is no difficulty in replacing the contract. However, if one party has performed his/her obligations, the situation is more complicated. For the new contract to be valid, the other party must do or promise to do something that is a benefit to the co-contractor and which he/she is not already bound to do. In other words, he/she must provide fresh consideration.

3 One party could, acting unilaterally and without consideration, release the other party from the obligations of the contract by deed. Remember that contracts by deed do not require consideration. The doctrine of *promissory estoppel* – whereby a promise to release a party from the strict contractual obligations may be binding so long as the other party acts upon it – may also play a role in this context.

16.3 Frustration

When parties to a contract agree on the terms, they assume that it will be perfectly possible to keep their promises. But circumstances could arise which make it impossible for the parties to carry out their agreement.

In the 17th century, parties to a contract were under an absolute duty to perform their contractual obligations. This was a harsh rule, because performance may be rendered impossible by events beyond the control of the parties. As is often said, 'Man proposes but God disposes'.

Starting with the case of *Taylor* v. *Caldwell* (see below), the courts recognized that contracts could be frustrated because of an event over which the parties had no control. In time, this became known as the *doctrine of frustration*. Frustration terminates the contract and frees the parties from their respective promises.

> *Taylor* v. *Caldwell* (1863)
>
> Taylor hired a music hall from Caldwell for a series of concerts. Tragedy struck after the agreement was signed. Before the date of the first performance, the hall was destroyed by fire. Taylor then sued Caldwell. The court said that since it was impossible to perform the contract, then the contract was discharged and the parties freed of their obligations.

There are some circumstances which render contracts frustrated. These are described below.

Physical impossibility

This might happen where something or somebody essential to the performance of the contract is unavailable. The case of *Taylor* v. *Caldwell*, cited above, is a good example.

If the presence of a person is absolutely essential and that person dies, then the contract is discharged. Illness, internment or imprisonment could also frustrate a contract. Consider these facts:

> *Shabba Man* v. *Musical Promotions*
>
> Shabba Man, a leading St Lucian cadence artist, was engaged by Musical Promotions of Dominica to give a performance. On the night of the performance he did not show up. Later, it turned out that Shabba Man had been ill just before the performance and had to be hospitalized so could not take his flight to Dominica. The reputation of Musical Promotions was ruined.

If Musical Promotions sued, they would not succeed because Shabba Man's illness made it impossible for him to fulfil his contractual obligations.

Subsequent illegality

The legislature may amend an existing law or enact a new law after a contract is made. The law could affect the contract and make its performance impossible. Alternatively, it could render the contract illegal. One circumstance which could automatically render a contract void is the outbreak of war.

Basis of the contract removed by non-occurrence of an essential event

The parties to a contract may have made the occurrence of a future event the basis of their agreement. If the event does not take place, then the main purpose of the contract cannot be achieved. For the contract to be frustrated, the event that does not take place must be so substantial that the main purpose of the contract has no possibility of being achieved. Consider these two examples, which are based on actual cases.

> *Krell* v. *Henry* (1903)
>
> Henry agreed to hire a flat from Krell to view the coronation procession of King Edward VII. However, the King fell ill and the coronation was cancelled. It was held by the court that the contract was frustrated. It was true that it was possible for Henry to come and sit in the room, but the main purpose of the contract to view the coronation procession was destroyed.

Contrast this case with *Herne Bay Steam Boat Co.* v. *Hutton*:

> *Herne Bay Steam Boat Co.* v. *Hutton* (1903)
>
> Hutton agreed to hire a boat from Herne Bay Steam Boat Co. to view the naval review and cruise around the fleet planned in honour of the coronation of King Edward VII. The review was cancelled because the coronation was cancelled. The court found that the contract was not frustrated because the fleet was still anchored in the bay and in any event the cruise could have taken place.

Interference by the government

It is possible for a government by its acts and policies to interfere with the performance of a contract. If the interference is temporary and has altered the contract so that what the parties have to perform is radically different from what was originally agreed, then it is likely that the contract would be held to be frustrated. Such events are rare.

Effects of frustration

Frustration has the effect of bringing a contract to an immediate end. In some islands, it is still a rule that all moneys paid to either party before the performance of the contract are not recoverable and sums not yet paid remain payable. This rule often produced hardship, particularly on the party who had done a considerable amount of work on the contract. Legislation has been introduced to ensure greater fairness between the parties. However, the legislation does not affect (a) contracts for the carriage of goods by sea, (b) contracts of insurance, or (c) contracts for the sale of goods in specified circumstances. Where legislation has been enacted, all sums paid are recoverable and sums not yet paid cease to be payable. However, the party to whom the money was paid or payable may now retain or recover an amount out of the sums paid or payable before frustration to cover expenses. The parties remain free to exclude the terms of the legislation by express agreement.

16.4 Breach

The performance of a contract is affected if a party refuses to perform his or her side of the agreement. Such refusal is usually described as a *breach of contract*. If a party states in advance that he/she does not intend to perform the obligations under the contract, or puts him or herself in a position where he/she cannot perform the obligations, then that party commits *anticipatory breach*. On the other hand, if the party accepts the contract but in its course fails to perform the obligations then the party is said to have committed an *actual breach*. Consider these two situations.

> **Situation 1:** Germain agrees to paint a portrait of Johanna for $5,000 in six months. He receives a down-payment of $2,000. Before Germain starts, he tells Johanna that he has changed his mind and will no longer do the portrait.
>
> **Situation 2:** Germain completes the painting but instead sells it to Redden, an admirer of Johanna, for $10,000.

In situation 1, Germain committed *anticipatory breach*, but in situation 2 Germain committed an *actual breach* of the contract. The breach occurred after he had embarked on the contract.

The nature of the breaches vary. A party may fail to perform one or more obligations under the agreement. Some terms of the contract are major, others are relatively minor. Where a major term is breached then the act is described as *a breach of condition*. If the term that is breached is minor, then it is said to be *a breach of warranty*.

Remedies

Where a party has breached a contract, the usual remedy is the award of damages – that is, monetary payment for the loss that has been suffered. Sometimes the parties agree at the outset and stipulate in the contract a sum that will be received if there is a breach. If the parties so state, then the sum payable is known as *liquidated damages*. If they have not agreed on a sum to be paid, the quantum of damages is described as *unliquidated damages*. The objective of unliquidated damages is to put the party who has suffered the breach in the position he/she would have been if the contract was performed according to the agreed terms.

It is important to bear in mind that the loss which is claimed by the injured party must have *arisen naturally from the breach*. Where not arising naturally, the loss must be said *to have been in the minds of the parties when they made the contract*. If these rules did not exist, then an injured party could claim for every conceivable loss which may have been suffered. Equally, it would be unfair if the injured party deliberately allowed the loss to become more severe so that heavy damages could be claimed. For this reason, once there is a breach the injured party has a duty to minimize the resulting loss. This is known as the *duty* to mitigate damage.

Sometimes a breach is so serious that it destroys any possible benefit to be gained from the contract. Obviously such a repudiation of a contract would be serious breach. So too would be a breach of a condition. In these circumstances, the injured party may wish to avoid the contract completely and bring it to an end. If the breach is not so serious, the injured party may elect to continue, suffer the defective performance by the party in breach, but seek to recover damages. If the party decides to terminate the contract, he/she must do so promptly, otherwise it could be concluded that he/she affirmed the contract despite the breach.

Other remedies are available, provided that specific circumstances exist to justify them. For example:

Quantum meruit claim If one party prevents another from performing the other's side of the bargain, then the affected party may claim a *quantum meruit*. This is usually awarded where a party has done some work but has not earned the agreed fee. In other words, he/she is paid the amount he/she has earned for the work that has been done.

Injunction This is an order that is obtained on application to the court. It prevents the party at fault from proceeding on any act that would be in breach of the contract.

Specific performance An order for specific performance is also obtained from the court. It compels a defaulting party to carry out obligations under the contract.

Orders for injunction and specific performance are only granted at the court's discretion and are not available in respect of certain types of contract.

16.5 Limitation of actions

Finally, it must always be remembered that a party cannot sleep on his or her rights. An injured party must seek redress within certain time limits.

An action on a contract that was not done by deed must be brought within six years of the establishment of the cause of action. If the contract is in the form of a deed, then the action must be brought within 12 years from the date when the cause of action arose. The periods may be extended at the court's discretion if there is evidence of fraud, concealment or mistake, which could not be discovered with reasonable diligence.

Key Points

- A contract may be discharged:

  (a) on performance by the parties of their obligations

  (b) by agreement

  (c) in consequence of frustration

  (d) on the commission of serious breach by a party to the contract which is treated as the end of the contract by the other party.

- Where a party has substantially performed his or her obligations, the party is only entitled to recover for the work done.

  If performance is only partial then the party is entitled to partial recovery of the benefit of the contract.

- If one party prevents the other from performing his/her side of the bargain then the party so affected can recover for the part of the work that has been completed.

- Where it is agreed that payment is to be made in stages, then the party entitled to payment could recover for the stage that is completed.

- A contract could be discharged by agreement in the following ways:

  (a) where the parties have agreed that the contract would be discharged on the occurrence of a certain event or on a certain date

(b) where the parties have agreed to replace an existing contract with a new contract

(c) if one party agrees to release the other party of his/her obligations by deed

(d) through promissory estoppel.

- Frustration may discharge a contract where:

  (a) it is physically impossible for the contract to be performed, eg a party dies

  (b) an existing contract has been rendered illegal by legislation or by war

  (c) there is serious interference by the state

  (d) the event which causes the frustration is outside the control of the parties.

- Breach may be actual or anticipatory. An actual breach usually occurs while the contract is being performed. Anticipatory breach usually occurs if a party declines to perform obligations at the very outset of the contract. A breach may be major or relatively minor.

- An aggrieved party may recover damages for breach. The injured party could only claim for losses that arise naturally from the breach, and must have been in the minds of the parties when they made the contract. The injured party has a duty to mitigate his/her loss.

- Where a breach is fundamental, an aggrieved party may have the option of bringing the contract to an end, or accepting defective performance and seeking damages.

- Provided that the circumstances justify them other remedies are available. These include:

  (a) *quantum meruit* claim

  (b) injunction

  (c) specific performance.

Questions

1 Explain, with the aid of examples, the ways in which a contract could be discharged.

2 Dimes Construction Company Ltd agreed to build a home for Madge Morgan, within six months. The building was completed eight months after the scheduled date of completion. Madge decided to sue. Consider the following defences offered by Dimes Construction Company:

(a) the foundation could not be completed on time because of persistent rain for three months

(b) a new Act passed by Parliament imposed new building standards and restrictions

(c) there was a 'flu epidemic and most of the employees had to be sent home.

3 Will a contract be discharged by frustration in the following circumstances?

(a) The Pathfinder Drama Society booked the City Hall for three concerts. They sold all the tickets for the show. The day before the first show the City Hall was destroyed by fire.

(b) Petrus, a resident of St Lucia, booked a room in the Blue Haven Guest House in Bridgetown in order to attend a reggae festival. He paid a deposit of a sum of money for the room. The festival is cancelled. Petrus now wishes to recover his deposit. Advise him.

Chapter 17 Some Types of Special Contract

When someone buys a car, agrees to pay for an item on a monthly or weekly basis until payment is complete, buys a lot of land, purchases an insurance policy or enters into an agreement to work for another person, that person is, in each instance, a party to a contract of a special type. The contract to purchase the car may be described as a contract for the sale or supply of goods; the contract to pay for an item by instalments is likely to be a hire purchase contract; the contract for the purchase of the lot of land is a contract for the sale of land; the purchase of insurance is simply known as a contract of insurance; and in respect of the agreement to work for another, the contract is usually described as a contract of employment.

All of these contracts are governed by the basic principles discussed in Chapters 15 and 16. However, each has evolved special rules and practices, some of which have been codified in legislation. Under each type of contract there may be subtypes. For example, if no money changes hands but items are exchanged, such a contract is a contract of barter. It is, therefore, extremely important to identify the different types of contract in the business world, and the basic legal principles that apply to each. This chapter provides an overview of the different kinds of business contract and the sources of the rules that regulate them.

17.1 Contracts for sale or the supply of goods

The commonest type of contract is the contract for the sale of goods. The law relating to the sale of goods in the Commonwealth Caribbean is to be found in statutes and is derived in the main from a British statute, *The Sale of Goods Act, 1893*.

Identifying a sale of goods contract

What is a contract of sale of goods? Most of the Acts define a contract of sale of goods as one

> 'whereby the seller transfers or agrees to transfer the property in goods to the buyer for a money consideration, called the price'.

This definition contains several elements which require clarification. *Property* means 'the general property in goods' and not merely a special property. It does not include property that is held to secure a loan, or property that is held for a limited period.

General property really means the full rights of ownership in the property. *Goods* include a variety of tangible items of personal property, for example cars, food, clothes, furniture, electronic equipment. Intangible property, that is property you cannot handle or touch, such as stocks, shares in companies, and copyright are excluded. The goods referred to do not include money or land. Thus crops grown for industrial purposes, for example sea-island cotton, could only be described as goods when they have been removed from the land.

A contract for the sale of goods could be about future goods. Such goods mean 'goods to be manufactured or acquired by the seller after the making of the contract of sale'.

It is important that you identify a contract for the sale of goods from other types of contract. One way of doing that is to identify some contracts that are not covered by the Sale of Goods Acts in the various islands. For example:

Contract of barter: The Act does not apply; there is no money consideration (the *price*).

Contract of hire: The Act does not apply; no ownership passes to the hirer.

Contract for work or skill: The Act does not apply; the buyer is purchasing the skill of the craftsman or professional. So the employment of an artist to paint a portrait does not fall within the Act. However, if the painting is purchased in a shop, that would be a contract for sale of goods.

What if the contract is one that involves a part exchange or trade-in? Consider this example. Brichem Appliances Ltd offers its customers a new 'Waverley' washing machine for the value of their old washing machine plus the difference in cash between the two. Here, a specific sum is derived from the trade-in of the old item. Since a price consideration is involved, such a contract will fall within the terms of a contract for the sale of goods.

Rights and obligations of the parties

Each party to a contract has certain rights and obligations. Subject to the law, the parties are free to agree on their terms. However, the legislation governing sale of goods automatically includes in every contract certain conditions and warranties.

The seller's obligations

These may be itemized as follows:

1 The seller has a right to sell the goods.

2 If the contract describes the goods, then there is an implied condition that the goods shall correspond with the description provided.

3 If the buyer in the course of the transaction makes known to the seller that the buyer is relying on the seller's skills or judgement, and the subject matter of the contract is of a description which is in the course of the seller's business to supply, there is an implied condition that the goods shall be reasonably fit for such purpose. This obligation does not apply if the article is sold under a patent.

4 The seller must ensure that the goods supplied to the buyer are of merchantable quality. Whether the goods satisfy this condition is a question of fact and common sense.

5 If the contract is for sale of goods by sample then it is subject to the following implied conditions:

(a) The bulk of the goods supplied must correspond with the sample in quality.

(b) The buyer must have sufficient opportunity to compare the bulk with the sample supplied.

(c) The goods supplied must be free from any defect which renders them unmerchantable. Such defects should not be apparent on reasonable examination of the sample.

6 It is the duty of the seller to deliver the goods to the buyer.

The obligations of the buyer

The major obligation of the buyer is to accept and pay for the goods delivered in accordance with the contract of sale. If the buyer has not seen the goods before delivery then the buyer is entitled to examine the goods before accepting them. Delivery may take one of several forms:

- actual handing over of the goods to the buyer
- handing over the means of exercising control and possession of the goods, eg handing over documents indicating title
- confirmation by a third party – that is, a person other than the seller and the buyer – that the goods are being held on behalf of the buyer.

What if a buyer claims that he/she has not accepted the goods, so a valid contract does not exist? Statutes say that acceptance has taken place if the buyer:

- intimates to the seller that he/she has accepted the goods, or
- does anything to the goods that is inconsistent with any suggestion that the seller retains ownership in the goods (eg if the buyer immediately resells the goods)
- retains the goods after the lapse of a reasonable time and does not tell the seller that he/she has rejected the goods.

In respect of the last point, consider the following scenario.

> Banfield decided to buy Audrey's car for $10,000. The parties agreed that Banfield would pay Audrey $8,000 on delivery and the other $2,000 in one month. Banfield took possession of the car, kept it for three weeks and drove some 300 kilometres. Banfield decided that the car was too slow for his purposes and returned it to Audrey. He claimed a refund of $7,000 and offered Audrey $1,000 for the use of the car. Audrey refused.

If Audrey sued, it is likely that she would succeed. A court will conclude that enough time had run against Banfield, so he could not reject the car. Clearly, Banfield sought to break his agreement with Audrey. In more technical terms, Banfield committed a *breach*. What can a seller or buyer do if either commits a breach? Either party can seek a remedy for the wrong that has been suffered. The remedies of the seller and buyer are contained in the legislation governing sale of goods.

The seller's remedies

The seller has the following rights of action:

1 The seller could sue for the price in these circumstances:

(a) Where the property of the goods has passed to the buyer, and the buyer neglects or refuses to pay for the goods on the agreed terms.

(b) If the parties agreed that payment would be made on a certain day, and the buyer neglects or refuses to pay – in this case the seller can sue for the price even though the property in the goods has not passed to the buyer.

2 The seller can also seek *damages* – that is, a sum of money as

compensation for the seller's loss or injury. Damages may be claimed if the buyer wrongfully neglects or refuses to accept and pay for the goods.

These remedies are of little help if the buyer has no money. In that event it may be better to seek remedies against the goods. There are three possibilities here:

1 The seller could hold on to the goods until the buyer pays. This is called *a right of lien*.

2 If the goods have left the seller and are on their way to the buyer, the seller may stop the goods on discovering that the buyer is *insolvent* – that is, the buyer is unable to pay his/her debts as they fall due. In technical language this action is referred to as *a right of stoppage in transit.*

3 If the seller has exercised his/her right of lien (as in (1)) or has stopped the goods in transit (as in (2)), then the seller may resell the goods where

- the goods are perishable
- the seller gives notice to the buyer that he/she intends to resell the goods and the buyer still does not pay for the goods within a reasonable time
- where the parties expressly agreed in the contract that the seller had a right to resell the goods if the buyer defaulted.

If on reselling the seller earns more profit than would have been earned in the original contract price, then he/she is entitled to keep such profit. What happens if it is the seller who wrongfully sells the goods to another buyer? In that event, buyer B acquires a good title in the goods, but the seller is accountable to buyer A for any profit that might have been made on the contract price originally agreed with buyer A.

17.2 Hire purchase contracts

Hire purchase contracts are very popular in the Commonwealth Caribbean. Most major business establishments offer options to purchase items on hire purchase, and there is legislation to regulate hire purchase agreements.

Definition of a hire purchase contract

A hire purchase agreement is an agreement expressed in writing under which a person hires goods and may buy the goods upon payment in full of the credit price. The legislation in most of our islands states that a hire purchase agreement is:

> 'an agreement for the bailment of goods under which the bailee may buy the goods or under which the property in goods will or may pass to the bailee'.

This is a rather cumbersome definition. A *bailor* is a person who entrusts an item or several items to another person. The recipient of the item or items is described as the *bailee*. The bailor retains the ownership in the property held by the bailee. *Bailment*, therefore, is an agreement to deliver goods by one person (the bailor) to another (the bailee) for a specific purpose, on the condition that when the purpose has been accomplished the goods shall be returned to the bailor. Thus hire purchase agreements are contracts of bailment in the sense that a store (the bailor) hires an item or items to a customer (the bailee) on condition that after the customer has paid a certain number of instalments for hiring the goods, the customer has the choice of buying the item. The distinguishing feature of these contracts is that the customer (or hirer) takes possession of the goods for immediate use and enjoyment, but does not become the owner of the goods unless and until a specified number of instalments have been paid. A customer who is a party to a hire purchase agreement cannot sell the goods while the agreement is alive because he/she is not the owner of the goods.

It is important to distinguish contracts of hire purchase from other kinds of consumer credit agreements (Table 17.1).

Table 17.1
A comparison of hire purchase contracts and other types of consumer credit agreement

Sale of Goods Buyer is committed to purchase the item from the very outset of the agreement; has no option of returning item. **Conditional Sale** Ownership is transferred some time in the future. **Credit Sale** The customer purchases the goods and agrees to pay for them later. Ownership is transferred to the buyer at the very start of the agreement.	**Hire Purchase** The customer obtains use and enjoyment of the item in return for paying regular instalments. Ownership is delayed until a specified payment is made. The customer is a hirer of the goods until a specified payment is made. The hirer is not bound to buy. He/she could pay the instalments and then refuse to purchase the goods. The instalments may be treated as the rental fee for the use of the goods.

Elements of hire purchase agreements

In most islands, a hire purchase price must not exceed a certain sum. For example, the maximum sum in Barbados is BDS $12,000, in Antigua EC $20,000 and in Trinidad & Tobago TT $15,000. A hire purchase price usually means the total sum payable by a hirer. This includes the cost of the item, interest, and sometimes handling and transportation.

Entering into an agreement

Before the agreement is entered into, the owner must state in writing, to the customer, the cash price of the item. This is to give the customer an idea of the difference between the cash price and the hire purchase price. The latter is usually made up of the cash price plus the interest on hiring the item. It is usually sufficient if the customer inspects the item and sees a ticket or label disclosing the price of the item. A failure to provide a price ticket could render the agreement unenforceable.

If the agreement is to be valid then the hirer as well as the owner or other persons acting on the owner's behalf must sign the agreement. The agreement, sometimes referred to as a *memorandum*, must contain the following:

- the hire purchase price – that is, the cash price plus interest
- the cash price
- the amount of each instalment
- the date on which each instalment is payable and the method of payment
- the identity of the goods
- a prominent notice of the terms prescribed in the schedule to the agreement.

In some countries, statutes may prescribe a fixed down-payment. It is, however, mandatory for the owner to send or deliver a copy of the agreement or memorandum to the customer at his/her address as recorded in the agreement, within seven days of the agreement. That requirement, as well as the obligation to state the cash price of the goods and to include specified information in the agreement or memorandum, may be waived by a court if it thinks it is just and equitable to do so.

Major terms of the agreement

In the Commonwealth Caribbean the terms to be included in hire purchase agreements vary from one country to another. The statutes

Figure 17.1
A hire purchase agreement

COMMON TERMS OF A HIRE PURCHASE AGREEMENT

1. The amount of the down-payment if any, and the monthly payments.
2. The total amount which must be paid to make the item the sole and absolute property of the hirer.
3. The address at which the hirer will keep the item under his possession and control and for inspection by the owner.
4. The obligation of the hirer to pay the rents, rates and taxes of the premises where the item is kept and the duty of the hirer to insure the item against loss or damage by fire and to protect it from seizure.
5. The right of the hirer to terminate the agreement and to return the item subject to any liability for arrears of hire, rent and for any damage to the item.
6. The effect on the agreement if the hirer becomes bankrupt and the conditions under which the owner may, after issuing the prescribed notice, terminate the agreement and repossess the item.
7. The effect of the hirer's unemployment or illness on the agreement.
8. Approval of the agreement by the owners to be confirmed by the delivery of the item.
9. Expenses of the owner which must be met by the hirer in the event that the hirer changes his address without notification and the owner incurs expenses in locating the hirer.
10. The interest to be paid by the hirer on due and outstanding payments.
11. The rights and obligations of the owner and hirer on the termination of the agreement by the hirer.
12. Restriction on the right of the owner to recover the item where a specified amount of the hire purchase price has been paid (usually 66.6 per cent).
13. Restriction of owner's right to recover the item where less than a specified amount of the hire purchase price has been paid (usually less than 66.6 per cent).
14. The description of the item which is the subject of the hire purchase agreement, its cash price and the hire purchase price.

specify a number of provisions which must not be included in any agreement. For example, in Antigua and Barbuda, Barbados, Grenada & Carriacou, and Trinidad & Tobago, agreements should not include any provision permitting the owner or his/her agent to enter the premises of the hirer by force and take possession of the goods. If the owner does so, then he/she is liable for this act. The owner or agent may enter the premises only if permitted to do so by the hirer or by a court. In Jamaica, Belize and The Bahamas, the rule is wider. No term in the agreement may authorize entry whether by force or otherwise.

Some other provisions which may not be included are as follows:

1 (a) Any provision restricting or preventing the hirer from terminating the agreement as permitted by the legislation.

(b) The imposition of any additional liability on the hirer because the hirer brings the agreement to an end.

2 In some islands, the owner is not permitted to include any provision restricting or excluding the right of the hirer to remedy the breach of the agreement by the owner.

3 Any provision that if the hirer brings the agreement to an end, he/she would face liability that is greater than that which is established by the legislation in question.

Except in Bermuda, Acts in the Commonwealth Caribbean prevent owners from including a provision that a person who handles a hire purchase agreement on behalf of the owner is to be treated as an agent of the hirer or buyer. Likewise, the owner is not liable for the wrongful acts or defaults of an employee engaged in the negotiation and completion of an agreement.

All the Acts in the Commonwealth Caribbean establish certain rights and duties on the parties to a hire purchase agreement.

Duties of the owner

The major duty of the owner is to supply certain information and documents to the hirer. An implied duty is the obligation of the owner to ensure that the goods are delivered to the hirer.

Duties of the hirer

The hirer, on the receipt of a written request from the owner, must indicate the whereabouts of the goods. Failure to do so without reasonable cause within 14 days could lead to a fine. It must be remembered that until a specified payment is made, the goods do not belong to the hirer. The hirer also has a duty to take delivery of the goods as promised when he/she signed the agreement. Of course, the instalments must be paid as agreed. The hirer also has a duty to take reasonable care of the goods and to insure them. Most hire purchase agreements make provision for automatic payment of insurance in the monthly instalments.

Rights of the owner

The major right of the owner is to recover possession of the goods from the hirer if the hirer breaches the terms of the agreement. The methods by which the owner can recover possession depend on the total amount the hirer has paid. In the islands listed in Table 17.2, if the hirer has paid more than the percentage of the total payment indicated, then the owner can recover the goods only through the courts.

Table 17.2 Recovery of hire purchase goods through the courts

Island	% paid
Antigua and Barbuda	70
Bahamas	50
Barbados	66.6
Belize	33.3
Bermuda	50
Grenada	70
Trinidad & Tobago	70

In certain circumstances it is possible for the owner to recover possession without court action. For example, if the hirer sells or gives away the goods or attempts to sell or give away the goods contrary to the terms of the agreement or to the law, the owner can recover the goods without court action. However, if the hirer has paid a certain percentage of the hire purchase price then he/she enjoys protection in the goods. Similarly if the hirer opts to terminate the agreement in accordance with his/her legal right to do so, recovery can be effected without court action.

Usually, if the hirer fails to pay an instalment that is due, the owner cannot repossess the goods unless the owner gives the hirer at least 21 days' notice of intention to do so.

Rights of the hirer

The hirer has a statutory right to bring a hire purchase agreement to an end before the final payment becomes due. If the hirer decides to terminate, then he/she must do certain things. First, notice of termination must be given to a person entitled or authorized to receive the instalment payments. Secondly, at the time of giving notice, or before giving such notice, the hirer must return the goods to the owner. Thirdly, the hirer must pay all outstanding payments, or any lesser amounts specified in the agreement. If the hirer has failed to take reasonable care of the goods while they were in his/her possession, then the hirer is liable to pay damages. The voluntary termination of the agreement by the hirer does not mean that the goods can be returned in any condition. The same responsibility applies if the hirer has been requested to return the goods. If the hirer unreasonably refuses to deliver the goods the hirer is under an obligation to take care of the goods until they are returned.

17.3 Contract of employment

Most of us begin our working lives by serving as an employee to another person, firm or public authority. A few people may actually start by being employers – that is, by employing others to work for them.

Creation of a contract

A contract of employment is created when one person (the *employee*) provides labour and skill to another (the *employer*) in return for wages. The nature and duration of the employment vary.

Of course, if such contracts are to be valid, the ordinary principles of law must apply. The contract must not be illegal. There must be *agreement*, *intention* to create legal relations, *consideration* and *capacity*. Equally, the contract must not arise from mistake, misrepresentation, undue influence or duress.

Types of employment contract

A contract of employment need not be written; it can be made verbally. Increasingly, however, legislation requires contracts to be in writing. Just as in a contract for the sale of goods statute implies a number of conditions, statute also compels employers to include certain terms in contracts of employment.

Types of employee

The law makes a distinction between *employees* and *independent contractors*. The independent contractor contracts to do a specific job, and on completion leaves and goes elsewhere to sell his/her skills, labour and services. The distinction between the two is often expressed as: *an employee has a contract of service, while the independent contractor has a contract for service.*

To determine the type of employee, the courts have created three major tests: the control test, the organization or integration test, and the multiple test.

The control test

The control test seeks to determine the degree and extent of the control of the employee by the employer. An employee is told what to perform, how to perform the function and even when to perform it. On the other hand, how the independent contractor performs a contract is his/her concern. He/she is paid for the completed job.

As companies became larger and more complex and employed diverse forms of highly skilled labour, the control test was found to be inadequate. A second test evolved.

The organization or integration test

This test seeks to determine if the person performing the labour is an integral part of the organization. Does the employee belong to the organization, and is the employee integrated with others within the organization? If the employee performs work for the organization but is not part of the organization then it is likely that he/she is an independent contractor.

The multiple test

More recently, the courts have considered *all* the relevant factors. These include:

- power to appoint, discipline, suspend and remove
- method of payment
- whether national insurance and income tax are deducted by the employer
- type of work performed
- the hours of work and flexibility of hours
- whether the person provides his/her own tools or works on the premises.

Some might rightly ask why it is important to make the distinction between an employee and a contractor. There are four reasons. Firstly, an employer is only liable for the damage caused to another person by the negligent act of an employee under a contract of service, provided that the act was caused by the employee in the course of employment – that is, while the employee was doing the job. This is called *vicarious liability*. If the employee is an independent contractor or an employee of an independent contractor, then it is the independent contractor who is liable, not the employer of the independent contractor. Secondly, the benefits, rights and remedies provided by employment legislation are mainly available to employees, not to independent contractors. Thirdly, certain responsibilities of the employer depend on the type of employee. An employer must deduct income tax and national insurance payments for employees. An independent contractor pays the tax liabilities directly. Finally, if the employer's business becomes insolvent, and the employer is unable to pay his debts, then employees usually enjoy a right of preference to be paid their unpaid wages and redundancy payments out of the remaining assets ahead of other creditors. Independent contractors, on the other hand, must rank as ordinary creditors.

Form of contracts

The parties to a contract are, subject to the law, free to agree to the terms of the contract of employment. However, some islands have enacted legislation which specifies the particulars to be included in a written contract. For example, Section 5 of the Contracts of Service Act of St Lucia states that the following particulars shall be included in written contracts and statements:

(a) the names and parties entering into the contract

(b) the date on which the employment began or is to begin and, in the case of a contract for a fixed term, the date on which the contract expires

(c) the scale or rate of remuneration and the method of calculating such remuneration

(d) the intervals at which remuneration is to be paid

(e) any terms and conditions relating to hours of work (including any terms and conditions relating to normal working hours)

(f) any term and condition relating to:

- holidays and annual vacation
- payment during illness, or
- pensions or National Insurance Scheme

(g) the length of notice which the employee is obliged to give and entitled to receive to terminate his contract of service.

If no particulars are to be stated under paragraph (f) or paragraphs (a) to (e) and (g), then the employer must state that fact. If any term of the contract contravenes any provision of the applicable legislation, then the statutory provision is to be substituted in the place of the term.

Even if no legislation exists to govern contracts of service, most written contracts include some of the terms itemized in the St Lucian legislation – see Figure 17.2.

Figure 17.2
An example of a written contract

Layne, Samuels and Anthony Ltd, Cave Hill, P.O. Box 8197, Bridgetown, Barbados

Our Ref: Telex: (809) 433-2197
Your Ref: Tel: (809) 433-2199

Dear Mr. Clement,

I write to offer you the post of Secretary to the Manager on the following terms and conditions:

(1) This offer must either be accepted or declined in writing within one week of the date of this letter. On acceptance, this letter constitutes the contract of employment.

(2) The effective date for the commencement of your appointment is July 1st, 1994. Initially, you will be appointed on a probationary period of three months, and on satisfactory completion of your probationary period you will be employed for an indefinite period.

(3) During your probationary period either party may terminate the employment with or without cause, without notice and without redress.

(4) During the period of your probation, your salary will be at the rate of $3,000.00 per month. Thereafter your salary shall increase to $3,500.00 per month.

(5) Subject to your entitlement of one hour per day Monday to Friday for meals, your hours of work are as follows:
(a) Monday to Friday excluding public holidays 8.00 a.m. to 4.30 p.m.;
(b) Saturday, excluding public holidays 8.00 a.m. to 12 Noon.

(6) Your vacation leave entitlements are as follows:
(i) 15 work days if employed for less than one year;
(ii) 20 work days if employed for more than one year but less than ten years; and
(iii) 25 work days if employed for more than ten years.
Vacation must be scheduled at a time convenient to the company and yourself and must be taken every year.

(7) You are entitled to a maximum of twenty days sick leave per year. Subject to the number of days of sick leave available to you in any one year, the company will pay you in full for the first three consecutive sick days. Thereafter, the company will pay the difference between the benefits paid by National Insurance and your base rate of pay.

(8) (a) The Company reserves the right to terminate your employment for gross misconduct without notice or pay in lieu of notice. Where termination does not arise from misconduct, indiscipline or other specified cause then the Company shall give six weeks notice or pay in lieu of notice. You may, however, waive the right to notice or pay in lieu of notice.
(b) Where you voluntarily terminate your employment with the Company, four weeks notice shall be given.

(9) Other terms and conditions not specified in this letter of offer are contained in the Company Personnel Guide, a copy of which is enclosed. The Personnel Guide does not form part of the contract of employment.

(10) I should be grateful if you would sign and return the attached copy of this letter as indication that you accept the post under the conditions offered.

Yours sincerely,

Mr. Havelock K.N. Liverpool
Personnel Manager

- -

I accept the post under the conditions offered.

Signature ______________________ Date __________

Applicable legislation

The contract of employment will be affected by numerous statutory enactments. These enactments import a number of provisions into the contract. Some items covered by legislation include:

- holidays with pay
- national insurance contributions and benefits
- severance payments
- redundancy payments
- trade union membership
- health and safety
- maternity leave
- unfair dismissal.

Provisions of the applicable statutes are automatically implied in the contracts of employment. However, other terms, particularly in respect of the rights and duties of the parties, may also be implied in the contract by the courts. A breach of an implied term by an employee could lead to termination of the employee's contract. Likewise a breach of the contract of employment by an employer may entitle the employee to claim damages, for example the amount of wages that the employee would have received had not the breach occurred. In some cases the employer could breach the contract by wrongful dismissal. Re-instatement may be possible in an appropriate case.

Duties of the parties

Every employer has certain duties:

(a) To pay the agreed wages or a payment that is reasonable in the context of the custom of the trade, industry or profession.

(b) To provide work – if an employee is paid a salary but is not given a reasonable opportunity to use the skills for which he/she was employed and to enhance his/her reputation, then that individual's future career could be jeopardized.

(c) To provide a reasonably safe system of work and to comply with statutory provisions aimed at enhancing safety at the workplace.

(d) To behave reasonably and responsibly to employees – the employer behaves unreasonably if unilateral changes are made to the agreed conditions of service, or if he/she exerts excessive pressure on employees to conform to unreasonable work practices.

(e) To reimburse a worker who incurs personal liabilities that are reasonable, necessary and unavoidable in the course of the performance of duties.

The employee also has obligations:

(a) To avoid acts of misconduct at the workplace and elsewhere. Depending on the nature of employment, such acts could constitute misconduct, absenteeism, lateness, dishonesty, insolvency, being under the influence of alcohol and drugs, disobedience to lawful instructions, and immorality.

(b) To carry out the agreed work personally. In other words, the employee cannot independently delegate the work to someone else.

(c) To serve the employer loyally and in good faith. The employee must not

- take bribes or make secret profits
- work for him/herself or for another party in spare time if the work competes with that of the employer and the employer suffers damage as a consequence
- declare to third parties secrets or confidential information that has to do with the employment and that was acquired in the course of employment.

(d) To exercise reasonable care and skill in the performance of his duties. This means that the employee must take reasonable care of the property of the employer, and be careful that his/her conduct does not harm co-workers and others so as to make the employer liable in damages. The employee must also work competently and efficiently.

(e) To obey all reasonable and legitimate instructions provided that they are within the agreed terms of employment. Disobedience may be justified if the order is unlawful, or is so unreasonable that no reasonable employee could be expected to obey the instruction.

Breaches of these duties could, in appropriate cases, lead to the termination of employment.

Termination of employment

A contract of employment can be terminated in several ways, for example:

- by notice
- by agreement
- by frustration

- by unfair dismissal
- by wrongful dismissal
- by dismissal for misconduct
- by redundancy
- in consequence of liquidation, bankruptcy or dissolution of a partnership.

Termination by notice

Usually a contract of employment states the period of notice which an employee must give to terminate the contract. The contract will also state the period of notice the employer is obliged to give. An employee does not have to give reasons when giving the agreed notice. If the contract is for a fixed period of time, for example one year, the employee cannot complain if no notice is given or if the contract is not renewed.

Termination by agreement

As in any other contract, both parties to the employment contract can end the contract by agreement. For example, the parties could enter into a new contract on new terms and conditions. In that event, the former contract is discharged. An employee could also be persuaded to bring the existing contract to an end on the payment of certain benefits. Note too that termination by notice is a form of termination by agreement.

Termination by frustration

Through no fault of the parties, a contract may be brought to an end by frustration. For example, if an employee is incapacitated by illness or injury then the contract cannot be performed. Likewise the death of either party could discharge the contract from the date of the death of the party so affected. So, too, if an employee is sentenced to a term of imprisonment, the contract is frustrated.

Unfair dismissal

It is a basic principle of employment law that where the employment is not governed by a written contract or by statute, an employer who gives reasonable notice can dismiss an employee at any time, without stating the reasons for the action. In the eyes of the law, dismissal is only wrongful if there is a failure to give adequate or reasonable notice. The law also imposes a burden upon the employee to prove that the dismissal was wrongful.

These principles are often abused, particularly by employers. In some countries, for example the United Kingdom, legislation was introduced to minimize and control unfair dismissals. Under these provisions, unfair dismissal could occur where the employment contract is terminated with or without notice, or the employer fails to renew a contract for a fixed term, or the employee leaves the employment voluntarily because the employer behaves in a manner that makes it impossible for the employee to perform the duties of employment.

In the Commonwealth Caribbean, the following countries have enacted unfair dismissal legislation: Antigua, British Virgin Islands, Cayman Islands, Dominica, Jamaica, Trinidad & Tobago, Turks and Caicos Islands, and St Vincent and the Grenadines. In these countries an employer must show that the dismissal was reasonable in all the circumstances.

Wrongful dismissal

Sometimes, challenges for wrongful dismissal may co-exist with unfair dismissal. For example, if an employee cannot claim under the unfair dismissal legislation, then an action for wrongful dismissal may be possible.

In principle, if an employer does not give adequate notice of termination, he/she could be in breach of the contract. Adequate notice depends on the terms, conditions and customs associated with the particular employment. An employer can dismiss a worker without adequate notice if the employee commits a serious breach of the contract. In that instance the dismissal may not be wrongful.

The most important remedy of the employee who has been wrongfully dismissed is damages. The amount of damages is normally the wages which the employee would have received had proper notice been given. In some cases, other regular earnings such as bonuses, tips, service charges or commissions may also be included.

Dismissal in consequence of misconduct

An employer is justified in dismissing an employee and thereby terminating the contract of employment for serious misconduct. If misconduct is of a grave kind, summary dismissal may be justified. The following are examples of misconduct justifying dismissal:

- lack of adequate qualifications, and capability
- incompetence
- serious disobedience to a lawful order
- repeated negligence in the course of the performance of duties

- breach of good faith, for example making a secret profit
- unacceptable immorality or moral turpitude
- persistent drunkenness
- serious physical attack on a co-worker or superior.

- ### *Termination by redundancy*

A contract of employment may be terminated where an employer ceases to carry on business. In that event, the employee is made redundant and becomes entitled to compensation based on the number of days or years of employment. In some countries, the compensation payment is styled 'severance payment'.

Usually severance payments are authorized by legislation – a good example is the Severance Payments Act of Barbados (see Figure 17.3).

Figure 17.3 Severance Payments Act of Barbados

Severance Payments for Redundancy in Barbados

Section 3(3)

For the purposes of severance payments, an employee who is dismissed shall be deemed

a) to be dismissed because of redundancy if his dismissal is wholly or mainly attributable to

(i) the fact that his employer has ceased or intends to cease to carry on the business for the purposes of which the employee was employed by him or has ceased, or intends to cease, to carry on that business in the place where the employee was so employed; or

(ii) the fact that the requirements of that business for employees to carry out work of a particular kind or for employees to carry out work of a particular kind in the place where he was so employed, have ceased or diminished or are expected to cease or diminish;

b) to be dismissed because of a natural disaster if his dismissal is wholly or mainly attributable to the destruction of, or damage caused to, the employer's place of business by fire, flood, hurricane, earthquake or other act of God whether or not similar to any of the foregoing causes.

The various Acts also specify the employees who are eligible for redundancy payments, the amount of redundancy payment, the procedure for handling redundancies, and the length of employment which qualifies an employee for payment.

Termination in consequence of liquidation, bankruptcy or dissolution of a partnership

Termination of employment may occur if (a) an employer becomes bankrupt, (b) the employer is a company and it is liquidated, (c) the employer is a partner in a firm and the partnership is dissolved.

Bankruptcy
Bankruptcy occurs when a debtor is no longer able to meet financial obligations. The state appoints a person to take possession of the property so that it may be realized and the proceeds distributed among creditors on the basis of preferable claims and priorities.

Bankruptcy does not automatically terminate the contract of employment. It will only do so if there is a term to that effect in the contract of employment. In theory, the employee could continue under the new management but it may not be possible to pay the usual wages. It may also be possible for the new employer to claim redundancy payments and wages which may have accrued from those with the responsibility for looking after the bankruptcy.

Liquidation
Liquidation of companies may be compulsory or voluntary.

Compulsory liquidation is ordered by a court, usually on the petition of a creditor, because the company cannot pay its debts. The court may appoint an individual known as a *liquidator* to manage the company's affairs. If the business of the company ceases, then the winding-up order could have an effect of wrongful dismissal. What is the position if the liquidator decides to continue the business to facilitate the winding-up? One view is that the liquidator may function as an agent of the company so that the contract of employment continues to be in force. Another view is that the appointment of the liquidator gives the employee notice of termination because for all practical purposes the liquidator is a new employer. Most writers prefer the view that employees should regard the order for liquidation as a dismissal and that a new contract may be negotiated with the liquidator.

Voluntary liquidation is initiated by the members of the company. If the business of the company comes to an end, then the employees may treat the closure as dismissal or termination of the contract of employment. If the business of the company continues to ensure an orderly winding-up then the position is generally similar to that described above in respect of compulsory liquidation.

Dissolution of a partnership
A partnership is a special kind of firm. It legalizes a relationship between people carrying on business in common with a view to make profit. Once a partnership is dissolved, the employees are regarded as being dismissed from employment. Usually, dissolution occurs if one partner dies, leaves the firm, or becomes bankrupt. The dismissal is treated as wrongful so the employee could claim damages. The damages would be reduced if the business continues under new arrangements and the employee is rehired.

17.4 Contracts for the sale of land

Most people, at some point in their lives, seek to purchase a parcel of land with a house built on it or, simply, a parcel of land with the intention to build on it in due course. Others buy land for investment purposes. Once the owner of the property, usually described as the *vendor*, has agreed to sell and the purchaser has agreed to buy, then the two parties may be said to be ready to enter into a contract for the sale or purchase of land.

Contracts for the sale of land must satisfy the usual rules of contract relating to capacity, invitation to treat, intention to create legal relations, offer and acceptance, consideration and so on. However, there is one feature which makes them different from other contracts: *it is a legal requirement that the contract must be in writing or evidenced in writing*. This requirement is aimed at preventing fraud, and disputes over land.

But merely agreeing to sell and buy land is not enough to convey the ownership or title of the land to the purchaser. The parties must also execute a *deed of conveyance* to complete the contract. The deed must then be registered to give notice to the whole world of proof of ownership.

One reason for entering into a contract before the vesting of title is to permit the purchaser to conduct certain preliminary enquiries about the land and property.

Important preliminary enquiries

Even before the parties sign the contract, the purchaser should seek to obtain from the vendor information on the following:

- whether there are existing disputes about the property
- ownership of the boundary walls, hedges and fences, if any
- rights of way to and from the property

- planning rcstrictions
- ownership and maintenance of roads to and from the property
- the existence of public utility services such as water, telephone, gas
- any covenants, for example possible restrictions on effecting physical changes to the property.

The more enterprising purchaser may also commission a structural survey of the property. Banks or institutions which offer loans to purchase property often insist on an independent survey in order to be sure that the property is in good condition.

The written contract

With the exception of St Lucia, the property legislation in force in the Commonwealth Caribbean requires that the agreement to sell and buy land should be supported with written evidence.

The minimum legal requirement is that the contract should be *evidenced* in writing, not that the entire contract itself should be in writing. Thus a memorandum to evidence an agreement to sell land has been held to include a letter, a clause in a will, a signed receipt, a telegram, and in one English case even an entry in a diary. In general, however, a good agreement should provide a clear description of the property, the identity of the parties to the contract, and any terms in the contract which the parties deem as essential. In some countries, statute law may require the parties to include or exclude certain terms in the contract. For example, in Barbados and Trinidad & Tobago the legislation forbids any attempt by the vendor to restrict a purchaser from retaining a lawyer of his choice.

A contract for the sale of land need not be complicated. Usually it contains the information indicated under the following headings:

1. *Definitions and interpretation*
   Here the terms used in the agreement are defined.
2. *Agreement for sale*
   This section confirms the agreement for sale. It identifies the nature of the contract.
3. *Deposit*
   This section states the deposit to be paid on or before signing the contract, and the grounds on which the purchaser could lose the deposit.
4. *Completion*
   This section specifies the date on which the actual sale and purchase is to be completed.

5 *Capacity*
This section defines the capacity in which the vendor – that is, the seller of the land – is contracting to sell the land.

6 *Possession*
Here provision is made for the property to be vacant on completion of the sale so that the purchaser can acquire possession.

7 *Title*
This section describes the title to the property, which is the subject of the contract.

8 *Incumbrances*
This section itemizes any special conditions or burdens attached to the property.

9 *Matters affecting the property*
This provision confirms that the property is sold subject to satisfying official requirements relating to town and country requirements or planning laws.

10 *Disclaimer*
This provision confirms that the purchaser has inspected the property and purchases it with full knowledge of its actual state and condition. It seeks to protect the vendor.

11 *Chattels*
This indicates whether the purchase price includes any special items usually described as chattels.

A contract for the sale of land may be made the subject of certain conditions. Great care must be exercised in agreeing to these conditions because they can be so vague that the agreement is virtually denied contractual force. Sometimes, a contract could only come into effect after a specified condition has been satisfied. Consider this example.

> Carlyle Gray agrees to sell his mansion, Beacon House, to Henry Birds. The agreement provides that the contract is subject to the sale of the purchaser's property at 55B Crescent Hill. Carlyle Gray would not be able to enforce the contract against the purchaser, Henry Birds, unless and until the latter sells his house.

Remedies for breach of contract

If either party to the contract for the sale of land refuses to complete the contract according to its terms, then the party who is prejudiced could explore several contractual remedies. These are summarized below.

Forfeiture of deposit
Most contracts usually stipulate that the purchaser must pay a deposit upon signing the contract. The deposit is intended to bind the purchaser. If the purchaser defaults, then the deposit may be forfeited. If it is the vendor who defaults then the deposit may be returned to the purchaser.

Specific performance
If a party defaults, then the other party could seek an order from the court to compel the other party to do what was promised – that is, execute the deed of conveyance. This remedy is only available at the discretion of the court.

Damages
If one party refuses to complete the contract, then it is open to the aggrieved party to rescind the contract and seek monetary compensation *instead of* specific performance. Monetary compensation, or *damages*, may be awarded for the recovery of the sums paid, the expenses incurred, and also for loss of bargain. The sums awarded must be for loss arising naturally from the contract and from special circumstances which the plaintiff knew or ought to have known when the contract was made.

Rescission
Just as was seen above, if one party to the contract defaults, the other party could seek to rescind the contract in order to be placed in the position which that party enjoyed before the contract was signed. In other words, the aggrieved party seeks to be restored to a position *as if* the contract did not exist. A party could seek rescission on any of these grounds: fraud, undue or excessive influence, misrepresentation as to an important fact, non-disclosure of an important fact, misdescription of the property subject to the contract, mistake, a defective title, failure to complete the contract.

Completion and registration

If the parties to the contract perform all their obligations, then the contract may be completed by the execution of a deed of conveyance. The *deed of conveyance* is required to transfer title in the land to the purchaser to enable possession of the property. Of course, the balance of the purchase money must be paid on signing the deed. The deed must be signed by the parties, sealed and delivered. *Delivery* means any act by the parties to indicate that the deed has been adopted by them.

In most islands it is a requirement that the deed is registered in the Land Registry in order to protect the title of the purchaser.

17.5 Insurance contracts

Life without risks is virtually impossible. On any given day, a person could sustain loss as a result of a fire, an accident, disease or in consequence of a crime. Then too natural perils such as hurricanes, lightning or even earthquakes may strike.

One of the simplest ways to protect oneself from loss is to enter into a contract of insurance. A contract of insurance allows a person who is subject to a risk to pay a small contribution, usually known as a *premium*, to an insurer who promises in return to compensate in proportion to the loss incurred, should the misfortune occur.

Types of insurance

One may distinguish between a contract for first-party insurance and a contract for third-party insurance. Under a first-party insurance one insures one's own life, house, car, jewellery, furniture, etc. A contract for third-party insurance insures one against the potential liability in law to pay damages (money) to another. In the event that the other party suffers loss then the insurance company would pay the other party damages on behalf of the party who had caused the loss.

In a book entitled *What Goes On In Insurance*, H. A. L. Cockerrell offers the following classification of insurance contracts:

1 *Personal*
One type provides benefits if the insured person dies. This is often referred to as *life insurance*. This category also includes insurance contracts to provide financial benefits to people who have suffered injury or disablement by accident or sickness, and expenses consequent on illness.

2 *Property*
This type of insurance protects against loss or damage to insured property such as motor vehicles, aircraft, ships, jewellery, and buildings and their contents.

3 *Liability*
This type of insurance contract is entered into by individuals, businesses and other organizations to protect them against being liable in law to pay compensation to another party who has suffered injury or damage. Third-party insurance falls into this category.

4 *Monetary losses*
This type of insurance contract is not common. The insured is protected against monetary losses. This classification also includes *fidelity guarantee insurance*, a type of insurance contract that protects the insured against embezzlement by dishonest employees. There is also *credit insurance* which protects against the risk that a party who has obtained a loan will fail to repay the loan.

It is important to bear in mind that the field of insurance is diverse. One can get an insurance contract for practically anything. For example, one type of life insurance policy is the *whole life insurance*. Under this policy, the insurer gives an undertaking to the insured to pay an agreed sum of money to the estate or beneficiaries of the insured on the death of the insured whenever that may be. Then there are *endowment policies*, which allow the insured person to receive a stated sum once he or she survives beyond a certain age. There are also various combinations of these policies for the enterprising client.

The insurance contract

Just as we saw in the case of other specialty contracts, a valid insurance contract must satisfy the requirements of offer, capacity, acceptance, consideration, and an intention to create legal relations. However, some practices are unique to insurance contracts.

Negotiations begin when the insurer, through its agents, presents the prospective client with a proposal form. The completion of the form usually constitutes the offer. If a premium is paid and submitted along with the proposal, the understanding is that the insurer will retain it pending a decision as to whether the offer will be accepted or rejected. However, until a decision is made, the offeror – that is, the person making the proposal – is entitled to withdraw the offer and recover the premium. If no premium is paid at the time of the offer, then the insurer will indicate that acceptance is subject to the payment of the premium by the proposer. In that event, the contract will come into effect upon payment of the premium.

The situation could be different if the proposal form states that the contract is not completed until the insurer issues the policy. In that event, it would seem that there is agreement between the parties that the issuance of the policy signifies acceptance of the offer of the party seeking insurance. An alternative interpretation is that the parties have agreed that it is a term of their negotiations that there is no binding contract until a formal document containing the terms of the agreement is signed by one of them.

Cover notes

It may take some time before an offer is accepted. Meanwhile, the proposer would wish to be covered and protected from liability. In this situation the insurer may agree to provide temporary cover upon receipt of the proposal pending full consideration of the offer and the issuance of the policy. The insurer then issues a *cover note*, which is fully effective as an insurance contract. The device of the cover note is used in many different types of insurance, but particularly motor vehicle insurance.

Repudiation of contracts

Even though parties have entered into a contract of insurance, circumstances may entitle the insurer to repudiate the whole contract or to avoid liability in respect of a particular claim under a contract of insurance. A contract could be repudiated for one of the following reasons:

1 The insured may not possess *an insurable interest*. This is required by statute. According to H. A. L. Cockerrell, 'For an insurance to be valid the insured person must be so related to the subject of insurance that he stands to lose by the occurrence insured against.' In that case he is said to have an insurable interest.

2 One or both of the parties may have entered into the contract to achieve a purpose that is illegal or contrary to the public policy of the state. For example, a contract of insurance on the property of a national of an enemy state would be illegal.

3 The insured property may be put to unlawful use. For example, in marine insurance law it is an accepted principle that the use of an insured ship for an unlawful voyage may render the contract illegal.

An insurer may have the right to repudiate a contract of insurance if the insured person (a) is guilty of fraud, (b) makes a statement that misrepresents the true state of the fact, (c) does not disclose a fact that could affect the decision to enter into the contract, or (d) breaches a term of the contract, and the breach is so serious that when the term is interpreted, it entitles the insurer to repudiate the whole contract. Fraud, non-disclosure and misrepresentation are so important that it is worth considering each in greater detail.

Fraud

Usually it is difficult to prove fraud. It occurs when a proposer makes a statement to the insurer which is false. The proposer knows the statement is untrue, or makes it recklessly and does not care whether it is true or false.

Misrepresentation

It is an insured's duty to answer honestly and in good faith all the questions on a proposal form. So if an insurer is induced to accept an insurance contract because the proposer, in the offer, makes a statement of fact that is false in a material particular, then if the insurer can prove the misrepresentation, the insurer can avoid the contract. Misrepresentation of a fact is perhaps a lesser form of dishonesty than fraud, but is dishonesty nonetheless. It is irrelevant whether the proposer, in making the statement, acted negligently or even innocently.

Non-disclosure

It is a fundamental principle of insurance contracts that before a contract is agreed the parties to the contract are bound to disclose to each other all information which is material to the contract and within their knowledge. The insurer does not and cannot be said to know all the facts. This principle is often described as *uberrima fides*, meaning 'utmost good faith'. The principle places an important responsibility on the proposer. Since insurance is really a contract premised upon speculation, it is only fair that an insurer should have enough information to decide whether to accept an offer of insurance and if so, the terms upon which the offer may be accepted.

Some examples will help to clarify the principle here. A proposer would be guilty of failing to disclose a material fact if he/she proposed any of the following:

(a) A whole life policy, but did not tell the insurer that he/she had made a recent visit to a specialist and after the contract was agreed, the proposer turned out to have cancer. It is immaterial that the proposer did not know something was seriously wrong at the time the offer of the contract was made.

(b) To insure a car, but did not disclose that he/she had had several road accidents. Several accidents suggest that the proposer is accident-prone and therefore a high risk. The insurer needs the information to decide whether the proposer should be charged a higher risk premium.

(c) A life policy but failed to inform the insurer that he/she had a serious heart condition. The proposer would be at high risk since such a person is likely to die prematurely.

Failure to disclose a material fact could provide a reason for the insurer to refuse to pay a claim under the policy.

The duration of a contract

The duration of a contract of insurance depends on the type of policy. For example, a life insurance contract is different from a contract for motor vehicle insurance. Once the insured pays the premiums the contract cannot be terminated by the insurer and remains in force until the death of the insured. A contract for a motor vehicle insurance policy is usually for one year. If it is renewed then a new contract comes into effect. The rules regarding disclosure apply to every new contract.

Indemnification

The insured is entitled to be indemnified once risk for which he/she took out the insurance has occurred. There are two very important rules here. First, in the case of a life policy, the insurer must pay the amount stated in the policy. This sum is called the *sum assured*. Second, in the case of insurance on property, the insured must prove the monetary value of the loss sustained. The insurer will then pay this amount and no more, even if a higher sum is stated in the insurance contract. The reason for this is that insurance on property is meant to compensate the insured for the loss sustained and not to enable a profit to be made from the loss. Otherwise the insured might be tempted to bring about the loss. So if, having been compensated by the insurer, the insured receives additional monies from another source to compensate the same loss, those additional monies will go to the insurer by what is known as *the doctrine of subrogation*.

17.6 Contract for a mortgage

Borrowing money is sometimes unavoidable. Indeed, banks exist to encourage people to save and to seek loans. But making loans can be a risky business. A lender would be at a serious risk if there was no reasonable guarantee that a borrower would repay. To ensure repayment a lender insists on some kind of security for the loan.

Where the loan of a substantial amount of money is involved, the lender often insists that the borrower provides security for the loan. One way of providing security is to confer on the lender certain rights or interests in an item of property belonging to the borrower so that if the borrower is unable to repay the loan on the agreed terms, the lender can make a claim on that property. This form of business transaction is described as a *mortgage*. One may, with the aid of a recent case (Re Bond North Ltd [1979] 3 All E.R. 919, 939), define a mortgage in the following terms:

> 'Any contract which, by way of security for the payment of a debt, confers an interest or a right in property which ceases to exist or is destroyed on payment of such debt, or allows for the appropriation of such property for the discharge of such debt, may be described as a mortgage.'

A form of contract

As a form of contract a mortgage involves an agreement between two parties. It contains a number of promises which the parties agree to observe or comply with during the existence of the mortgage. The promises are usually described as *covenants*. The borrower (or debtor) is referred to as the *mortgagor*, and the lender (or creditor) is described as the *mortgagee*. Usually, the agreement is written. It transfers the title or interest of the mortgagor (ie the borrower) to the mortgagee (ie the lender) and contains the terms and conditions of the debt. The transaction may be represented in this way:

Mortgagor (the borrower, debtor and owner of the property)	→	Transfers the title in the property to	→	Mortgagee (creditor or lender)

All mortgages contain a provision described as a *proviso for redemption*. This *proviso* means that once the mortgagor has repaid the loan, including both principal and interest, the mortgagee will reconvey the title of the property to the mortgagor. This may be represented thus:

Mortgagor (borrower or debtor)	←	Reconveys the title of the property to	←	Mortgagee (lender or creditor)

There are some transactions which are similar to mortgages but are not identical. See Table 17.3.

Table 17.3 Mortgages and similar transactions

Other transactions	Mortgage
Lien A person retains another's property until a debt is repaid, eg a vehicle that is sent to be repaired.	A mortgagee has a right to sell the property if the mortgagor defaults, but the holder of a lien does not.
Pledge A person gives items of property, called chattels, eg chairs, jewellery, to another to hold in possession until the debt is repaid.	A pledge is confined to chattels. A mortgage may include chattels. A mortgagee has ownership of the property; the person who holds the pledge only has possession.
Charge The creditor takes security rights in the property. This does not involve ownership or possession.	The mortgagee acquires ownership of the property that is the subject to the mortgage.
Bill of sale This resembles a mortgage but is confined to chattels or personal property that is unconnected with land. The lender acquires a right in the property, eg a vehicle, up to a certain amount of the loan that is repaid.	Mortgages are usually not controlled by special legislation with specific terms and conditions.

The method by which mortgages are created is usually prescribed in legislation.

A difference in St Lucia

In St Lucia, though lawyers speak of a mortgage, the instrument that is used is a *hypothec*. Like a mortgage, a hypothec secures a debt. The hypothec gives the creditor a security interest in the land of the borrower (or debtor) but does not confer title or ownership in the land. However, if the borrower defaults in repaying the loan, the law permits the land to be sold to recover the outstanding balance. A hypothec is in many ways similar to a mortgage.

The rights and duties of the parties

While a mortgage is in existence, the mortgagor remains in possession of the property that is subject to the mortgage, provided that the mortgagor observes the terms and conditions set out in the mortgage and agreed to by the parties. Once repayment is complete, the mortgagee is under a legal duty to reconvey the title of the property to the mortgagor.

Parties to a mortgage are free to include in the mortgage document certain terms and conditions. One of the most important conditions of a mortgage is the right of the mortgagor to redeem the mortgage by repaying the loan after a certain period of time has elapsed. In other words, a mortgagee (the lender) cannot compel a mortgagor (the borrower) to retain a mortgage over a period of time so that the mortgagee could earn as much interest as possible. This right to the mortgagor is described as the *equity of redemption*.

There are other terms and conditions which impose obligations on the mortgagor. Generally, the mortgage will state that the mortgagor must:

(a) make agreed instalment payments

(b) pay taxes, for example land and house taxes if they exist

(c) ensure that the property, if it includes a building, is insured with a reputable and approved insurance company – the mortgagor would wish to ensure that fire or a hurricane or other natural disasters do not destroy the investment in the property

(d) not commit waste on the property – waste refers to any act or inaction that alters the physical character of the property and in consequence reduces the value of the property

(e) seek the approval of the mortgagee to engage in specified transactions. For example, it may be a requirement that the mortgagor obtains the written consent of the mortgagee if the mortgagor proposes to lease the property while the mortgage is in existence.

What are the consequences if the mortgagor defaults by failing to pay the mortgage instalments? The remedies of the mortgagee depend on the terms of the mortgage agreement. The standard mortgage gives the mortgagee the following choices:

1 *Sale of the property*
If there is a serious default by the mortgagor, the mortgagee could exercise the power of sale. The mortgagee may do so under the terms of the mortgage or after obtaining an order from the court. Three conditions must be satisfied before the power could arise. These are established by statute and usually include:

(a) the mortgage must have been done by deed

(b) instalments of the mortgage money remain due

(c) the mortgage agreement does not have a provision disallowing the power of sale.

The three conditions must exist for the power of sale to arise. The mortgagee can then exercise the actual power once it can be proved that one of the conditions has been met. The proceeds of the sale are normally used to clear the outstanding balance. The surplus, if any, would go to the mortgagor.

2 *Foreclosure*
Foreclosure is a drastic step. A foreclosure order is issued by the court. On an application to the court, a final order of foreclosure,

described technically as a *foreclosure absolute,* may be issued. It extinguishes all the rights which the mortgagor enjoyed in the property. However, it is not unusual for a court, before making a final order, to permit the mortgagor an opportunity to settle the outstanding amount within a stipulated period. If the mortgagor fails to settle the outstanding amount, then the court may issue the foreclosure absolute, the equivalent to a final order.

3 *Suing on the personal promise to pay*
As noted above, a mortgage is essentially a contract of loan. If the mortgagor fails to repay the loan and interest, then the mortgagor has breached a term of the agreement. The mortgagee could therefore sue the mortgagor for breach of a promise to pay. However, the option to sue only arises after the date on which the mortgagor has the right to redeem or repay the mortgage.

4 *Possession of the property*
Since the title of the mortgaged property is vested in the mortgagee, the mortgagee has the power to take possession as owner should the need arise. It is, however, extremely rare for a mortgagee to do so. Where this step is taken, it is done to facilitate the sale of the property, or to acquire any rents or profits from the property to pay interest accruing on the loan. In addition, a mortgagee who takes possession of the property has to give an account to the mortgagor. Generally speaking, mortgagees do not like to be burdened with this responsibility.

Entering into a mortgage agreement is, therefore, a serious step. When someone wants to buy a house and land, careful thought must be given to the decision. A mortgage entails numerous costs. The banks usually require the prospective house owner to have at least 10 per cent of the cost of the property. If the land is not owned then the title deeds to the land must be prepared and executed. Also, a mortgage agreement must be prepared and executed. Usually, both documents are prepared by lawyers on behalf of the parties. Above all, the prospective mortgagor must ensure that the instalment payments can be met comfortably from the family income.

Key Points

- All special contracts must satisfy the general rules requiring offer, acceptance, consideration and an intention to create legal relations in order to create an enforceable legal contract. However, each type of special contract has its own rules and customs.
- A contract for the sale of goods is a contract whereby a seller of goods transfers or agrees to transfer the property in the goods to a buyer at an agreed price. Such a contract must be distinguished from a contract of barter, a contract of hire, and a contract for work or a skill.
- The rights, obligations and remedies of the buyer and seller are defined in legislation governing the sale of goods. However, subject to the law, the parties are free to agree on their own terms.
- A hire purchase contract permits a person to hire goods and to acquire the ownership of the goods upon payment in full of the credit price. A hire purchase contract must be distinguished from (a) a contract for the sale of goods, (b) a conditional sale and (c) a credit sale.
- In most islands there is a ceiling on the price of goods that may be made the subject of a hire purchase contract. The contract must be expressed in writing. Usually, the legislation in each island provides for the rights and obligations of the respective parties.
- A contract of employment is created when one person provides labour and skill to another in return for wages. A contract may be verbal, but increasingly the tendency is towards providing written contracts.
- A clear distinction must be made between an employee of service and one who has a contract for service. To identify the employee the courts use three tests: the control test, the organization or integration test, and the multiple test.
- The contract of employment is subject to numerous statutory enactments. These are automatic terms of the employment contract.
- The law imposes duties and obligations on both the employer and employee. A breach by either party may lead the aggrieved party to seek a remedy permitted by law.
- A contract of employment could be terminated by (a) notice, (b) agreement, (c) frustration, (d) in consequence of unfair dismissal, (e) wrongful dismissal, (f) dismissal for misconduct, (g) redundancy, or (h) by liquidation, bankruptcy or dissolution of a partnership.
- It is a fundamental legal requirement that a contract for the sale of land must be evidenced in writing.

- If a party to a contract for the sale of land breaches the contract, the following remedies are available to the aggrieved party: forfeiture of deposit, specific performance, damages, rescission.
- On completion of the contract, a deed is executed and then registered.
- There are different kinds of insurance contract. A first-party insurance provides coverage for the insured. A third-party insurance contract is intended to benefit a party other than the insured. Some other types of insurance are personal insurance, property insurance, mobility insurance and insurance against monetary losses.
- A temporary insurance policy may be issued in the form of a cover note.
- It is a cardinal principle of insurance contracts that parties to an insurance contract must disclose to each other all information that is material to the contract. This is known as the principle of *uberrima fides*.
- An insurance contract may be repudiated if:

  (a) the insured does not have an insurable interest

  (b) the purpose of the contract is illegal or contrary to public policy

  (c) the insured property is put to unlawful use.
- An insurer may be entitled to repudiate an insurance contract because of:

  (a) fraud

  (b) misrepresentation

  (c) non-disclosure

  (d) a breach of a term by the insured.
- A mortgage is created to provide security for a lender. A mortgage confers on the lender (the *mortgagee*) certain rights or interests in an item of property belonging to the borrower (the *mortgagor*) so that if the mortgagor defaults the mortgagee could lay claim to the property.
- Liens, pledges, charges and bills of sale must be distinguished from a mortgage. Unlike a mortgage, none of these transactions confers the right of ownership on the lender.
- In St Lucia a *hypothec* is used to secure a debt of property.
- The mortgage imposes obligations on the mortgagor. Some of these include a duty to:

(a) pay regular instalment payments

(b) pay taxes on the property

(c) insure property

(d) avoid waste on the property

(e) seek the approval of the mortgagee for certain transactions involving the property.

➤ If the mortgagor defaults, the mortgagee has several remedies, including:

(a) sale of the property

(b) an order of foreclosure from the court

(c) suing for breach

(d) possession of the property.

Questions

Sale of goods

1 What options does an unpaid seller have against the buyer in a contract for the sale of goods?

2 Brazen Enterprises Ltd sells Jiffy Appliances Ltd their entire stock of napkins held in their warehouse. It was agreed that Jiffy Appliances would take delivery in another week. Two days later, the warehouse is destroyed by fire. The property was not insured. Advise Jiffy Appliances.

3 Adella purchased a set of pans from Home Center Appliances. They are packed in a large box on which is written: 'Made in England. Non-scratching. Non-sticking. Stainless.' Advise Adella in each of the following situations:

(a) On the bottom of one of the pans she finds a label which says 'Made in Korea'.

(b) After two months, food sticks to the bottom of the pans, which must be soaked for two days to remove it.

(c) After one month the pans show signs of rust.

Hire purchase contracts

4 Distinguish a hire purchase contract from (a) a contract for the sale of goods, (b) a conditional sale and (c) a credit sale.

5 Michelle entered into a contract of hire purchase with Wonderland Appliances for the purchase of a television. It was agreed that Michelle would pay for the television by monthly instalments of $100. The total cost of the television was $1,000. Advise Wonderland Appliances in the following circumstances:

(a) Michelle has defaulted after two payments.

(b) Michelle has defaulted after paying $700.

(c) Michelle sells the television to Paul and the sale is discovered.

Contracts of employment

6 Explain the distinction between *a contract of service* and *a contract for services.*

7 Mercury is employed by Sentinel Security Ltd as a guard. Sentinel Security Ltd discovers that Mercury takes drugs. Sentinel Security Ltd immediately dismisses Mercury. Advise Mercury.

8 Explain the requirements that are necessary to render a contract of employment valid.

9 Advise Armstrong Builders and Engineers Ltd (the employer) whether it is entitled to dismiss the following employees:

(a) Busboy has been absent through illness for four months.

(b) Belinda has been repeatedly late for eight days.

(c) Joey repairs a radio for his friend Kombo during normal working hours without charge.

(d) Spike, well known for his temper, curses the Manager in the presence of other employees and accuses him of being a slave driver.

10 What remedies are available against Armstrong Builders and Engineers Ltd if all the employees are dismissed?

Contracts for the sale of land

11 What is meant by the requirement that a contract for the sale of land must be evidenced in writing?

Contracts for mortgages

12 Antasia and Redmond entered a mortgage agreement with Bankers International Ltd for the purchase of a house and land in Wonderland. Redmond loses his job. Antasia and Redmond are

unable to repay the mortgage. Explain the options available to the mortgagee.

13 What is meant by *the equity of redemption*?

14 Explain the difference between a *mortgage* and a *charge*.

Insurance contracts

15 What is an *insurable interest*?

16 Why is the principle of *uberrima fides* important to insurance contracts?

17 Kendra made a proposal to an insurance company for a whole life policy on his life for $500,000. He answered all the questions asked by the agent of the company. A few days later Kendra fell ill and was diagnosed with pneumonia. Unaware, the company accepted the proposal and the first premium was paid by Kendra's wife. Five days later Kendra died. Is the company liable to pay $500,000 to Kendra's wife, who is the beneficiary?

Other questions and activities

18 Identify for your island the legislation which governs (a) sales of goods, (b) hire purchase contracts, (c) employment contracts and (d) mortgages.

19 Trace the steps that must be followed in obtaining a mortgage to (a) build a house on land owned by the mortgagor and (b) purchase a house and land in a housing scheme.

20 What does the legislation of your country provide for employees in respect of the following:

(a) holidays and annual vacation

(b) payment during illness

(c) maternity leave

(d) pension

(e) severance or redundancy payments

(f) safety at work

(g) unfair dismissal

(h) contracts of employment?

21 With the assistance of your teacher, select a store that offers items on hire purchase. Assume you wish to purchase a selected item on hire purchase. Write a report on:

(a) the procedure involved, from the selection to the delivery of the item to your home

(b) the major terms of the agreement

(c) the cost of the item and the total interest that must be paid during the agreement

(d) the consequences that would follow if the agreement is breached (i) by you and (ii) by the company.

Before presenting the report to your class, discuss it with the selected firm to ensure its accuracy. Perhaps you can invite the representative of the firm to hear your report and to help you by responding to questions.

22 Phillip and Mary wish to obtain a mortgage of $300,000 for 25 years, to buy a house and land in a housing development.

(a) What fees would they have to pay to execute the necessary legal documents?

(b) What kind of income must Phillip and Mary earn to justify the mortgage?

(c) If the mortgage is offered at an interest rate of 10 per cent per annum, what would (i) the total interest, and (ii) the principal be?

Chapter 18 Social Accounting

In this chapter we look at the standard of living of a society. We define the standard of living and show how it is measured. One measure of the standard of living is the average national income of the country. We will look at its measurement in detail. We also look at the distribution of income between members of the society.

An increase in the level of national income is one of the goals of economic development. Other factors are life expectancy, a clean environment, improved health care and a more equitable distribution of income. Here we discuss economic growth and development and show the role of saving and investment in this process.

18.1 The standard of living

The standard of living is the level of material well-being of an individual or household. It is sometimes referred to as the level of economic welfare. It is determined by the amount of both social and private goods and services the individual consumes. It includes the amount of leisure the individual enjoys and the benefits from a better environment. A given level of consumption will result in different standards of living depending on the circumstances of the household. For example, a large family will need to consume more to achieve the living standard of a small family.

One indicator of the standard of living is the level of income measured by the *gross national product* (GNP). It has two drawbacks. First, it does not take account of the things which cannot be measured in the form of money, for example a clean environment, a low crime rate, more leisure hours, better health care, higher standards of education and better housing. To deal with this the Overseas Development Council in the United States has developed a *physical quality of life index* (PQLI) which is an index number based on the percentage of literacy, infant mortality rate and the life expectancy rate of a country.

Second, the level of income does not take into account that a given level of income will buy less when prices rise. To adjust for this the level of real income is calculated. *Real income* is a measure of the amount of goods and services that a given amount of money (nominal income) can buy.

To calculate the level of real income it is necessary to calculate the *consumer price index* or the *implicit price deflator*. The consumer price index is usually called *the cost of living index*. It is made up of the prices of a standard basket of goods which the average household buys on a regular basis. It includes things like food and beverages, clothing, transportation, housing, medical and health care products. The products which take up a larger portion of the household's income have a higher percentage (weight) in the calculation of the price index.

The weights for the various items in the consumer price index are determined by a consumer expenditure survey. The year of the survey is called the *base year*. The base year is given an index of 100. If prices increase, the price index rises and if prices decline, the price index decreases. The rate of inflation is the percentage change in the price index over a given period, say one year. If the price index was 104 in 1988 and 116 in 1989, the inflation rate can be calculated in the following way:

$$\text{Inflation rate} = \frac{116 - 104 \times 100}{104} = 11.5\%$$

This calculation shows that the cost of living increased by 11.5 per cent.

When there is inflation the household's real income decreases. To find the household's real income we divide its money income by the consumer price index and multiply by 100. If the household money (nominal income) was $1,000 in both 1988 and 1989 then the real income was:

$$\frac{\$1{,}000 \times 100}{104} = \$962 \text{ in 1988}$$

and

$$\frac{\$1{,}000 \times 100}{116} = \$862 \text{ in 1989.}$$

When these calculations are made, it is said that the household's money income has been deflated by the consumer price index. Thus the household's real income is its nominal income or money income deflated by the consumer price index. If its real income falls, its standard of living also falls. This is usually true of people with a fixed income, like old-age pensioners.

Other effects of inflation:

- Inflation reduces the value of assets which have a fixed money value like savings and life insurance policies.

- It forces income earners into a higher income tax bracket, resulting in higher income tax payments.
- It redistributes income from wage earners to people who earn profits, because wages do not increase as fast as inflation.
- The value of money declines continuously and people will try to hold goods rather than money.

The implicit price deflator

In measuring the level of real income for the country as a whole it is better to deflate the level of national income by the implicit price deflator. The *implicit price deflator* is an index of prices used to deflate the level of national income of the country. The weight for the implicit price deflator is the size of the various sectors in the economy. The real income of the country is the *gross domestic product* (GDP) of the country deflated by the implicit price deflator (see page 286 for a definition of GDP). If the base year of the implicit deflator is 1980 then the deflated income for each year is said to be given in 1980 dollars.

If the real income of the country increases it does not mean that the standard of living of the country increases. If the population of the country increases faster than the level of real income then the standard of living falls. To find out if the standard of living increases we calculate the level of per capita income – the income per head of the population. It is found by dividing the level of real income by the population.

$$\text{Real per capita income} = \frac{\text{Real national income}}{\text{Population}}$$

18.2 The measurement of national income

There are three basic ways of measuring national income: the income method, the expenditure method, and the output or value-added method.

The income method

The income method sums all the incomes earned by households in the economy during the period. Households receive income from the sale of factors of production or resources. The factors of production include land, labour, capital and entrepreneurship. The various factors of production receive income in the following forms:

land : receives rent
labour : receives wages and salaries
capital : receives interest and dividends
entrepreneurship : receives profits.

When we sum all of the incomes received by the factors of production we get national income at factor cost, for it tells us how much it costs in terms of factor payments to produce the goods and services.

The expenditure method

The expenditure method sums the value of all the expenditure on final goods and services produced in the economy during the accounting period. Only expenditure on final goods and services is included. Goods are regarded as final goods and services when they are purchased by the final user. Expenditure on final goods and services includes household consumption expenditure (C), government expenditure (G), investment expenditure (I) and net exports, ie exports minus imports (X – M).

The expenditure method gives the equation

$$Y = C + I + G + (X - M)$$

Households use a part of the income they receive to buy goods and services in the form of consumption. Another portion of the income they receive is saved in the commercial banks. This is borrowed by firms and they use it to buy investment goods. A third portion of the income that households receive goes to the government in the form of taxes, and this the government uses to finance government expenditure. Foreigners also buy our goods when we export to them but some of the income that households receive is not spent on domestically produced goods and services. It is spent on imported goods. Therefore we must subtract expenditure on imports to find out the value of expenditure on goods produced in the economy: (X – M).

The output method

The output method sums all of the output of final goods and services produced by firms in the economy during the year. There are too many firms in the economy to treat each firm individually, so the firms are usually aggregated into sectors/industries, for example agriculture, mining, manufacturing, etc. If the output of all the firms in the economy is added, there will be double-counting, because some firms produce intermediate goods, which are used by other firms to produce final goods. This is why the value-added method is used. This can be illustrated with the following example:

Firms/product	Output	Value added	Sector
The farmer – cane	$ 300	$300	agriculture
The sugar factory – sugar	$ 500	$200	manufacturing
The confectioner – sweets	$ 850	$350	manufacturing
The supermarket – sweets	$1,000	$150	distribution
Total	$2,650	$1,000	

If the output of all the firms is summed we get a total of $2,650, which is much more than the value of the final goods which the household purchases from the supermarket. In this figure we have counted the value of the cane produced by the farmer four times, the sugar three times and sweets twice. To get the correct figure we need to add the value added by the firms at each stage of production. The value added is found by subtracting the value of the goods purchased from the previous stage from the output of the firm in the present stage. Therefore the value added of the confectioner is $850 – $500 = $350. When all of the value added is summed we get national income via the output method. This method gives national income at factor cost.

The output method gives us the same value as the expenditure method. The value $1,000 from the output method is identical with the figure which consumers pay at the supermarket for the final goods. This is true in general if there are no indirect taxes or subsidies. The income method also gives the same figure, because the income which households receive is used to buy the goods and services produced by the firms. Therefore the three methods should yield the same result.

18.3 Different concepts of national income

In discussing the different concepts of national income it is perhaps best to get an understanding of the basic ideas behind the concepts, rather than thinking of them in terms of what is to be added and what is to be subtracted. It is therefore helpful to distinguish between the concepts of domestic product and national product; gross and net; factor cost and market price.

Domestic product refers to the goods and services produced within the physical confines of the country during a specified period. *National product* refers to the product which accrues to residents of the country. For example, 20 tonnes of sugar and 15 tonnes of vegetables may be produced in Barbados for the year. That is the domestic product. However, a Trinidadian firm may have invested capital to produce the output, the profits of which are paid to the Trinidadian investor, not to Barbadians. Therefore that amount must be deducted from the domestic product to find how much goes to Barbadians, ie the national product. Similarly, Barbadians may have invested in St Lucia and the profits received have to be added to the domestic product to find the national product. In general, all income/factor payments made to foreigners are deducted and all income/factor payments received from abroad are added to the domestic product.

We also need to distinguish between the terms *gross* and *net*. *Gross* refers to the total of goods and services produced. However, in order to produce these goods some of the country's capital stock is used up. If we calculate how much goods and services were produced after we have adjusted for the capital goods we have used up, we have calculated the *net* product. A measure of the amount of capital used up is depreciation or *capital consumption allowance*. Thus if we subtract depreciation from gross product we get net product.

The final two concepts to be distinguished are *market price*s and *factor cost*. The product measured at factor cost tells how much it costs in terms of factor payments to produce the product – that is, how much in terms of wages, rent, profits, etc. The product measured at market prices tells us how much the goods and services are sold for on the market. When these goods are sold on the market, three things may happen:

1 The government may find it necessary to impose indirect taxes on the goods (eg stamp duty or consumption taxes). These indirect taxes will raise the price on the market above the factor cost.

2 Government may give a subsidy to producers so that they can lower the price of essential goods to the consumers. In this case the subsidy reduces the price on the market below factor cost.

3 The government may impose neither taxes nor subsidies, in which case the market price and factor cost are the same. Therefore to convert from market prices to factor cost we need to add indirect taxes and subtract subsidies. To move from market prices to factor cost we do the opposite.

Given these distinctions we can look at the various concepts like gross domestic product (GDP) at factor cost and immediately see what they mean. Gross domestic product at factor cost is the total of product produced within the physical confines of the country, measured in terms of factor payments before any deduction for depreciation is made.

One very important concept is national income. In general terms, *national income* refers to all the important national accounting aggregates. However, the strict definition of national income is *net national product* (NNP) at factor cost. This is calculated by adding net factor payments abroad to GDP at factor cost to get gross national product (GNP) at factor cost, and then deducting allowances for depreciation.

There are also two other aggregates which are usually calculated. *Personal income* refers to all income received by households. It consists of that part of national income which goes to households before personal taxes are paid, and also includes transfer payments. *Disposable income* refers to all income over which households have discretion to dispose of as they wish. It is calculated by deducting personal direct taxes and levies from personal income.

18.4 The distribution of income

If the level of real per capita income increases, then the standard of living of the country as a whole increases. This does not mean that the standard of living of every person in the country increases. A per capita income of $3,000 does not mean that everyone in the country gets $3,000. The rich will get much more than the poor and in most cases the rich get richer and the poor get poorer. To see what is happening at the individual level we can look at the personal distribution of income.

The *personal distribution of income* refers to the distribution of income between members of a society. It can be represented by a *Lorenz curve*, which shows the percentage of income that a given percentage of the population receives. Figure 18.1 shows a Lorenz curve calculated for St Vincent and the Grenadines for 1983. It shows an unequal distribution of income. The lowest 20 per cent of the households received only about 8 per cent of the total income while the top 20 per cent received about 46 per cent. The diagonal of the graph frame represents equality of income distribution. The further away the curve is from the diagonal the more unequal is the distribution of income. Governments in the Caribbean have to try to reduce the inequality in the distribution of income to increase the standard of living of the poor.

The distribution of income can be improved by government policies. These include the following:

Taxation Progressive direct taxes which tax the rich at a higher rate than the poor tend to reduce income inequality. The income tax

Figure 18.1
Lorenz curve for St Vincent, 1983

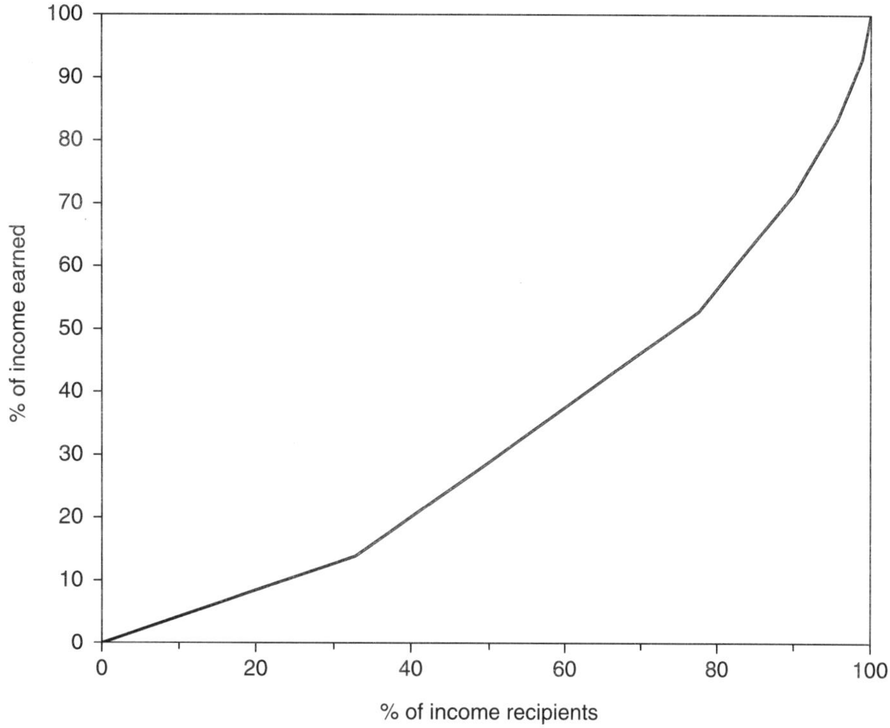

structure of most Caribbean countries is progressive, the major exception being Jamaica, which has a proportional income tax.

Government expenditure Government expenditure programmes which tend to benefit the lower income households more than upper income households also reduce income inequality. These include welfare programmes and health schemes.

The redistribution of income Taxing the rich to support the poor leads to a redistribution of income. This can be effected by a combination of taxation and government expenditure.

The redistribution of wealth Wealth can be redistributed by the government acquiring land and selling it to the poor. Governments in many Caribbean countries have acquired estates and helped poor people to buy their own land. They also help poor people to set up their own businesses.

Promoting balanced economic growth and development Economic management which promotes growth and development and reduces distortions in the economy tends to reduce income inequality. More opportunities are created for poor people to find better jobs.

18.5 The role of saving and investment

The development of the economy requires an increase in the capacity of the economy to produce output. This increase in capacity is only possible if the capital stock of the country increases. The capital stock is the total amount of capital goods that a country has. For the capital stock of the country to increase, there must be investment. There are many definitions of investment – it can mean putting money in the bank, or buying financial assets. Here, investment refers to an increase in the capital stock – the purchase of new plant and machinery. This type of investment increases the capacity of the country to produce goods and services.

It is necessary to have funds available to invest. Some investment funds come from abroad in the form of foreign investment. But a country must be able to generate some of its own funds for investment, by saving. Saving is possible when households abstain from consuming part of their income. Individual households in the economy save and put their money in financial institutions like commercial banks and finance houses. These institutions lend the money to firms that are willing to invest. Households can invest directly in firms by buying shares or bonds issued by firms (see Chapter 5). They can buy government bonds or treasury bills and the government will use the money to invest in the country's infrastructure. People can also use their savings to set up their own businesses.

Saving and investment interact to create a process of continuous growth. If people save more, then more funds are available for investment. Investment increases the capital stock of the country which increases the capacity of the economy to produce more. This results in higher (growth in) income. With higher income people are able to save more. Businesses can invest more, resulting in greater capital formation and more growth in income and output. This is a continual process, which is only broken if people consume all their income. It is therefore important for people to save in order to help the growth and development of the country.

18.6 Economic growth and development

The terms *economic growth* and *economic development* are sometimes used interchangeably. However, they do not mean the same thing. *Economic growth* is an increase in the level of real income or output of the country as measured by the real gross domestic product (GDP). Real GDP is GDP at factor cost deflated by the implicit price deflator. If we say that the economy grew by 4 per cent, we mean that the real GDP increased by 4 per cent during the time period under consideration.

Economic development refers to the changes in the underlying structure of the economy, changes in the institutional framework, and improvement in the quality of life. If the economy grows and there is little impact on the mass of the people of the country because the growth is confined to just a small sector, that cannot be called development. Economic development will result in growth, but growth need not mean economic development. So as well as growth in real GDP, other things affecting the quality of life have to be considered, for example the number of doctors and hospital beds, access to running water, access to electricity, food intake, the level of literacy, the distribution of income and housing.

Economic development can be defined as *the process through which the real per capita income of the country increases*. The general population of the country must benefit from the increases. There must be improvement in the distribution of income. The rise in real income must be accompanied by changes in basic conditions like improved diet, better health, clothing and housing, rising literacy, and an improved physical and cultural environment.

The distinction between growth and development means that governments in the Caribbean must use a 'basic needs' approach to development. This approach argues that the most basic requirements of people must be satisfied before the less essential needs of a few are met. It involves raising the income earning opportunities for the poor, and public assistance in the provision of good health, education and sanitation services and clean water. The aim is to improve the standard of living of the poor in a shorter time than if there was growth alone.

Key Points

- The standard of living is the level of material well-being of the individual or household. It can be reduced by inflation.
- Per capita income is the level of income per head of population. It is not a good measure of the standard of living because it ignores the distribution of income.
- Economic development refers to changes in the structure of the economy and improvement in the quality of life.
- Economic growth is an increase in the level of real income. Economic development implies economic growth but economic growth does not imply economic development.

- National income is the value of final goods and services produced in a country during a given period. There are several concepts, but the two most widely used are gross domestic product (GDP) at factor cost, and net national product at factor cost.
- There are three methods of measuring national income: the income method, the expenditure method and the output method.

Questions

1 Explain what is meant by *the standard of living*. How does inflation affect the standard of living?

2 Suppose that the consumer price index was 105 in 1988 and 120 in 1990. If Mr Layne's pension was fixed at $100 per week, what was his real income in 1990? By how much did his real income decline?

3 Define *economic growth*. What is the relationship between economic growth and economic development?

4 Distinguish between *economic growth* and *economic development*. What role does saving and investment play in the development process?

5 Describe the three methods of calculating national income.

6 Distinguish between:

(a) *gross domestic product* and *net national product*

(b) *personal income* and *disposable income*

(c) *GDP at market prices* and *GDP at factor cost*

(d) *gross investment* and *net investment*.

7 (a) State *five* ways in which people invest in their country.

(b) Show how foreign investment could affect the development of a country.

(c) Explain three of the problems which your country could face if there was a shortage of foreign investment.

Chapter 19 International Trade

Caribbean economies are small, open economies which have significant contact with the rest of the world mainly through international trade. International trade is defined as *the exchange of goods and services between countries*. It can be divided into import trade and export trade. *Import trade* is the purchase of goods and services from a foreign country. For example, if Barbados buys cars from Japan and rice from Guyana, then Barbados is said to import cars from Japan and rice from Guyana. *Export trade* is the sale of goods and services to foreign countries. For example, St Vincent and St Lucia export bananas to the United Kingdom, and Grenada exports vegetables to Trinidad & Tobago.

International trade exists because of differences in the distribution of resources between countries. Some countries have large quantities of some resources while others have none. For example, Kuwait and Saudi Arabia have large deposits of oil while the Caribbean countries have very little. Jamaica has bauxite while Dominica has none. Due to the differences in distribution of resources, the demands of different countries for goods and services vary according to their ability to produce them.

Bauxite storage at Discovery Bay, Jamaica

If resources could be easily transferred from one country to another, there would be no need for international trade. Resources would simply be transferred to where the goods are needed. However, most resources are relatively immobile (cannot easily be moved), so the goods made from these resources are traded. Countries specialize in the production of those goods in which their resource base gives them a comparative advantage.

The advantages of specialization:

1 Just like people, countries are able to specialize in those activities which they can perform best and so increase the level of welfare.

2 Countries can reap economies of scale internationally. The larger international market allows firms in the country to expand their scale of production and so receive the benefits of large-scale production. The markets in the individual Caribbean countries are quite small and local firms need to export to make the most of economies of scale.

3 International trade exposes local firms to greater competition and so increases the efficiency of their use of resources. Most of the exports of Caribbean countries are sold under protective agreements which limit the amount of competition these countries face. Sugar and bananas are both sold under highly protective arrangements.

4 International trade promotes growth in Caribbean countries. Because the economies are so small, the countries need to export more in order to grow. The local market cannot provide sufficient stimulus for growth.

5 The commercial links established through international trade have many beneficial effects on consumption and production. The quality of goods and services consumed increases. More efficient methods of production are used because there is access to better technology.

6 International trade promotes valuable political links between the Caribbean and other countries, and also between the Caribbean countries. Links between the Caribbean and developed countries like the United States, the United Kingdom and Japan enable us to receive development assistance from these countries. Within the Caribbean, the Caribbean Community (CARICOM) provides the basis for economic and social cooperation (see page 308).

19.1 International trade and specialization

In Chapter 1 we discussed the advantages of specialization of the individual. From that analysis we concluded that individual specialization increases the welfare of the society. International specialization also increases the welfare of the society. This can be demonstrated by *the theory of comparative advantage.*

Assume there are two countries, for example St Lucia and Barbados, and they produce two goods, sugar and bananas. Suppose further that using one-half of their resources in each line of production, they can produce the following:

Country	**Bananas**	**Sugar**
Barbados	100	200
St Lucia	200	100
Total	300	300

The total output of the two commodities would be 300 tonnes of bananas and 300 tonnes of sugar. Now suppose Barbados shifts all of its resources into the production of sugar, it would produce 400 tonnes of sugar and no bananas. Similarly, if St Lucia specializes in the production of bananas it would produce no sugar and 400 tonnes of bananas. The total output would now be 400 tonnes of sugar and 400 tonnes of bananas – a net increase in production of 100 tonnes of sugar and 100 tonnes of bananas. This increase in output can be distributed between the two countries to increase their welfare. This law was demonstrated by Adam Smith and was called *the theory of absolute advantage.*

Quite a lot of international trade is explained by absolute advantage, where one country has the advantage in one or the other of the two goods. But what happens if one country is more efficient in the production of all commodities? This is probably true of the Caribbean, because we are high-cost producers of all goods. In this case, trade can still be beneficial to both countries.

Assume the production relations for Barbados and Dominica are as follows:

Country	**Oranges**	**Sugar**
Barbados	200	300
Dominica	600	500
Total	800	800

We note that Dominica is more efficient in the production of both goods than Barbados. It would seem from this example that no trade exists. To demonstrate that trade is beneficial to both countries we calculate how much of each item the countries would have to give up (forgo) in order to produce one more unit of the other item. This is called the *opportunity cost* or *comparative cost of the good.* To produce 200 tonnes more oranges, Barbados would have to give up 300 tonnes of sugar, so the opportunity cost of one tonne of oranges is (300/200) = 1.50. Similarly, to produce 500 tonnes more sugar, Dominica would have to give up 600 tonnes of oranges, giving an opportunity cost of sugar of (600/500) = 1.20. The opportunity costs of the two goods in the two countries are:

Country	Oranges	Sugar
Barbados	(300/200) = 1.50	(200/300) = 0.67
Dominica	(500/600) = 0.83	(600/500) = 1.20

From these relationships we see that Barbados has the lower opportunity cost for sugar (0.67) and Dominica has the lower opportunity cost for oranges (0.83). This means that Barbados should specialize in the production of sugar, and Dominica in the production of oranges.

As long as the exchange rate lies between 1.20 and 0.83, both countries can benefit from trade. Suppose that the two countries exchange the goods at 1 tonne of oranges for 1 tonne of sugar. Barbados can exchange 1 tonne of sugar for 1 tonne of oranges from Dominica. If it chooses to produce oranges at home it would have to give 1.5 tonnes (the opportunity cost) of sugar. Thus Barbados is better off trading with Dominica. Similarly, if Dominica chooses to produce sugar at home it would have to give up 1.2 tonnes of oranges to produce 1 tonne of sugar, whereas if it trades it could exchange only 1 tonne of oranges for 1 tonne of sugar. Thus Dominica is also better off trading with Barbados. As long as there are differences in comparative cost, countries can benefit from international trade.

Comparative advantage explains the pattern of international trade based only on production considerations. The trade pattern may be modified by a number of factors:

Demand The demand for the product can reverse the conclusions of comparative advantage. The demand for a product in a country can be so large that the country becomes a net importer even if it has a comparative advantage in its production. This happens if the country does not produce enough to satisfy its own demand, or a large demand in that country makes the price very high.

Transport cost When transport cost is added to the cost of production, the price of the product may not be competitive in other countries.

Changes in technology In the world today there are very rapid changes in technology which make production processes more efficient. Countries with new inventions can take away the comparative advantage from less inventive countries.

Historical trade links Caribbean countries still continue to buy goods from the United Kingdom, even though they can be obtained from cheaper sources. This is because the Caribbean has historical trade links with Britain. Similarly the UK still continues to buy Caribbean sugar and bananas although they could get them cheaper from other places.

Preferential agreements Trade in some commodities is under preferential agreements. Our exports of sugar to the United States and the UK, exports of bananas to the UK, and many manufactured products to Canada, the United States and the UK, come under these preferential agreements.

Government intervention in international trade Countries interfere with the free movement of goods, for example by means of tariffs, quotas, licences, exchange controls and outright prohibition (see Chapter 20).

19.2 The balance of payments

One of the most important policy issues in relatively open economies is how to get rid of a surplus or deficit in the balance of payments. However, before looking at the balance of payments policy it is helpful to understand how transactions are recorded on the balance of payments, and what is meant by a deficit or surplus in the balance of payments.

The balance of payments is a systematic record of the transactions between residents of the home country and residents of the rest of the world. These transactions include:

- merchandise trade
- trade in services
- unilateral transfers
- capital movements
- official reserve transactions.

Merchandise trade refers to the import and export of goods such as rice, bananas, razor blades and pencils. *Services* include tourism, shipping, banking, insurance and dividend payments. From time to time, countries and individuals receive gifts from abroad for which no payment is made. These are referred to as *unilateral transfers* or *unrequited receipts and payments*. These include government grants, remittances and pensions from abroad. *Capital movements* refer to long-term and short-term movements of money between countries. Examples of such capital movements are government-to-government loans and movement of money abroad to take advantage of higher interest rates. *Official reserve transactions* are transactions undertaken by the monetary authority to bring about balance of payments equilibrium. These include the purchase and sale of gold and foreign assets such as US dollars and pounds sterling.

Balance of payments book-keeping

Any transaction which normally gives rise to the purchase of foreign currency is recorded as a debit entry of the balance of payments, and any transaction which normally gives rise to a sale of foreign currency is recorded as a credit entry. Put another way, any transaction that uses up foreign currency is a debit item and any transaction that earns foreign currency is a credit item.

Exports of goods, therefore, are credited because they earn foreign exchange, while imports of goods are debited. Similarly, exports of services are credited and imports of services are debited. The recording of these transactions is illustrated in Table 19.1: exports of goods amount to $550 and are listed under credits, while imports amount to $700 and are debited. Similarly, exports of services ($250) and imports of services ($150) are recorded under credits and debits respectively. Unilateral receipts bring in foreign currency and are therefore credited. Unilateral payments, on the other hand, use up foreign exchange and are therefore debited.

Capital imports increase our holdings of foreign currency. For example, if the government of Barbados borrows $1 million from the United States, it receives an equivalent amount of US dollars, which increases the government's holdings of US dollars by one million. Therefore capital imports must be credited. Capital exports are listed under debits, for in order to invest abroad you need to purchase (use up) currency.

We can treat capital and goods in a similar way if we think of importing capital as exporting a financial claim. For example, if the government of Barbados borrowed money from the United States, it would have to give an IOU in exchange for the money.

We can therefore regard capital imports as exporting IOUs and capital exports as importing IOUs. Viewed this way, exports of IOUs have to be credited and imports of IOUs have to be debited. In Table 19.1 we see that long-term and short-term capital imports amount to $100 and $150 respectively and are listed under credits. Capital exports of $50 and $300 for long-term and short-term capital respectively are debited.

Table 19.1 The balance of payments account

	Credits (+)	Debits (–)	
Current account			
Exports of goods	550		
Imports of goods		700	
Balance of visible trade			–150
Exports of services	250		
Imports of services		150	
Balance of invisible trade			+100
Unilateral receipts	100		
Unilateral payments		80	
Errors and omissions		90	
Current account balance			–120
Capital account			
Long-term capital			
Long-term imports	100		
Long-term capital exports		50	
Short-term capital			
Short-term capital imports	150		
Short-term capital exports		300	
Balance private capital movements			–100
Official settlements balance			
Official reserve transactions			
Official reserve movements			+220
Reduction in gold	30		
Reduction in foreign assets	70		
Borrowing from IMF	120		
Total	**1,370**	**1,370**	

Official reserve transactions are undertaken to provide the public with the foreign exchange they need to undertake private transactions. Therefore if the private sector, including the government, wishes to spend more foreign currency than it receives, the monetary authority will have to run down its holdings of gold and other foreign assets. In other words, it exports gold and foreign assets. Therefore decreases in the assets of the monetary authority must be listed under credits. Similarly, increases in its stocks of gold and foreign assets must be listed under debits. In the example given in Table 19.1, stocks of gold are reduced by $30 and foreign assets are reduced by $70, and borrowing from the International Monetary Fund (IMF) ($120) is listed under credits, because the private sector spent more foreign assets than it received.

The items 'Errors and omissions', amounting to $90, states the errors that have been made in recording the transactions. For example, tourist expenditure cannot be accurately recorded, because no one knows exactly how much each tourist spends in the country. Since the overall balance of payments must balance, the errors and omissions is the amount that is needed to make the total debits equal to the total credits. In Table 19.1, total credits are $1,370 but total debits without errors and omissions are $1,280. The difference between the two is $90 – the figure for errors and omissions.

The balance of payments is just another type of account, and transactions are recorded by double entry. If all transactions are recorded accurately, the total of debits will equal the total of credits. Put another way, every unit of foreign currency sold must be bought by someone, and every unit of foreign currency bought must be sold by someone. Since the actual amount of foreign currency bought must be equal to the amount of foreign currency sold, the overall balance of payments must always be equal. That is, in an accounting sense the balance of payments always balances.

Balance of payments imbalances – deficits or surpluses – refer to the balance in a particular part of the accounts. For example, we can look at merchandise trade and obtain the balance of visible trade. The merchandise trade balance is called *the balance of visible trade* because it deals with goods which one can see (visible) and touch (tangible). This account has a deficit of $150, because the imports of goods ($700) exceed the exports of goods ($550). Debits carry a negative sign (–) and credits carry a positive sign (+) and we therefore end up with –$150 when we take exports and imports together.

The balance of invisible trade is found by taking exports of services and imports of services together. Services which include things like banking, insurance and tourism are not visible or tangible – hence the name *invisible trade*. This account yields a surplus of $100 (ie exports $250 minus imports $150).

If we add the balance of visible trade (–$150) to the balance of invisible trade (+$100) we get the balance of trade, which has a deficit (–$50). The balance of trade is therefore the balance we obtain when we look at trade in both goods and services. It is the difference between the imports and exports of goods and services.

One of the more important accounts is *the current account*. Current account transactions are those that directly affect the level of income in the country. The current account also measures the amount the country is borrowing (deficit) or lending (surplus) abroad. Included in this account are trade in both goods and services and unilateral transfers. In the final column of Table 19.1, the current account balance shows a deficit of –$120, made up of a visible trade balance of –$150, an invisible trade balance of +$100, an excess of unilateral receipts over unilateral payments of +$20, and errors and omissions –$90.

The *capital account* shows the inflow and outflow of money from the country for investment purposes. These movements of money can be in the form of loans, investment in stocks or shares, or even money flows to set up a new business or to buy an existing business. Other forms of foreign investment are discussed in the final chapter.

Because the balance of payments must balance overall, a surplus (or deficit) on the current account must be matched by an equal deficit (or surplus) on the capital account. In fact this is true for any part of the balance of payments and all the other transactions taken together. Therefore the deficit of –$120 on the current account must be matched by a surplus of +$120 on the capital account.

On the capital account we note that there is a deficit of –$100 for the balance of private capital movements. Under official reserve transactions we have a surplus of +$220 on the official reserve movements which makes an overall surplus on the capital account of +$120. This can be expressed as *the balance of payments equation*:

$$C + K + R = 0$$

where C is the current account balance, K is the capital account balance and R is the official reserve movements.

The official settlements balance tells us by how much the monetary authority has to increase or decrease its assets in order to accommodate the rest of the economy. Therefore one can view the official settlements balance as a good measure of disequilibrium in the balance of payments. In fact this is the balance that the International Monetary Fund (IMF) looks at in determining if a country's balance of payments is in equilibrium.

The *balance of payments* of a country is therefore equivalent to the official settlements balance. It measures the difference between the total international receipts and total international payments undertaken by people or organizations other than the monetary authority. This includes the private sector and the government. It differs from the *balance of trade,* which includes only payments and receipts with respect to goods and services. The balance of payments also includes receipts and payments for capital account transactions.

The causes of balance of payments deficits

The balance of payments is in disequilibrium if there is a deficit or surplus on the official settlements balance. Both deficits and surpluses on the balance of payments are bad. However, persistent deficits are a bigger problem, for a country has to keep running down its foreign reserves in order to finance deficits. Since foreign reserves are limited, if deficits persist, sooner or later the country will have to borrow from the International Monetary Fund.

Deficits can arise for a number of reasons, for example:

Excess domestic credit creation If the local banking system creates excess credit then people have excess money balances which they spend mainly on imported goods and services.

Excessive government expenditure Increases in government expenditure increase the level of spending in the economy, but because the economy is open, most of the increased spending falls on imported goods and services.

Excessive wage increases These can also lead to balance of payments deficits. With higher wages people can spend more, because most of what we consume and a large part of investment is imported.

Reduction of export earnings Reduction of export earnings can arise from three sources: (a) natural disasters, (b) loss of export markets and (c) a fall in export prices. A natural disaster like a hurricane can reduce the quantity of goods available for export, as when hurricane David destroyed much of Dominica's banana crop. Loss of export markets means that the country cannot sell its goods abroad – for example, furniture manufacturers can no longer sell in the Trinidad market because of trade restrictions. A fall in export prices also reduces export earnings. For example, the fall in the price of oil and low bauxite prices in the international markets have significantly reduced the export earnings of Trinidad and Jamaica respectively.

Balance of payments policy

Temporary deficits can be financed in the following ways:

1 By running down the country's foreign assets and monetary gold.

2 By borrowing from the central banks in other countries.

3 By borrowing from commercial banks in other countries.

4 By using up the credit facilities offered by foreign firms.

5 By borrowing from the International Monetary Fund (IMF).

If an adverse balance of payments persists, the country will have to use corrective measures, which means adopting various policies, for example monetary policy, fiscal policy, incomes policy, devaluation and direct controls.

Monetary policy

Monetary policy is manipulating the money supply to bring about some economic goal, in this case the goal is balance of payments equilibrium. We noted that domestic credit creation can lead to a balance of payments deficit, so to get rid of a deficit, domestic credit can be controlled.

Either the general level of credit in the economy can be controlled or controls can be applied selectively to credit for imported consumer durables like cars, stoves and refrigerators. The conventional tools of monetary policy – reserve ratio, open market operations, discount rate, etc – will not be very effective because the structure of these economies inhibits the effective use of these policies.

Fiscal policy

Fiscal policy refers to the use of the government budget to achieve some economic goal. If the government spends excessively, government expenditure would exceed government revenue, yielding a deficit on the government budget. Excessive government spending also leads to a balance of payments deficit, so cutting the government budget deficit will lead to a reduction in the deficit on the balance of payments. Increasing direct taxes also reduces disposable income, so consumption will fall. Given the high import content in our consumption goods, imports will also fall off.

Incomes policy

Incomes policy refers to control on prices and incomes in the economy, ie wages and profits. Profits are usually not restrained, as they are seen as an incentive to produce, so an incomes policy usually becomes a policy of wage restraint. Wage restraint affects the balance of payments in three ways:

1 Smaller wage increases imply that workers' purchasing power does not increase as quickly and spending on imports will not rise as quickly, preventing the balance of payments deficit from getting worse.

2 Wages represent a large part of government expenditure, since government is the largest employer. So if wages can be restrained it will be easier for the government to meet its fiscal targets.

3 If wages are restrained in the face of inflation caused by devaluation, workers' real wages fall and the cost of producing goods for export will fall, making them more competitive on international markets. However, if prices rise faster than wages, people's real wages will fall causing people to reduce their work effort, which means that fewer goods will be produced for export.

Devaluation

Devaluation is the reduction in the value of the domestic currency with respect to foreign currencies. The effect of this is to make foreign goods more expensive to domestic consumers so that imports are reduced. At the same time domestic goods become cheaper to foreigners, who buy more of them, and domestic exports increase. If imports fall and exports rise, the balance of payments should improve.

For example, the exchange rate between the Barbados dollar and the US dollar is currently (at the time of writing) BD $2 = US $1 (ie BD $1 = US 50 cents). If the Barbados dollar is devalued, its value would be reduced to, say, BD $3 = US $1 (ie BD $1 = US 33 cents). Barbadians will now have to pay more Barbados dollars for the goods they have to import: before the devaluation a car which cost US $10,000 would cost BD $20,000, and after devaluation the same car would cost BD $33,000. Devaluation increases the price of imports and people buy fewer imports.

However, imports may not fall if imports consist mainly of necessities and goods for which there are no local substitutes. Also, with a devaluation the price of domestically produced goods will rise and exports will no longer be cheaper to foreigners, so exports may not rise either. In the case of the Caribbean, therefore, devaluation may not be an effective tool for dealing with balance of payments deficits.

Direct controls

Direct controls refer to trade restrictions which aim to reduce the level of imports. These include import quotas, licences and exchange controls. In terms of the theory of international trade these are referred to as *non-tariff barriers* and include the following:

Tariffs (customs duties)	These increase the price of the imported commodity above the production cost.
Quotas	Quantitative limitations on the amount of goods imported or exported.
Licences	The importer or exporter needs to get permission (a licence) from the Ministry of Trade before the goods can be imported/exported.
Exchange controls	Controls put in place by the central bank or ministry governing the sale of foreign exchange.
Outright prohibition	The government bans the importations of certain goods.

If such measures are successful in reducing the level of imports, they will help in curing the balance of payments deficits. These controls impose a cost on the economy in terms of inefficient allocation of resources and should only be used as short-term measures.

Key Points

- International trade increases the welfare of the country and helps to generate economic growth.
- The theory of comparative advantage is one explanation of international trade but is not a complete explanation. It has to be adjusted for things like transport costs, changes in technology and preferential agreements.
- The balance of payments is a record of transactions between the home country and the rest of the world. It records merchandise trade, trade in services, unilateral transfers, capital movements and official reserve transactions.
- There are several balances which can be calculated for the balance of payments. The most important ones are the trade balance, the current account balance and the official settlements balance.

- A balance of payments deficit results if the country is spending more abroad than it is earning. It can be financed by running down the country's foreign assets, borrowing, and buying on credit.
- A persistent balance of payments deficit can be corrected by monetary policy, fiscal policy, incomes policy, devaluation or direct controls.

Questions

1. Explain the advantages of international trade. Why is trade important for the Caribbean?
2. Outline the theory of comparative advantage and explain why it cannot fully explain the pattern of international trade.
3. Discuss the major influences on the pattern of trade of Caribbean countries.
4. What is *the balance of payments*? Say what transactions are recorded in the balance of payments and how they are recorded.
5. If the balance of payments always balances, how can there be deficits or surpluses on the balance of payments?
6. How can deficits on the balance of payments be financed?
7. Discuss the measures which can be used to correct an adverse balance of payments.
8. What are non-tariff barriers to trade? Explain how they
   (a) affect the pattern of trade
   (b) can improve the balance of payments.
9. (a) State *five* methods used by governments of any Caribbean country to restrict foreign imports.
   (b) Select *two* of the methods you have named in (a) and give reasons why it was necessary to introduce them in that country.
   (c) Show how effective these two methods have been.

(CXC June 1985)

Chapter 20

Regional and International Business Environments

The small size of Caribbean economies makes them very dependent on developments in the rest of the world, which in turn quite quickly have an effect on the Caribbean economies. A decline in income in the United States, Canada or the United Kingdom has an exaggerated effect on the Caribbean countries, since they depend on these countries for tourism and remittances from Caribbean immigrants living there.

20.1 Local/regional economic institutions

There are a number of local and regional institutions which assist businesses or affect them in some way. Among the local institutions are the following:

The Chamber of Commerce This is an association of business people from all branches of commercial activity. It tries to improve the business environment in the country and represents the position of the business community to the government and external agencies.

The Manufacturers Association This is an association of business people engaged in manufacturing activity. Like the Chamber of Commerce it tries to improve the economic environment for businesses and represents the position of its members to the government. In some countries the two groups form a single association called the Association of Industry and Commerce.

The Small Business Association This is a grouping of small businesses which tries to improve the position of the small business in the country. One of its aims is to influence government policy towards small businesses.

The Employers Federation This is an association of employers which is concerned with matters of employment and labour relations. It tries to promote the position of employers in relation to labour, and represents the position of the employers to the government.

Table 20.1 Membership of economic associations

Caribbean Community (CARICOM)	Antigua & Barbuda, The Bahamas, Barbados, Belize, Dominica, Grenada, Guyana, Jamaica, Montserrat, St Kitts-Nevis, St Lucia, St Vincent & the Grenadines, Trinidad & Tobago
Organization of Eastern Caribbean States (OECS)	Antigua & Barbuda, Dominica, Grenada, Montserrat, St Kitts-Nevis, St Lucia, St Vincent & the Grenadines
Caribbean Basin Initiative (CBI)	All CARICOM countries except Guyana, and also: Aruba, Dominican Republic, Haiti, Netherlands, Antilles, Costa Rica, El Salvador, Guatemala, Honduras, Panama
British Commonwealth	All former British colonies on becoming independent
CARIBCAN	All British Commonwealth countries in the Caribbean, and Canada
European Union (EU)	Belgium, Denmark, France, Germany, Greece, Ireland, Italy, Luxembourg, Netherlands, Portugal, Spain, United Kingdom

The Caribbean Community

There are also economic institutions at the regional level. The most important of these is the Caribbean Community (CARICOM), which is a regional integration movement between 13 English-speaking Caribbean countries. Its goal is to further the economic development of the region through closer economic cooperation. The movement started in 1968 as the Caribbean Free Trade Area (CARIFTA). It abolished import duties on goods produced by the member countries of CARIFTA.

The integration movement was further deepened with the signing of the Chaguaramas Treaty in Trinidad & Tobago, which established CARICOM in 1973. The objectives of CARICOM are economic cooperation through the Caribbean Common Market, the coordination of foreign policy, and functional cooperation in areas such as health, education and culture, youth and sports, science and technology, and tax administration.

The Common Market To establish the Common Market the free trade provisions of CARIFTA were continued. Member countries also decided to have discussions on the removal of non-tariff barriers to trade. The countries also established a Common External Tariff (CET). Although there are no tariffs between the countries, they planned to maintain the same level of tariffs against goods imported from non-CARICOM countries. Member countries have tried unsuccessfully for many years to establish the CET. As at May 1994, only Antigua and Barbuda are still able to implement the CET.

Coordination of foreign policy The countries try to put forward the same stance on international matters. The countries' ambassadors consult one other when voting in international institutions.

Functional cooperation The countries cooperate in the provision of common social services like education, health, meteorology, sports and culture, science and technology and tax administration. Three institutions which provide these services are the University of the West Indies, the Caribbean Examinations Council (education) and the Caribbean Meteorological Organization (meteorology).

Membership

At present the member states of CARICOM are Antigua & Barbuda, The Bahamas, Barbados, Belize, Dominica, Grenada, Guyana, Jamaica, Montserrat, St Kitts-Nevis, St Lucia, and St Vincent & the Grenadines. Of these states, only Montserrat is not independent. Membership is open to any state in the Caribbean that is willing to exercise the rights and assume the obligations outlined in the Treaty.

Organizational structure

The Heads of Government Conference The most important institution of CARICOM is the Heads of Government Conference. This is the final authority of the Community and determines policy. It is responsible for the conclusion of treaties on behalf of the Community and entering into relationships between the Community and international organizations and states.

The Common Market Council This is the next most important institution. The Council is made up of ministers of government who are designated by each member state. The Council is responsible for the development and smooth running of the Common Market and for the settlement of any problems arising out of its functioning.

Other institutions

There are many other institutions of the Community relating to cooperation in specific areas: health, education, labour, foreign affairs, finance, agriculture, mines and natural resources, industry, transport, science and technology. Each member state is represented by the minister of government responsible for that area.

The CARICOM Secretariat

The CARICOM Secretariat is the body responsible for carrying out the decisions made by the Heads of Government Conference, the Council of Ministers, and Committees of Ministers responsible for the various areas (see above). It looks after the day-to-day activities designed to achieve the goals of the Community, and is located in Georgetown, Guyana.

The activities of the Secretariat are divided into five sections:

- trade and agriculture
- economics and industry
- functional cooperation
- legal
- general services and administration.

The head of the Secretariat is the Secretary-General.

Associate institutions

The following bodies are designated Associate Institutions in the Treaty:

Caribbean Development Bank

Caribbean Examinations Council

Caribbean Investment Corporation

Caribbean Meteorological Organization

Council of Legal Education

University of Guyana

University of the West Indies

West Indies Shipping Corporation

The Caribbean Development Bank

The Caribbean Development Bank (CDB) was established by the English-speaking Caribbean countries to provide development finance to member countries. It makes loans to the governments and to the private sector in these countries. The loans usually offer a lower rate of interest than the commercial banks, and borrowers have a period of grace before they are required to begin repayments on the loan. This type of lending is called *concessionary lending* or *soft loans*. The bank also provides technical assistance to borrowers to help them establish their businesses.

The CDB receives its funds from international lending institutions like the International Bank for Reconstruction and Development (IBRD – popularly known as the World Bank), and the Inter-American Development Bank (IDB). The CDB also receives funds from the developed countries such as the USA, UK, France and Canada, which are all members of the Bank but are not permitted to borrow from it.

The Caribbean Association of Industry and Commerce (CAIC)

The Caribbean Association of Industry and Commerce (CAIC) represents the interest of businesses at the regional level. It is an association of business people from the English-speaking Caribbean countries. It has the same goals as the associations of industry and commerce in the individual countries, but it also tries to increase cooperation between business people across the region and represents their interests at the regional and international levels. It is made up of representatives of the business associations in each territory.

The Organization of Eastern Caribbean States (OECS)

The OECS is an institution which promotes greater cooperation between the Eastern Caribbean countries. These countries are Antigua & Barbuda, Dominica, Grenada, Montserrat, St Kitts-Nevis, St Lucia, and St Vincent & the Grenadines. The Organization was established by the OECS treaty in 1981. It covers foreign affairs, defence and security and economic affairs.

The most important body is the OECS Authority, which is made up of the heads of government of the member states. The Authority makes all the major policy decisions and meets twice a year. There is also a Foreign Affairs Committee which coordinates foreign policy, and an Economic Affairs Committee which deals with economic matters.

The OECS Central Secretariat, located in St Lucia, performs the daily administrative tasks. The Economic Affairs Secretariat is in Antigua, and looks after economic matters.

The major activities of the OECS are:

- The promotion of economic and political integration.
- The management of a common currency – the Eastern Caribbean dollar through the Eastern Caribbean Central Bank.
- The coordination of legal matters through a joint supreme court.
- The establishment of joint embassies abroad.
- The promotion of cooperation in areas like health and education.

The World Bank (IBRD)

The World Bank is an international financial institution which was established in 1944 to provide development finance to the less developed countries of the world. The funds of the World Bank are provided by the developed countries. The Bank provides soft loans to the least developed countries through the International Development Association (IDA). Since only the least developed countries can benefit from IDA funds, countries 'graduate' when their level of per capita income reaches a certain level. Trinidad & Tobago has graduated, and Barbados is on the verge of doing so.

The Inter-American Development Bank (IDB)

The IDB is similar to the World Bank and was established to service the needs of the independent countries in North and South America and the Caribbean, providing development finance to countries in those areas. The majority of its funds are subscribed by the USA and Canada. The OECS countries have not sought to become members of the IDB.

20.2 International trading agreements

The Caribbean's international trade is governed by a number of agreements. Some of the more important ones are described here.

The General Agreement on Tariffs and Trade (GATT)

The GATT agreement was signed at the Geneva Conference in 1947 and came into effect in January 1948. It is a multilateral trade agreement which sets out the rules for the conduct of international trade. It also provides a forum for negotiations on the solution of international trade problems and the gradual removal of tariffs and non-tariff trade barriers.

The major trade negotiations were carried out in three 'rounds' of negotiations: the Kennedy Round (1964–67), the Tokyo Round (1973–79) and the Uruguay Round (1985–93). The levels of tariffs have been reduced significantly by these negotiations. The Uruguay Round is the most wide-ranging set of trade negotiations. Progress has been slow because agreement could not be reached on the reduction of protection for agriculture in the United States and the European Community.

The basic principle of GATT is that tariffs should be non-discriminatory – that is, a country should maintain the same level of tariffs to all the members of GATT. The principle was amended to allow economic integration movements and a system called Generalized Trade Preferences (GSP) was offered by the developed countries to less developed countries like those in the Caribbean. The GSP allows duty-free access of most manufactured products of less developed countries into the markets of the developed countries.

The Lomé Convention

The Lomé Convention is a trade and aid agreement between the countries of the European Community (EC) and 68 countries in Africa, the Caribbean and the Pacific Ocean. These 68 countries are called the African, Caribbean and Pacific (ACP) countries. The Caribbean countries are the CARICOM countries, Suriname and the Dominican Republic. The agreement covers three areas: trade, aid and export earnings stabilization. The first three conventions lasted five years, but the present agreement lasts for ten years.

Trade The ACP countries are allowed duty-free access of manufactured products into the EC countries. Products like sugar, rum and bananas are also imported into the EC countries on a preferential basis.

Aid Development aid is provided to the ACP countries through the European Development Fund (EDF). It finances projects like roads and schools which have been identified by the governments of the ACP countries.

Export earnings stabilization If the export earnings of the ACP countries received from the EC decline below a given level, the EC will compensate the producers of those commodities. For example, if a hurricane destroys the bananas in St Lucia, the EC will compensate the banana farmers.

The European Union (EU)

The European Community, or *European Union* as it is now known, is an integration movement between most of the countries of Western Europe. Current member countries are Belgium, Denmark, France,

Germany, Greece, Ireland, Italy, Luxembourg, the Netherlands, Portugal, Spain and the UK. The EC was established by the Treaty of Rome in 1957. Its aim is to harmonize the economic and social policies of the member countries.

The European Union is now a single market, which means that goods circulate freely between the member countries. Some of the preferential treatment of ACP products will be removed as a result, and this will have a damaging effect on the export of Caribbean products to Europe, especially bananas. However, the Single European Market also provides a larger market for Caribbean products in Europe.

The Caribbean Basin Initiative (CBI)

The Caribbean Basin Initiative is a trade agreement similar to the Lomé Convention, between the United States and countries in the Caribbean and Central America. It allows the duty-free importation of over 90 per cent of Caribbean goods into the United States. It excludes textiles, clothing and leather goods. Sugar is imported into the United States under a quota system. The sugar quotas are revised annually by the US government. In recent years the sugar quotas for the Caribbean countries have been reduced drastically.

There is no export earnings stabilization programme and the aid package was a one-time lump sum, in contrast to the Lomé Convention which is an on-going programme. The CBI also has a programme which encourages US firms in Puerto Rico to set up factories in the Caribbean.

Caribbean Canadian Free Trade (CARIBCAN)

This is a trade agreement between the English-speaking Caribbean countries and Canada. It is similar to the Lomé Convention and the CBI. It allows the duty-free import of 98 per cent of Caribbean goods into Canada, but excludes bauxite, bananas and leather goods. Bauxite and bananas are important exports of the Caribbean.

Organization of Petroleum Exporting Countries (OPEC)

OPEC is an association of oil-producing countries which was established in 1974 to increase the revenue from oil for the producing countries and conserve their deposits of oil, which is a finite or exhaustible resource – that is, one day it will all be used up. OPEC restricts the production of oil to force an increase in the price. Such an organization is called a *cartel* – a formal agreement between companies to cooperate in matters dealing with price setting and output restrictions. OPEC assigns production levels to all of the member countries based on their historical levels of production.

The increase in oil prices creates inflation and balance of payments problems in all of the Caribbean countries except Trinidad. The increase in oil prices increases the price of gasoline, electricity and cooking gas, and in fact can affect the price of all goods and services. Trinidad is the only Caribbean country to benefit from an increase in the price of oil because it is an oil producer.

20.3 Socio-economic problems of the Caribbean

Since their independence, Caribbean countries have had to implement their own strategy of economic development. The strategies have met with modest success and have helped to reduce some of the economic problems of the region. However, many problems still exist and more emerge with economic development. For example, the development of the tourist sector causes environmental damage. Some of the major economic problems of the region are described here.

High rate of population growth The population of all of the Caribbean countries except Montserrat is growing fast, and particularly the number of young people. This puts pressure on the government to create employment opportunities, housing and social services. Some countries like Barbados have managed to reduce the rate of population growth, but all the Caribbean countries will have to pay greater attention to family planning as a means of reducing the growth rate of the population.

Unemployment The high rate of population growth creates unemployment problems, as governments are unable to provide enough employment opportunities. The rate of unemployment in the Caribbean ranges from about 15 per cent in Barbados to about 40 per cent in St Vincent and the Grenadines. The unemployment rate is even higher among young people. A reduction in unemployment can only be achieved by increased economic development, which depends on increasing exports.

Migration International migration reduces the population pressures on limited resources. It also reduces unemployment pressure. However, it removes large numbers of skilled people who are needed to help in the development of the country. Rural–urban migration increases the number of people living in the cities. This puts pressure on housing and social services. It also reduces the amount of labour available for agricultural production. Economic development will create more local employment opportunities and reduce the incentive to migrate.

Shortage of capital The countries of the Caribbean have a relatively large amount of labour but very little capital. The shortage of capital restricts the development of the economy. This shortage can be alleviated by increasing the level of domestic saving, by grants from foreign countries, foreign borrowing, direct foreign investment and foreign portfolio investment.

The high level of imports The high bill for imports, especially for consumption goods, limits economic development in the region. Scarce foreign exchange which can be used to purchase capital has to be used to buy consumption goods. Large amounts of food which can be produced locally are imported. This problem can be relieved by *import substitution* – that is, by producing goods locally instead of importing them.

Natural disasters The Caribbean countries are prone to natural disasters. Each year, hurricanes and storms affect the region. In 1988 hurricane Gilbert devastated the Jamaican economy and one year

Hurricane damage

later hurricane Hugo did the same to Antigua, Montserrat and St Kitts-Nevis. Volcanic eruptions and earthquakes are also occasional hazards. Little can be done about natural disasters except to prepare for them.

Unfavourable international developments The Caribbean countries are so dependent on the rest of the world that any unfavourable international economic development may affect these economies adversely. A recession in the developed countries causes a recession in the Caribbean. The increase in oil prices following Iraq's invasion of Kuwait meant higher prices in the Caribbean. Not much can be done to avoid such situations except for Caribbean countries to put policies in place to offset any adverse effects.

Economic dualism The inflow of foreign capital into the Caribbean sometimes creates a technologically advanced sector that receives high wages while the rest of the economy remains underdeveloped and receives low wages. The economic development in this modern sector does not spill over into the more backward sector. Thus a dual economy is created. The modern sector is called an *enclave*. The petroleum industry in Trinidad is a good example. To deal with this problem the government of the country must use the revenue it receives from the modern sector to develop the rest of the economy.
Rising crime rate Economic development is usually accompanied by an increase in the crime rate. The spread of illegal drugs has also increased the crime rate. This can affect the tourist industry adversely. The police forces will have to increase their efforts at fighting crime. Governments will also have to establish education programmes which teach people about the effects of using illegal drugs.

Environmental degradation As economic development takes place, the natural resources of the region are depleted and too fast a rate of depletion may result in the destruction of the environment. For example, uncontrolled expansion of the tourist industry may lead to problems with sewage discharged into the sea, killing the coral reefs and polluting the beaches. Excessive logging may destroy the forests and reduce water resources, and the use of chemicals in agriculture may pollute the rivers. Countries therefore need to be careful with their natural resources, and manage them so that the environment is not degraded or destroyed.

20.4 Education and economic development

Human resources is the most abundant resource in the Caribbean. It must be developed and properly managed to achieve the maximum benefit. Education and training are necessary to develop human resources. The education and training that the population acquires is called *human capital*. Human capital is a very important element in the development process. Studies have shown a strong relationship between education and economic development in less developed countries. Part of the gap between rich and poor countries can be explained by differences in education.

Education and skills increase the productivity of labour and make people more employable. The entrepreneurial skills acquired by business people and managers increase their ability to efficiently utilize limited resources. Skilled personnel are required to operate and service capital equipment. Education allows a country to adapt new technology to suit the structure of the economy, and even to invent new technology.

Education alone does not result in economic development. To be of any use, education must be relevant to the needs of the society. An education system that is based on that of developed countries is of little use to the Caribbean. In his book *Economics for a Developing World*, Michael Todaro says, 'Clearly something is seriously wrong with a primary and secondary education system modelled upon its counterpart in economically advanced societies and transferred to an environment to which it has very little if any relevance.'

Governments in the Caribbean place great emphasis on human resource development. They are trying to improve the standard of education and to make it more relevant. The Caribbean Examinations Council (CXC) uses syllabuses which are more relevant to the Caribbean. Textbooks and educational aids are designed especially for the Caribbean. They have established technical schools to improve the occupational skills of the labour force. There are also adult literacy programmes to educate adults.

20.5 Foreign investment and technology transfer

In Chapter 18 we discussed the relationship between investment and economic development, and identified the ways of increasing investment. Among these was foreign investment. Foreign investment comes from two sources:

1 Selling securities to foreigners.

2 Direct foreign investment.

Issuing securities on the international market

Local firms can sell their shares to residents of foreign countries. In this way they are able to raise funds for investment. When this type of foreign investment takes place the foreign firm or individual does not have control over the local firm. This is called *portfolio foreign investment.*

Direct foreign investment

Direct foreign investment occurs when a foreign resident establishes a firm in the country. The foreign resident has control over the firm. Thus the distinction between foreign and portfolio investment rests on control of the firm. The most widespread form of foreign direct investment is the multinational corporation which has its head offices in one of the developed countries and has branches in many different countries. The foreign banks in all of the Caribbean countries are examples of multinational corporations.

In addition to the investment funds which the multinational company brings to the country, it also brings modern technology and management and marketing skills, and instructions about how the firm is to operate.

The advantages of foreign investment:

1 The country receives capital which is usually in short supply.

2 It receives management and marketing skills.

3 The balance of payments of the country improves when foreign capital comes into the country.

4 The level of income grows as the firm employs unused resources.

5 The rate of unemployment declines as more people are employed.

6 Government revenue rises through taxation of the multinational company.

Disadvantages of foreign investment:

1 The profits which the multinational earns in the country are sent back to the head office.

2 In the long term, the balance of payments deteriorates when profits are sent abroad.

3 Foreign investment can create a dual economy (see page 316).

4 Foreign firms may meddle in the affairs of a country. Because countries are dependent on them, a foreign company may embarrass the government by reducing exports and creating economic hardship. It is alleged that this tactic was used by bauxite-producing firms in Jamaica in the 1970s.

5 The technology used may be inappropriate. Technology that is created for conditions in developed countries is often not suited to local conditions. Often it is capital intensive, which does not create much employment.

6 Research and development is done at the head office and none is done in the Caribbean.

7 People are brought in to do the more technical jobs, and may not teach the local people to do these jobs.

8 Local branches are charged management fees and royalties.

9 Transfer pricing may be used, to reduce the tax the foreign company has to pay to the local government. The cost of inputs of the local branch from the head office is overstated, and the price of the outputs sent to the head office is understated, so the profits of the local branch are lower, as is its tax. Because the head office and the branches are one firm, they do not lose anything.

Given the shortage of capital facing the Caribbean countries, they will have to depend heavily on foreign investment to assist in economic development. They cannot develop without it. They will have to try to minimize the disadvantages to receive maximum benefit from foreign investment. They need to put policies in place to reduce exploitation by the multinational corporations.

Technology transfer

Technology transfer refers to the adaptation of technology to meet the specific conditions in the receiving country. It also involves the acquisition of skills by local people so that they can use, maintain and adapt the technology.

Technology transfer has been difficult for the Caribbean because the multinational firms which own the rights to the technology are only willing to share it at a very high price. They bring the technology to the region but do not teach local people to maintain and adapt the technology. Multinationals have invested millions of dollars in research and development (R & D), and the profits and royalties they receive are returns on their investment.

For technology transfer to take place, some way will have to be found to get the firms in the developed countries to share the technology. Technology will have to be adapted to suit conditions in the Caribbean. Also, resistance in the Caribbean to the new technology will have to be overcome. New technology often means a loss of jobs, and unions may try to resist its adoption.

Key Points

- Local private-sector organizations like the Chamber of Commerce, Manufacturers Associations and Employers Federations are groups that try to further the interests of the private sector.
- CARICOM is a regional integration movement between the countries of the English-speaking Caribbean. Its aims are the economic development of the region and the provision of common services.
- The Heads of Government Conference is the most important decision-making unit in CARICOM. The CARICOM Secretariat, located in Guyana, takes care of day-to-day administration.
- The OECS is a closer integration movement between the countries of the Eastern Caribbean.
- Much of the Caribbean's international trade takes place under preferential trading agreements. These include the Lomé Convention, the Caribbean Basin Initiative and CARIBCAN.
- Some of the economic problems facing the Caribbean countries are high unemployment, lack of capital, migration, high import bills and natural disasters.
- The education and skills of the population are called *human capital*. It is an important element in the economic development process. Education must be relevant to the development needs of the society.
- For economic development to take place, the Caribbean needs both local investment and foreign investment, which has many advantages and disadvantages. Countries have to try to minimize the disadvantages to receive the maximum benefit from foreign investment.

Questions

1. Describe the work of three organizations which further the interests of the business sector.
2. What is CARICOM? Describe its organizational structure.
3. What is the OECS? What are its major objectives?
4. Describe the work of three international financial institutions.

5 What is the Lomé Convention? How does it affect Caribbean trade?

6 Write short notes on:

(a) OPEC

(b) the European Community

(c) the ACP.

7 Explain *five* of the major economic problems facing the Caribbean and say how they can be solved.

8 Describe the role of education in economic development. Is education in the Caribbean geared to our economic development?

9 Explain the two types of foreign investment. What are the advantages and disadvantages of foreign investment?

10 What is *technology transfer*? Why has technology transfer been difficult in the Caribbean?

11 (a) List *five* major international trade and cartel agreements which affect the Caribbean, and state the main objectives of any *three* of them.

(b) Select *one* of the agreements named in (a) and show how useful that agreement has been to the economic development of the Caribbean. In your analysis, reference should be made to the structure and format of the agreement as well as to the principle of economic assistance.

(CXC June 1989)

Appendix The derivation of a simple cost equation

See Chapter 7.

Table A1 shows the production costs data for an accounting period. Column 1 shows the actual total costs incurred on the production of 500 units of output. The classification of the costs into fixed and variable elements is shown in columns 2 and 3.

Table A1 Production cost statement for an accounting period

	(1) Actual total costs ($)	(2) Fixed costs ($)	(3) Variable costs ($)
Material used	2,000		2,000
Direct labour	2,500		2,500
Supervisory labour	400	400	
Factory rent and rates	500	500	
Maintenance	500		500
Fuel and power	2,500		2,500
Office	1,100	1,100	
Depreciation	2,000	2,000	
	11,500	**4,000**	**7,500**

The variable cost (VC) per unit is calculated as follows:

$$VC = \frac{\$7,500}{500} = \$15$$

The total (TC) equation is

$$TC = 4,000 + 15(x)$$

Note that the equation can be used to estimate the total cost for any number of items to be produced. For example, assume an output of 600 units. What is the total cost?

$$\text{The new total cost} = \$4,000 + 15\ (600)$$

$$= \$13,000$$

Glossary

accounting variance analysis The difference between two (dollar) figures, the standard figure and the actual figure. A variance can be either favourable or adverse. Accounting variance analysis is not the same as statistical variance analysis.

aggregate demand A measure of the real purchasing power of the community. Commonly referred to as the total effective demand or total expenditure, it normally comprises private consumption (C), private and public investment (I), government expenditure (G) plus net exports ($X - M$).

autarky A closed economy that attempts to be completely self-reliant.

balance of payments (table) A summary statement of a nation's financial transactions with the outside world. See also *current account.*

barter transactions The trading of goods directly for other goods in economies not fully monetized.

brain drain The emigration of highly educated and skilled professional and technical workers from one country to another.

capital This term has a number of different meanings:

capital stock	– the physical assets of a business
equity capital	– an owner's called-up capital, or the total amount due from shareholders
capital employed	– the funds available to a business to carry on activities
capital expenditure	– expenditure that is expected to produce benefits in periods beyond that in which the original expenditure is incurred
capital gains	– an increase in the value of an asset over its original cost when realized by sale
capital loss	– a decrease in the value of an asset
capital reserve	– a reserve that is not available for distribution as dividend
capital transaction	– a transaction relating to capital expenditure
working capital	– current assets minus current liabilities, ie an investment measure required to finance the day-to-day operations of a business.

closed economy An economy in which there are no foreign trade transactions or any other form of economic contacts with the rest of the world.

collateral Also described as security, in the form of insurance policies, land titles or deeds, guarantees, shares or debentures. A guarantee is a promise to answer for the debt, default or error to another person.

comparative advantage A country has a comparative advantage over another if in producing a commodity it can do so at a relatively lower *opportunity cost* in terms of the forgone alternative commodities that could be produced.

control The application of policies and procedures for directing, regulating and coordinating production, administration and other business activities in a way that achieves the objectives of a business.

coordination A continuous process where the efforts of a group are harmonized so that the desired goal or a goal nearest to it is obtained. A lack of coordination in a firm usually results in disorder of its activities.

credit There are many kinds of credit. A *revocable credit* is one that can be cancelled. An *irrevocable credit* is guaranteed by the bank issuing it and cannot be altered without the consent of the exporting company. A *confirmed irrevocable credit* is one in which the bank joins in the guarantee. It is the safest method by which an exporting company can obtain payment for its goods. A *transferable credit* is one where the company that receives the goods has a right to give instructions to a bank to make the credit available to a third party. An *acceptance credit* is one where the exporter's bill is accepted by a bank.

current account That portion of a *balance of payments table* that portrays the market value of a country's visible (eg commodity trade) and invisible (eg shipping services) exports and imports with the rest of the world.

division of labour Allocation of tasks among workers so that each person engages in tasks that he or she performs most efficiently. Division of labour promotes worker specialization and thereby raises overall labour productivity.

economic growth A sustained increase in the level of national income of a country. On the other hand, *economic development* is growth accompanied by changes in the structure of the economy. *National income* is the total value of goods and services produced in the economy during the period of one year.

enterprise, entrepreneurship The ability to organize business and take risks. In every productive activity there is the chance that it may not be successful. Thus there is a chance of making profits or losses. This situation is referred to as *taking risks*. See also *risk*.

holding company A parent company that exercises control over a subsidiary company. A company is a subsidiary of another if (a) the board of directors is controlled by members of the parent company or (b) the parent company holds more than half in nominal value of the subsidiary's issued equity share capital.

increasing returns A disproportionate increase in output which results from a change in the scale of production. In traditional economic theory, increasing returns (and thus decreasing costs) will occur until a certian output level has been reached and thereafter diminishing returns (increasing costs) are assumed to set in.

indirect taxes Taxes levied on goods purchased by the consumer (and exported by the producer) for which the taxpayer's liability varies in proportion to the quantity of particular goods purchased or sold. Examples of indirect taxes are customs duties (tariffs), excise duties, sales taxes and export duties.

infant industry A term given to a newly established industry usually set up behind the protection of a tariff barrier as part of a policy of import substitution. Once the industry is no longer an 'infant', the protective tariffs are supposed to disappear, but they often do not.

interest Whenever there is a time-lag between the borrowing and the paying back of money, the question of interest arises. Interest can be regarded as the time value of money – today's dollar has a greater value than tomorrow's dollar – or as the cost of borrowing.

investment tax credit The business tax paid by a firm is reduced if it undertakes new investment during the year.

lease A contract by which the owner (the *lessor*) of a physical asset permits another person (the *lessee*) to use the asset for a stated time, in return for payment at an agreed price. The asset at all times remains the property of the lessor, although the lessee may be given an option to purchase the asset either during the time-span of the lease or at its termination.

market economy A free private enterprise economy governed by a price system and *market mechanism*.

market research A systematic study of data to which mathematical methods are applied to obtain information relevant to the marketing of products or services. *Quantitative research* is measured in figures. *Qualitative research* seeks information on reasons, images and motives

merchandising The physical process of stocking retail and distribution outlets with goods so that they are in the right place at the right time. The goods are assembled, arranged and displayed where they can easily be seen, reached, selected and transported to the place of payment.

mixed economic system An economic system that is a mixture of both capitalist and socialist economies. Mixed economic systems characterise most developing countries. Their essential feature is the co-existence of substantial private and public activity within a single economy.

model A way of looking at something. A model can be descriptive or quantitative. In a firm there are many models. A predictive model, for example, supplies answers to questions like 'If a certain course of action is taken, what will the consequences be, and how will the achievement of objectives or avoidance of constraints be affected?'

national income Total monetary value of all final goods and services produced in an economy over some period of time, usually a year.

primary products Products derived from all extractive occupations – farming, lumbering, fishing, mining and quarrying (foodstuffs and raw materials).

profit mark-up An arbitrary percentage figure on total cost which when added to the total cost gives the price.

progressive income tax A tax whose rate increases with increasing personal income, ie where the proportion of personal income paid by a rich person in taxes is greater than that paid by a poorer person. A progressive tax structure therefore tends to improve income distribution.

regressive tax If the ratio of taxes to income as income increases tends to decrease, the tax is called 'regressive'. Relatively poor people pay a larger proportion of their income in taxes than do relatively rich people.

research The continual search to discover improved ways of work performance, product creation or improvement in technology. Research calls for long-term finance and plenty of human creativity.

risk A general definition is *loss*. Risk is a general fact of life which can be predicted with some degree of accuracy, for example pilferage of a firm's goods. Non-insurable risks are of three types:

(a) marketing risk, which means that a person who sets up a business cannot feel entirely confident that the product will sell, perhaps because of a change in public taste or fashion

(b) uncertainty due to the success of rival products and changes in technology

(c) financial, legal and political uncertainties, for example a government may declare that a firm's products do not pass certain standards, or may not give permission to a producer to import raw materials or buy foreign exchange. Note that the reward to the business in operating in the face of risks is *profit*.

Insurance risk also includes defective products, personal health, pollution of air, water and the work environment, personal liability, nuclear hazards, earthquakes, floods, hurricanes, riots, crime. Note that some risks are financed by firms, for example bad debts, because any insurance premium would have to cover the loss *plus* the insurance company's administration costs and profits.

sample A proportion of the population relevant to a survey, for example a household. There are two different kinds of sample: quota and random. For a *quota sample* an interviewer is responsible for finding a certain number of people. The sample is usually small, and can be based on particular groups – people of a particular age, for example. For a *random sample*, names and addresses are selected at regular intervals from a list and the interviewer questions those people. Reserve names may be used if the orginal names on the list cannot be contacted.

solvency The ability of a person or a firm to repay debts and obligations when they fall due.

standard of living The level of material well-being of a society. It is determined by the quantities of goods and services (including leisure) consumed.

standards Qualitative or quantitative targets that a management function applies to certain work activities. When standards are expressed in money, they are called *standard costs*. Standard costs are measures of what costs should be, assuming that normal conditions prevail in the firm and in its business environment.

tariff A fixed percentage (eg 30 per cent) on the value of an imported commodity levied at the point of entry into the importing country.

tax holiday A period of time (usually 5–10 years) during which a firm pays no business income tax.

Useful references

Beckford, G. *Persistent Poverty*, ISER, Jamaica, 1970.

Brennan, Michael J. *Theory of Economic Statics*, Prentice-Hall, 1970.

Cockerrell, H. A. L. *What Goes On In Insurance,* Woodhead-Faulkner, 1982.

Crump, T. *The Phenomenon of Money*, Routledge & Kegan Paul, 1981.

Harvey, J. *Mastering Economics*, Macmillan, 1985.

Harvey, J. and Johnson, M. *Introduction to Macro-Economics*, Macmillan, 1983.

Howard, M. *Public Finance in Small, Open Economies: The Caribbean Experience*, Praeger, 1992.

Layne, W. A. *Cost Accounting Analysis and Control,* Macmillan Publishers Ltd, 1984.

Layne, W. A. *An Introduction to Accounting for CXC Students*, Cambridge University Press, 1990.

Leftwich, Richard H. and Eckert, Ross D. *The Price System and Resource Allocation*, Holt-Saunders, 1985.

Lewis, W. A. *The Principles of Economic Planning*, Allen and Unwin, 1949.

Lipsey, R., Purvis, C. and Steiner, P. *Economics*, Harper and Row, 1989.

Miller, C. J. and Palmer, N. E. *Business Law*, ICSA Publishing, 1991

Moggridge, D. E. *Maynard Keynes: An Economist's Biography,* Routledge, 1992.

Prest, A. *Public Finance in Developing Countries*, Weidenfeld & Nicholson, 1975.

Samuelson, Paul A. *Economics*, McGraw-Hill, 1976.

Skinner, A. *Adam Smith: The Wealth of Nations*, Pelican Classics, 1974.

Sunshine, C. A. *The Caribbean: Survival, Struggle and Sovereignty,* EPICA, 1988.

Riboud, J. *The Mechanics of Money*, translated by S. Harrison, St Martin's Press, 1980.

Todaro, M. *Economics for a Developing World*, Longman, 1979.

Walker, D. M. *The Oxford Companion to Law*, Clarendon Press, Oxford, 1980.

Index